Americans, Congress, and
Democratic Responsiveness

*Public Evaluations of Congress
and Electoral Consequences*

David R. Jones and
Monika L. McDermott

*With a New Afterword
to Include the 2008 Election*

THE UNIVERSITY OF MICHIGAN PRESS

ANN ARBOR

First paperback edition 2010
Copyright © by the University of Michigan 2009
All rights reserved
Published in the United States of America by
The University of Michigan Press
Manufactured in the United States of America
♾ Printed on acid-free paper

2013   2012   2011   2010   5   4   3   2

A CIP catalog record for this book is available from the British Library.

Library of Congress Cataloging-in-Publication Data

Jones, David R., 1968–
    Americans, Congress, and democratic responsiveness :
  public evaluations of Congress and electoral consequences / David R. Jones
  and Monika L. McDermott.
       p.   cm.
    Includes bibliographical references and index.
    ISBN-13: 978-0-472-11694-2 (cloth : alk. paper)
    ISBN-10: 0-472-11694-0 (cloth : alk. paper)
    1. United States. Congress—Public opinion.   2. United States.
  Congress—Elections.   3. Voting—United States.   4. Public opinion—
  United States.   I. McDermott, Monika L., 1966–   II. Title.

JK1041.J66   2009
328.73—dc22   2009004567

ISBN 978-0-472-03409-3 (pbk. : alk. paper)
ISBN 978-0-472-02213-7 (ebook)

To our parents

CONTENTS

ACKNOWLEDGMENTS

Our biggest debt in this project is to former Speaker of the House Newt Gingrich. It is extraordinarily unlikely we would have started on this line of research absent the 1994 Republican revolution, led by Gingrich, and the Republicans' policy-rich Contract with America. The Republican takeover of Congress, their subsequent policy actions, and the public's reactions sparked a conversation between the two of us about ideological Congresses and public evaluations of them. That conversation led to our first publications on this topic and eventually to this book.

Along the way, we have had generous support and invaluable help in collecting data. We would first like to sing the praises of the Time-sharing Experiments for the Social Sciences (TESS) project run by Diana Mutz and Arthur Lupia. This project is an incomparable resource for social scientists. Our experience with TESS could not have been better. We thank Diana and Skip for the project's existence, as well as for the efficient and helpful process they oversee. We also thank the Indiana University Center for Survey Research, specifically John Kennedy, for efforts in data collection. Other data were generously and efficiently gathered by the Center for Survey Research and Analysis (CSRA) at the University of Connecticut, under the direction of Sam Best. We thank him and everyone at CSRA for their efforts on our behalf. The Roper Center archives at the University of Connecticut were an invaluable data source for us. And Jennifer DePinto at the CBS News Election and Survey Unit spent time providing us with needed data.

Institutional debts are owed to Baruch College at the City University of New York, for research support for David, and to both the Dirksen Congressional Center and the Professional Staff Congress of the City University of New York, for seed money in the early stages of the project.

We also received indispensable advice and encouragement from colleagues and friends. Several people helped us with the book prospectus, including Tom Halper and Barbara Sinclair. Jeffrey Ladewig patiently read multiple parts of the book, offering helpful advice. We thank Chris Wlezien, who offered suggestions on the work, as well as a forum for its presentation, and Vince Hutchings for encouragement and the suggestion that we submit the manuscript to the University of Michigan Press. Keith Poole took the time to provide us with technical advice on his data and its use. Lyle Scruggs was always there when we needed to bounce statistical ideas off of someone. Sam Best, Janet Gornick, and Kristin Kelly offered advice navigating the world of book publishing. We also thank Oksan, Jeff, Aidan Kaan, and baby Batu for the pool and for helping us keep our priorities straight.

We have had the pleasure of working with several editors at the University of Michigan Press. We would like to thank Jim Reische for his enthusiasm for our project and his passing of the baton on his departure, Phil Pochoda for keeping us in the race, and Melody Herr for helping us across the finish line with grace and gusto.

Finally, each of us thanks our spouse for a significant contribution without which this idea would never have developed and this book would not have been written.

CHAPTER 1

Introduction

Prior to the 2006 congressional elections, conventional wisdom in political science suggested that the battle for control of the House would be close. Some academic forecasting models predicted that Republicans would hold on to a narrow majority, others that Democrats would gain enough seats to overtake them. Virtually none, however, predicted that Republicans would lose as many as the thirty seats they actually lost, giving the Democrats a majority advantage of thirty-one seats.[1]

Four years earlier, during the 2002 congressional elections, the American Political Science Association held a symposium of election experts one month before the vote. Every forecasting model presented in the symposium predicted that Democrats would retake majority control of the House from the Republicans.[2] On election day, however, not only did the Democrats not win a majority of seats, but the Republicans actually increased the size of their majority.

This clear discrepancy between political science theory and political reality is troubling and begs the question, why are these political forecasting models failing so consistently? A close look at both the models and reality points to an obvious shortcoming. Despite the fact that public approval of Congress's performance was near record lows just before the election in 2006 (26 percent in the Gallup Poll) and at record highs just before the election in 2002 (50 percent in the Gallup Poll), not a single academic model of the congressional elections took into account public evaluations of the institution.[3] Instead, these models focused on such factors as presidential approval ratings and the nation's economy.

If one believes that Americans care not just about the general performance of the president and the economy but also about the performance of Congress specifically, the results of these elections become understandable and even predictable. In 2006, the lowest public approval ratings of congressional performance in twelve years led to greater losses for the House majority party than expected (the greatest losses in twelve years). In 2002, record high approval ratings of Congress's performance helped the House majority to increase its seat margin—rather than decrease it, as predicted.[4]

Unfortunately, the failure of academics to seriously consider public evaluations of Congress in their 2006 or 2002 forecasts is illustrative of the current state of scholarly thinking in this area. In fact, no standard model of congressional elections has ever included public judgments of congressional performance. Why? Put simply, traditional political science theory and research suggest that Americans do not care much about what policies the collective Congress is pursuing and that even if they did care, Congress and its members are insulated from public judgments of the institution's performance.

This standard view that neither the public nor the Congress is responsive to the other is quite disturbing from the perspective of normative democratic theory. In the classic model of democratic responsiveness, citizens evaluate governmental institutions on the basis of their policy performance, then government institutions decide their policy behavior in light of public judgments—shifting their policy behavior in response to significant public disapproval and maintaining it when the public approves. According to the conventional scholarly portrait, then, Americans and their Congress fail the basic test of democratic responsiveness. If Americans' attitudes toward Congress have no basis in actual congressional policy behavior and if their evaluations have no electoral effect in any event, then Congress is free to act in any way it sees fit in terms of the policies it formulates and enacts.

We believe that the conventional academic view underestimates the democratic capabilities of both Americans and their Congress. The purpose of this book is to show that democracy is actually working better—in terms of the public-Congress relationship—than much of the existing scholarship portrays. We demonstrate how Americans use policy direction to evaluate congressional performance, how they use these judgments when voting in congressional elections, and how Congress is ultimately responsive to these judgments of its performance. In making our case, we challenge long-standing assumptions of scholarship on public opinion, elections, and congressional behavior. In the end, we tell a story that is quite different in both its assumptions and its conclusions from current evaluations of American democracy.

We are not arguing that the traditional factors the literature has found to be significant in explaining public opinion, voting, and congressional behavior are unimportant. Quite the contrary, we believe they are essential to any good explanation of these political phenomena. Nor are we arguing that the factors we choose to focus on are necessarily more important than the factors emphasized in existing research. We do, however, argue that the discipline's traditional explanations of the relationship between the public and Congress are incomplete. Our book seeks to address this gap in an effort to contribute a missing piece to this scholarly puzzle. Before we present our full argument, however, it is important to take a closer look at the existing research.

PUBLIC EVALUATIONS OF CONGRESS — THE CONVENTIONAL VIEW

The study of democratic responsiveness is fundamentally about the relationship between the government and the governed. Given the wide scope of this topic, questions about the democratic responsiveness of Americans and Congress necessarily relate to large and disparate bodies of research. Here, we are interested, first, in public opinion research related to the question of how Americans evaluate the performance of political actors generally and Congress in particular. Second, we are interested in behavioral research on how Americans vote in congressional elections and how Congress and its members perceive and react to public evaluations of the institution's performance.

How Americans Evaluate Congress

Do Americans respond to congressional policy behavior when evaluating the institution? By and large, the public opinion literature says no. It portrays American citizens as overwhelmingly uninterested and uninformed about the policy actions of government (A. Campbell et al. 1960; Converse 1964; Delli Carpini and Keeter 1996; Hibbing and Theiss-Morse 2002; Smith 1989). Looking at the 1956 presidential election, the authors of *The American Voter* (A. Campbell et al. 1960) famously find that only a small proportion—12 percent—of the electorate spontaneously and knowledgeably evaluated the parties and candidates in terms of their placement on a liberal-conservative policy spectrum. More than four decades later, in their book *Stealth Democracy,* Hibbing and Theiss-Morse argue that not much has changed: "The people as a whole tend to be quite indifferent to policies and therefore are not eager to hold government accountable for the policies it produces" (2002, 2).

This characterization of Americans as uninterested and uninformed about policy matters is considered particularly applicable in the case of Congress (Hibbing and Theiss-Morse 1995; Stokes and Miller 1962). In contrast to the single president, the 535-member Congress is seen as an institution too complex for citizens to understand or even consider. Fenno muses, "Most citizens find it hard or impossible to think about Congress as an institution. They answer questions about it; but they cannot conceptualize it as a collectivity" (1978, 245). Congress is also less likely than the president to receive coverage in the national news media (Jamieson 1988). Perhaps as a result, scholars note that the public's ability to answer seemingly simple survey questions about Congress is quite poor. According to Stokes and Miller, "the electorate sees very little altogether of what goes on in the national legislature. . . . and much of the public is unaware even of which party has control of Congress" (1962, 545). Summarizing the literature, Mondak and his colleagues state that "nothing in the empirical record suggests that citizens are at all well informed regarding the people, politics, and procedures of Congress" (2007, 34).

If Americans do not think in policy terms and do not have much information about Congress and its policy actions, it becomes difficult to imagine them evaluating Congress on policy or ideological grounds. Indeed, in their important work *Congress as Public Enemy,* Hibbing and Theiss-Morse find that "policy is rarely mentioned by people when asked about their dislikes of Congress" (1995, 48). Rather than reflecting Americans' concerns with the policy direction of Congress, public evaluations of Congress's job performance are thought to stem mainly from concerns with the style and pace of the legislative process (Hibbing and Theiss-Morse 1995) or from general concerns with national conditions, such as the state of the economy (Durr, Gilmour, and Wolbrecht 1997; Parker 1977; Patterson and Caldeira 1990; Stimson 2004).

Consequences of Public Judgments of Congress

Even if Americans' evaluations of Congress were related to policy concerns, the literature does not view public evaluations of Congress as providing any real impetus for responsiveness on the part of Congress (Fenno 1975, 1978; Mayhew 1974; Stokes and Miller 1962). In his seminal work *Home Style,* Fenno notes that in such a large and diverse body as Congress, "it is easy for each congressman to explain to his own supporters why he cannot be blamed for the performance of the collectivity" (1978, 167).[5] Fenno finds that House members feel so safely insulated from any negative public evaluations of their institution that they often "run *for* Congress by running *against* Congress"—actually denigrating the performance of the rest of the institution in their interactions with constituents (168). The notion that congressional evaluations do not affect the fortunes of individual members is supported mainly by a simple yet dramatic observation: despite the fact that a majority of Americans tend to disapprove of the collective Congress, individual members of Congress are regularly reelected at astonishingly high rates—an average of over 90 percent in House elections and only slightly less in Senate elections. That Americans appear to simultaneously "hate Congress" and "love their own member" is so widely known that it is often referred to simply as "Fenno's Paradox" (Fenno 1975; see also Cook 1979; Jones 2003; Mutz and Flemming 1999; Parker and Davidson 1979).

If incumbents can avoid individual responsibility for congressional performance, might Congress at least be subject to some sort of collective responsibility, with disapproval leading to electoral tides that produce institutional turnover? Mayhew suggests not, noting that "national swings in the congressional vote are normally judgments on what the president is doing . . . rather than on what Congress is doing" (1974, 28). Stokes and Miller concur that congressional performance considerations are "unlikely to bring down electoral sanctions" on the majority party (1962, 545). Hibbing and Tiritilli argue that the public generally does not attribute responsibility for Congress's performance to the majority party, so that "most of the time, even when people are quite disapproving of Congress, this disapproval does not have direct electoral repercussions" (2000, 128).[6]

Even some members of Congress seem to have accepted this conventional wisdom. Former Speaker of the House Thomas "Tip" O'Neill famously declared that "all politics is local." More recently, in the months leading up to the 2006 election, the chairman of the National Republican Congressional Committee, Representative Tom Reynolds, seemed to be (optimistically) channeling Richard Fenno.

> Congress's approval rating is a little flat. My self-esteem wants to see it a little higher. But it is what it is. The most important thing is people love their congressman, no matter what. (Reynolds quoted in Nagourney 2006)

At the time, prominent political consultants were advising Republicans that gerrymandered districts and a focus on local issues would protect them from any negative electoral effects of low congressional approval.[7]

Without a threat of electoral defeat when the public disapproves of Congress, there would also appear to be little strategic incentive for members to alter their policy behavior in response to public disapproval of Congress. Indeed, numerous studies find that members exhibit very little ideological change throughout their legislative careers (Carson et al. 2004; Lott and Bronars 1993; Poole and Romer 1993; Poole and Rosenthal 1997; Poole 2007).

Overall, the view that congressional performance evaluations do not affect Congress and its members is so dominant that few scholars have even thought it necessary to empirically test for such effects. Standard studies of individual voting behavior (e.g., Jacobson 2004), congressional election outcomes (e.g., Tufte 1975), ideological change among individual members (e.g., Poole and Rosenthal 1997), and collective congressional responsiveness (e.g., Erikson, MacKuen, and Stimson 2002) do not consider congressional approval as a possible causal variable.

REASONS FOR GREATER OPTIMISM

Despite the impressive weight of scholarly opinion reflected in the preceding discussion, there are important reasons to suspect that both Americans and their Congress are more capable of producing a responsive system than is traditionally argued. Certain politicians, pundits, and even some scholarly studies suggest that citizen capacity for policy-related evaluation of Congress is greater than commonly thought. Additionally, others suggest that members of Congress may not be as insulated from public judgments of their institution as has been traditionally believed.

Congressional Policy Direction and Congressional Approval

An initial issue in questioning the conventional wisdom in political science is establishing whether or not Americans actually have enough information about policy matters to effectively evaluate Congress along these lines. The standard academic view, based on survey data, is that they do not. This view has, however, been seriously challenged in other quarters as being far from conclusive (Kuklinski and Quirk 2001).

One prominent avenue of research suggests that the public has ways of dealing with information shortages. For example, literature on information shortcuts, or heuristics, argues that, in practice, voters mitigate against their relatively low levels of political sophistication by relying on familiar cues to guide them (e.g., Popkin 1991). Other literature shows that political information does regularly reach even politically inattentive citizens indirectly through their social networks—friends, family, and coworkers (Huckfeldt and Sprague 1995).

In the field of political psychology, research into online, or impression-driven, processing suggests that while Americans may not be able to readily recall specific political information when questioned by survey researchers—thereby scoring poorly on typical knowledge tests—they nevertheless do form general impressions of governmental actors based, at least in part, on such information (e.g., Gant and Davis 1984; Lodge, McGraw, and Stroh 1989; Lodge, Steenbergen, and Brau 1995; Lodge and Stroh 1993). According to this school of thought, individuals regularly come into contact with political information, even if inadvertently, and they absorb the information by updating their impressions of political actors as a result of it. Once they have updated their judgments, individuals have no more use for the specific information and are likely to forget it. In this way, Americans may well base their judgments about governmental actors on factual information—including policy—even if they cannot recall the information itself.

Although researchers have predominantly examined such theories in terms of individual candidates, this logic could potentially also apply to judgments of the collective Congress. Lipinski (2004) finds that in their mailings to constituents, approximately three-quarters of representatives send messages concerning Congress's collective performance. His research also shows that these messages about Congress focus primarily on congressional policy.[8] Lipinski claims that the content of these mailings are "an excellent proxy for all of a member's communications with constituents," be they through personal interactions or through the news media (9; see also Cannon 1999). Thus there may actually be a considerable amount of policy information about Congress available to citizens, either directly from members themselves or indirectly through the news media or via opinion leaders who closely follow Congress. Citizens could potentially use this information about the policy activity of Congress to update their general impressions of Congress—even if they cannot recall a single specific bill on which Congress has worked.

Even if citizens do absorb policy-related information about Congress,

to what extent do they actually use such information to evaluate government actors? While the traditional view is that Americans generally do
not think in policy or ideological terms, some scholars offer a less pessimistic assessment. Challenging the perspective put forth in *The American Voter,* Nie, Verba, and Petrocik (1980) argue that 1956 was a low
point of ideological distinction between presidential candidates and between political parties in government. According to this alternative view,
citizens who otherwise would use ideology to evaluate political candidates may not bother to dwell on this criterion when few ideological differences exist among political actors. But when ideology is salient and
differences are clear, ideology can be an important factor for ordinary
citizens (see also Wright and Berkman 1986). If Americans are more
likely to judge political actors on ideological grounds when policy differences are salient, they are almost certainly doing so more now than in the
past. American parties in government have become increasingly ideologically polarized over the past three decades (Aldrich 1995; McCarty,
Poole, and Rosenthal 2006; Rohde 1991). Many scholars argue that this
elite polarization has in turn increased both the awareness and the importance of ideology among the public (Abramowitz and Saunders 1998,
2000; Hetherington 2001; Levine, Carmines, and Huckfeldt 1997).

Consistent with this research showing a greater ideological orientation among the American public than traditionally thought, scholars have
found that citizens' performance evaluations of a variety of governmental
actors are based at least partly on ideological or issue proximity. Specifically, ideological discrepancy has been shown to significantly contribute
to Americans' performance evaluations of the president (Ragsdale 1991)
and of individual members of Congress (Binder, Maltzman, and Sigelman 1998). If the public can make policy-based judgments of the performance of individual members of Congress, it seems plausible that they
could do the same with regard to the performance of the collective Congress. Whether or not they actually do so remains an open question.[9]
However, some real-world evidence leads us to suspect this is the case.

In April 2005, public approval of Congress dropped significantly after
Congress passed legislation attempting to help keep Terri Schiavo—a severely brain-damaged woman—on life support. Polls conducted concur-
rently showed that over three-quarters of Americans opposed this policy
action. Given this evidence, several media commentaries speculated that
Congress's policy action with regard to Schiavo was partly responsible for
the drop in congressional approval (e.g., Harwood 2005). This was not

merely an isolated incident during the period of Republican control in Congress. In the late 1990s, some Republican representatives, such as Brian Bilbray, complained that while the right-wing agenda of the leadership in Congress delighted conservative citizens, it was hurting public approval of Congress among moderate Americans, such as those in his home district (Rosenbaum 1998). In July 1999, Representative Michael Forbes of New York cited this very reason in explaining his decision to leave the Republican Party to become a Democrat (Dao 1999).

Political Effects of Congressional Approval

Moving from the issue of how Americans evaluate Congress to the issue of whether such evaluations have any political impact, one again finds voices at odds with the conventional wisdom in political science. Many of these voices come from the political world itself, where members of Congress, the news media, and political pundits have begun to recognize the potential electoral importance of congressional approval ratings. This was particularly noticeable during the 2006 elections. In April 2006, Senator John McCain predicted, "We Republicans are going to have a tough race in 2006 because the country is not happy with us. We have a 25 percent approval rating in Congress" (Pierce 2006). In September, the *New York Times* ran a front-page story on Congress's low approval rating, noting the potential ramifications.

> Across the board, the poll found marked disenchantment with Congress, highlighting the opportunity Democrats see to make the argument for a change in leadership and to make the election a national referendum on the performance of a Republican-controlled Congress. (Nagourney and Elder 2006)

Other journalists were similarly broadcasting alarms for the Republican Congress that year, noting that the low levels of congressional approval were eerily similar to the levels prevailing prior to the electoral tidal wave that hit the Democratic Congress in 1994 (e.g., Traub 2006). The electoral implications of congressional approval ratings have also been noted in years where no major electoral tide was evident. One particularly astute observer of American politics, David Broder (1996), credited Republicans' relative success in the 1996 elections to a moderated legislative strategy that "boosted public approval of Congress and made it harder for Democratic challengers to press their case."

Even evidence in existing scholarly research provides reason to question conventional thinking in political science that congressional evaluations have no electoral consequences. To begin, we know that candidates
for Congress are not judged merely on their own individual merits. Literature on retrospective voting demonstrates that Americans' congressional
votes are partly based on their performance evaluations of the president
(Fiorina 1981). If Americans were to view the president as overwhelmingly responsible for national policy, it would make sense not to consider
the influence of other institutional evaluations. There is, however, ample
evidence that Americans actually view Congress as a more powerful institution than the presidency and as the branch that is more responsible for
a variety of policy areas (Hibbing and Theiss-Morse 1995; Rudolph
2003). Given Americans' belief that congressional performance is at least
as consequential as presidential performance and given that a winning
congressional candidate will have more impact on congressional performance than on executive performance, it would be strange if voters based
their congressional ballot solely on their evaluation of the president and
not on their evaluation of Congress. Yet there is minimal systematic research on whether and how voters use congressional evaluations when
making a decision in congressional elections.[10]

Finally, even if Americans consider congressional performance as
one factor when voting for Congress, is there any reason to think that this
would affect congressional behavior? While Fenno's impression from
traveling with House members in the early 1970s was of members almost
uniformly unconcerned about low institutional approval, more recent
research paints a very different picture. In a survey of House members
serving in 1997–98, Lipinski (2004) finds that over two-thirds of representatives themselves believe that low congressional approval harms the
reelection prospects of majority party incumbents. He goes on to argue
that member concern over congressional approval ratings helps drive at
least one aspect of congressional behavior: communications with constituents. Specifically, Lipinski finds that members of the majority party
actively try to improve the institution's image by portraying it in a positive light in the mailings they send to constituents.[11] For our purposes,
this finding has two important implications. First, as with John McCain's
comments previously cited, it suggests that politicians perceive a real
electoral threat from congressional disapproval, even though the academic world generally has not. Second, if congressional approval drives
incumbent behavior when it comes to communications, it seems logical
that it could also have an impact on their policy behavior.

In sum, although the prevailing academic view is that Americans do not seek policy responsiveness from the collective Congress and that Congress is unlikely to provide it in return, other political observers raise doubts about the accuracy of this portrait. Given the conflicting perspectives presented in the two previous sections and given the surprising dearth of empirical evidence specific to this question, it is simply impossible to say for sure what we know and what we do not know. What is missing is a specific theory about how Americans use policy considerations to evaluate the performance of Congress and how such evaluations lead to congressional policy responsiveness, with systematic empirical tests of each element of that argument.

OUR ARGUMENT

The idea that citizens think in policy terms and attempt to hold government accountable in elections is certainly not new (Downs 1957; Key 1966). What is new is applying these concepts to public evaluations of the collective Congress. Building on the strands of literature hinting that both the American public and Congress are more capable of forming a responsive democratic system than expected, we argue that Americans do make policy-based evaluations of Congress and do use these evaluations in elections. Additionally, in doing so, the public provides the electoral threat or reward necessary for Congress and its members to be responsive to the public's judgments and preferences. In the remainder of this section, we lay out the argument that we make throughout the course of this book.

We argue that, just as Americans prefer their president and their own member of Congress to be in sync with their personal political outlook, they also prefer that the collective institution of Congress be so. For citizens to gauge whether this is the case, they must have at least a basic understanding or knowledge level about Congress and its actions. If existing research is correct, this requirement is unrealistic—citizens cannot even name the majority party in Congress on a regular basis. However, consistent with research in political psychology, we argue that the public can have an overall impression of what Congress is doing even if they cannot cite relevant facts and details at a given point in time. While Americans may not pay close attention to the institution's daily actions, they nevertheless form a general sense of its policy direction based on bits of information absorbed in various forms, including from coverage of major policy actions in the media, from member communications, or indirectly through opinion leaders who are more attentive to public affairs.

Because Americans have the capacity to gauge the policy orientation of Congress, they also have the ability to compare it with their own ideological or policy preferences and make judgments of Congress based partly on how well they feel Congress represents their views. At the end of the day, when asked to evaluate congressional job performance, citizens who perceive the general ideological stance of Congress as distant from their own preferences will be more likely to give Congress low marks for performance, while those who feel that congressional actions match their preferences will be more likely to give the institution positive ratings.

Citizens use these evaluations of congressional representation, along with other factors, when voting in congressional elections. Retrospective voting theory contends that voters who are unhappy with the performance of government hold the party in power accountable during elections. While the prevailing view of retrospective voting in congressional elections is that these elections are a referendum on the performance of the president, we believe that voters also hold Congress accountable for its own performance during elections, much in the same way they do the president. In accord with retrospective voting theory, voters evaluate the performance of Congress, observe—either consciously or unconsciously—which party is in control of the institution, and then hold the majority party responsible for congressional performance. On election day, voters reward or punish candidates from the majority party based partly on their evaluations of Congress. In particular, voters who approve of the job Congress has done will be more likely to vote for congressional candidates from the majority party. Voters who disapprove of Congress's performance will be less likely to vote for congressional candidates from the majority party.

Voters' use of congressional evaluations in their electoral choices leads to larger systemic effects. First, public evaluations of Congress affect the decision making of strategic politicians who are considering a run for Congress. Existing literature finds that experienced politicians are alert to meaningful tides in public opinion that could affect their potential electoral fortunes (Jacobson and Kernell 1983). To date, the literature has not considered the possible effects of tides in congressional performance evaluations. But if politicians recognize that congressional approval affects voting, they will react strategically to this aspect of their electoral context. When public approval of Congress is low, this represents an electoral threat to majority party candidates. Therefore, politically experienced candidates will be more likely to challenge majority party incumbents, while majority party incumbents will be more likely to retire. Since disapproval of Congress does not represent a threat to minority party candidates, it will not increase challenges to or retirements by minority party incumbents.

Finally, public evaluations of one Congress significantly affect the ideological makeup of the next Congress. When approval of Congress is low, the combined effects of having less appeal among voters, sustaining more retirements, and facing stronger challengers will mean that more members of the majority party are replaced with minority party candidates who have distinctly different ideological outlooks than their predecessors. Furthermore, incumbents who do manage to win reelection when the public disapproves of Congress will recognize the change in the electoral landscape and react accordingly, shifting subtly away from the ideological positions taken by the majority party prior to the election. The collective result of majority party members being replaced with minority party members while incumbents move away from the majority party will be a shift in the overall policy behavior of Congress. Specifically, the more the public disapproves of Congress before an election, the more the next Congress will shift away from the previous majority party position.

While each piece of our argument is important, the most significant point is the larger story it tells about congressional policy responsiveness. When Americans register their disapproval with the performance of Congress, they do so in part because they are unhappy with the policy actions of Congress as run by the majority party. By factoring this policy-related institutional evaluation into their congressional votes, along with other political considerations, citizens are able to affect the overall ideological profile of their Congress. This entire process provides a portrait of both Congress and the American public that may prove surprising to some. Scholars in particular have found fault with both the citizenry and the government for not fulfilling their democratic responsibilities. Our theory argues that to some extent, they actually do.

METHODOLOGICAL APPROACH

Because our argument runs somewhat counter to standard expectations and because these specific issues have generally not been subjected to systematic empirical analysis, our methodological approach in this book is to test the predictions of our hypotheses at each stage of the argument, using a wide variety of data sources and research methods. We present both individual and aggregate empirical evidence covering more than three decades of congressional history and public opinion. Our data include not only traditional survey data but also a survey experiment, panel data, election returns, and roll call voting records, among other data.

This pluralistic empirical approach has two main benefits over the limited empirical work to date on this topic, much of which has relied on one type of analysis using data from one particular point in time. First, showing support for our arguments regardless of which method is used to test them provides a high degree of confidence that our claims are accurate, not merely an artifact of any one particular analytical technique. Second, showing support for our arguments across a large time frame and a wide range of historical contexts (e.g., Democratic as well as Republican majority Congresses) helps demonstrate that our findings are generalizable beyond any single period or political environment.

PLAN OF THE BOOK

In the remainder of this book, we systematically address each aspect of our argument and discuss the overall implications of our findings. Chapter 2 examines the basic question of whether or not Americans even care about the policy representativeness of the collective Congress. If they do not, there is no point in taking additional steps to explore their capacity to evaluate Congress along such lines. We begin by reviewing the limited empirical research on this specific question and find some evidence that is surprisingly supportive of our view. We then introduce a survey experiment we designed to test whether or not there is a causal relationship between the policies Congress pursues and citizens' evaluations of congressional job performance. We present original data from this experiment demonstrating that Americans do recognize and react to certain policy actions of the collective Congress. In particular, we find that self-described conservatives become substantially less approving of Congress after hearing about a specific liberal policy action Congress has taken, while liberals become a bit more approving.

Chapter 3 looks at the question of how much Americans really know about Congress. We begin by reviewing the scholarly debate over the informational capacity of the public. Building on existing work in this area, we present an argument explaining how it is possible for Americans to gain a general sense of the policy direction of Congress even while they may score poorly on factual survey questions about Congress. Our argument predicts that public evaluations of congressional performance will change systematically when salient aspects of Congress change—even among citizens traditionally viewed as less knowledgeable. Taking advantage of natural pseudoexperiments afforded by actual changes in party control, we analyze an American National Election Studies (ANES) panel survey conducted before and after the 1995 change in party control in the House and Senate, original surveys we commissioned before and after the 2001 midsession change in party control of the Senate alone, and media surveys of opinion changes during the early days of the 1995 and 2007 sessions of Congress. Our findings support the claim that most Americans—not just a small, politically savvy segment, as is typically thought—possess enough information about Congress to at least partly base their judgments of the institution on its policy orientation.

Chapter 4 elaborates on Americans' understanding and use of ideology and then puts discussion of this issue together with the parts of the story presented in the two previous chapters to test our full theory of how Americans judge congressional performance. We argue that Americans evaluate the job performance of Congress based partly on their perceived ideological distance from Congress as run by the majority party, with greater distance leading to less approval. We test this argument in two ways. First, to test the effect of ideological distance on an individual citizen's approval of Congress, we analyze ANES surveys from thirteen different Congresses with available data (1980–2004). Even after controlling for other important factors—including partisanship, presidential approval, congressional process concerns, and the national economy— we find that in each Congress, the more ideologically distant a citizen is from the majority party in Congress, the less likely it is that the citizen will approve of Congress's job performance. Second, we test whether the effect of ideological distance we find among individuals is replicated at the level of aggregate approval ratings of Congress. Using a quarterly time series of congressional approval ratings from 1974 through 2006, we demonstrate that increases in the overall ideological divergence between the public and Congress decrease the percentage of people who approve of Congress, while reductions in the ideological divergence between the public and Congress increase the percentage who approve of Congress.

Chapter 5 analyzes whether Americans take into account their retrospective evaluations of Congress when casting their congressional ballots.

We theorize that disapproval of Congress decreases voting for majority party candidates. We then test this prediction in two ways. First, we use ANES surveys from 1980 through 2004 to see whether individual voters who disapprove of Congress are less likely to vote for majority party candidates in House elections. Next, we use actual election returns from 1974 through 2006 to test whether individual majority party candidates for the House receive a smaller share of the vote when public disapproval of Congress is high, compared to when it is low. In both tests, the evidence demonstrates that across all race types—whether there is an incumbent from the majority or minority party or the seat is open—Americans are indeed less likely to vote for majority party candidates when they disapprove of Congress and more likely to vote for them when they approve.

Chapter 6 looks at the potential effect of congressional approval ratings on candidates' strategic decisions of whether or not to run for Congress. Specifically, we analyze the effect of congressional approval ratings on the decision of experienced candidates to challenge an incumbent and on the decision of incumbents to retire rather than run for reelection. We test our model at the level of the individual House race, using data covering every contested House election from 1974 through 2006. Consistent with our expectations, we find that incumbents from the majority party are more likely to face experienced challengers and more likely to retire when approval of Congress is low, while incumbents from the minority party are not.

Chapter 7 addresses a question at the heart of this book: is Congress responsive to public evaluations of its performance? We analyze two ways in which ideological responsiveness might be achieved: through incumbent replacement and through incumbent adjustment. First, adding congressional approval to a standard model of congressional seat swing, we find that greater disapproval of Congress significantly increases the number of seats lost by the House majority party. Using ideological scale scores of House members developed by Poole and Rosenthal (1997), we further show that partisan change in a seat almost always produces ideological change. Second, we demonstrate that greater disapproval of Congress also produces a greater shift by reelected House members away from the average ideological position of the majority party in the previous Congress—though this effect is much less dramatic. Finally, we demonstrate that the combined result of these two effects is that greater disapproval of Congress actually shifts the average ideological preference and average winning policy outcome in the House away from the position of the majority party in the previous Congress.

In chapter 8, we conclude with a reassessment of the conventional scholarly wisdom regarding public evaluations of Congress. We also discuss the broader implications of our findings for the study of public opinion, Congress, and democratic responsiveness.

CHAPTER 2

Responding to Congressional Policy

One of our main arguments in this book is that the public responds to congressional policy behavior when evaluating the performance of Congress. As we discussed in the introduction, this argument is consistent with the thinking of many political commentators and members of Congress themselves, but key elements of the argument may raise some eyebrows in the scholarly community. The first such element is our argument that Americans desire policy representation from Congress. The second is our argument that Americans are able to obtain reasonable information regarding Congress's general policy leanings. The final element is our contention that Americans are capable of processing this information and using it in a reasonable way to judge Congress. To demonstrate that our overall argument regarding policy concerns is valid, we need to provide evidence in support of each of these particular points.

In this chapter, we momentarily put aside questions of Americans' informational capabilities (addressed in chap. 3) and precisely how Americans process policy information (addressed in chap. 4). We here focus specific attention on the first question: do Americans care about policy representation by Congress? We review existing evidence and discuss some of the difficulties past studies have had in attempting to address this particular issue. We then introduce our own methodological approach: a controlled survey experiment. By specifically providing individuals with select policy information about Congress, we are able to isolate the question of whether or not they choose to use that policy information when evaluating Congress. After presenting the results, we conclude with a discussion of what we have (and have not) learned from this exercise, placing it in the larger context of our overall argument and our pluralistic research strategy.

EXISTING STUDIES

Existing research demonstrates that Americans use multiple criteria to evaluate the job performance of Congress. In particular, many studies find that citizens consider the state of the national economy when making their judgments about how well Congress is doing its job (Durr, Gilmour, and Wolbrecht 1997; Parker 1977; Patterson and Caldeira 1990; Rudolph 2003; Stimson 2004). Positive perceptions of the national economy can help to boost approval of Congress, while negative perceptions can lead to disapproval. At the same time, many studies find that citizens also at least partly base their evaluations of Congress on the *way* in which Congress does its job (Hibbing and Theiss-Morse 1995, 2002; see also Fenno 1975; Parker and Davidson 1979). If people perceive congressional processes to be too inefficient or too unfair (biased toward special interests), they are less likely to approve of Congress's job performance. Overall, there is strong evidence that both of these factors—economic concerns and process concerns—contribute to Americans' evaluations of Congress.

While we do not dispute the significant role played by economic and process concerns, we believe that there is another important factor contributing to Americans' judgments of Congress: a desire for policy representation. The idea that Americans might want their policy views to be represented in government is not new to scholars. As discussed in chapter 1, it is featured prominently in classic theoretical treatments of politics, such as in the work of Anthony Downs (1957). Empirical studies have confirmed that policy compatibility significantly affects public evaluations of the job performance of other political actors, including the president (Ragsdale 1991) and individual members of Congress (Binder, Maltzman, Sigelman 1998). Similarly, we believe that a desire for policy compatibility also contributes to public attitudes toward the collective Congress. The more information a citizen receives indicating that Congress is acting contrary to his or her own policy preferences, the less likely that citizen will be to approve of Congress, all else being equal.

The feature of our theory that distinguishes it from other theories of congressional evaluation is its focus on policy content. The idea is somewhat analogous to Mayhew's (1974) discussion of the public's interest in position taking on the part of their own individual member of Congress. Mayhew says that the most important aspect of position taking is that a member takes policy positions that align with the positions of his or her constituents, not that a member's positions necessarily carry the day or that a member devotes a great deal of effort during the legislative process: "The position itself is the political commodity" (62). In a similar fashion, we argue that citizens care about the policy representativeness of the actions of the collective Congress, independent of their other concerns about particular outcomes achieved or the manner in which those decisions are reached.

As we also noted in chapter 1, aspects of our argument about Americans' desire for policy representation by Congress appear to contrast with the basic thrust of earlier and more general research on the formation of political attitudes among the American public—in particular, the long-standing impression that Americans are not much concerned with policy (e.g., A. Campbell et al. 1960). However, other existing research suggests that the public does care about policy representation from Congress. While scholars have performed very few direct tests that are appropriate for evaluating our particular theory, what little evidence does exist is surprisingly supportive of our argument, given the skeptical tone of the prevailing scholarly wisdom.

In *Congress as Public Enemy*, Hibbing and Theiss-Morse (1995) present a regression analysis of congressional job approval. In a footnote to their analysis, the authors also report that in an alternative specification, a variable measuring a person's ideological difference from Congress behaves precisely as our argument would predict—with greater ideological difference from Congress leading to lower approval.[1] In a subsequent analysis of congressional approval, Hibbing and Theiss-Morse (2002) use a citizen's perceived difference from recent national policies as an explanatory variable.[2] Here again, consistent with our argument, they find this measure of policy difference to have a "highly significant" negative effect on approval of Congress. The effect is also quite substantive. While the authors' central focus is on the effect of their process variable (also significant), the results show that policy concerns have the strongest effect of any variable in their model, including party identification, economic concerns, and process concerns. Using a different model specification, Hibbing and Larimer (2005) find that a variable measuring whether respondents like recent policies has the most powerful effect in the model—greater than party identification or concern with processes. The authors conclude that "approval is undeniably connected to policy satisfaction" (73). Thus, even in studies that focus on elements other than policy concerns, the empirical evidence supports the idea that Americans care about policy representation.

Other cross-sectional analyses of congressional evaluations have tested different measures of policy compatibility and found strong effects. Wlezien and Carman (2001) find that the distance between a person's ideological self-rating and the entire sample's mean ideological rating of Congress significantly affects that person's favorability toward Congress on a hundred-point scale.[3] In previously published work (on which we expand in chap. 4), we have found that an individual's ideological distance from the majority party in Congress significantly contributes to disapproval of Congress (Jones and McDermott 2002; Jones 2003).

That results from multiple empirical studies—each using different data sources, different model specifications, and different measures of policy compatibility—all tend to find the same pattern of positive results provides solid support for our argument. At a minimum, one can safely conclude that policy compatibility with Congress, variously measured, significantly and consistently correlates with an individual's approval of Congress. These empirical results should not, however, be viewed as the last word on this question.

One common feature of the aforementioned studies, both those in support of and those in opposition to our argument, is that they rely exclusively on standard cross-sectional survey data. A negative consequence of this reliance is that such studies have no control over what information respondents have or do not have about the policy actions of Congress. As a result, researchers cannot be sure that the effects of self-reported policy differences on congressional evaluations can be definitively attributed to knowledge of actual policy actions taken by Congress. For example, it may be that individuals who do not approve of Congress for reasons unrelated to policy tell a pollster that they think Congress is distant from their own policy views, while those who approve of Congress merely project their own policy views onto it. If true, this could account for a statistical correlation between the variables even if policy difference was not a causal contributor to the opinion.

Put simply, because existing research on this subject does not—and cannot—fully control for actual respondent information about congressional policy, we cannot know whether or not policy compatibility truly contributes to evaluations of Congress. To demonstrate that part of what Americans want from Congress is policy representation, it is necessary to augment existing research with a method of analysis that provides the researcher with a greater degree of control over what information individuals actually have about Congress. In the next section, we discuss how experimental research methods are particularly well suited for this task.

EXPERIMENTAL METHOD

When researchers are interested in demonstrating that x leads to y—in our case, that congressional policy action leads to public attitudes or attitude change—they face various trade-offs between method of analysis and certainty of conclusions. Scholars have traditionally measured conclusion certainty through two concepts—internal validity and external validity. Internal validity is the extent to which the researchers can be certain that the conclusions they are drawing are actually causal.[4] External validity is the extent to which the results can be generalized over populations, situations, and stimuli. At one time, demonstrating both types of validity in one single study was considered nearly impossible, due to the nature of available methods. Attitude surveys, the dominant method in political science research from the 1940s through the 1990s, could hope only to offer external validity, not to establish causal connections. Laboratory experiments, a method that started to gain ground in the field in the late 1980s, were considered the only possible way to ensure internal validity, but their limited generalizability outside the lab led many to cast them a skeptical eye. As a result, a new, hybrid model has been gaining ground in the study of political science.

Given the strengths and weaknesses of both surveys and experiments, research in the last decade or so has taken to combining the two in an attempt to maximize study reliability, rather than accept the traditional trade-off (Sniderman and Grob 1996). One such hybrid is the telephone survey experiment. In a common version of the telephone survey experiment, survey respondents are randomly assigned to groups that are each read different information by the interviewer before all answering the same attitudinal question. In this survey design, any significant differences in measured attitudes among the groups can definitively be attributed to the stimulus presented to each group—or not presented, in the case of a control group. In other words, one can establish a causal connection. Furthermore, as with standard telephone surveys, subjects are at home in their natural setting rather than in a lab. If the stimulus is modeled after real-world stimuli and the researcher takes some minimal steps to disguise its true purpose, it is possible to minimize potential concerns about experimental artificiality, while at the same time increasing the researcher's ability to draw causal inferences.

Because of the benefits provided by telephone survey experiments, we chose such a design to test whether policy concerns causally contribute to public evaluations of Congress. Through an in-kind grant of telephone survey time from Time-sharing Experiments for the Social Sciences,[5] our survey was conducted by Indiana University's Center for Survey Research between October and December 2004. The basic design of the experiment measured citizens' evaluations of congressional performance following exposure to stimuli delivered randomly to separate samples of respondents. The experiment also included a control group that received no stimulus. The stimuli were brief synopses of actual news stories relating to congressional actions. To avoid signaling the true purpose of the experiment to participants, the stimuli were presented in the guise of a question about how much the subject had heard or read about a recent news report on Congress.

To address our central research question, our experimental design included three possible conditions, to which the survey randomly assigned respondents. The first condition was the control condition—respondents in this condition received no story about the government or Congress before being asked to evaluate congressional job performance. To test our argument regarding public responsiveness to congressional policy behavior, we created two stimulus conditions, one liberal policy condition and one conservative policy condition. Table 2.1 contains the text of the statements used as experimental stimuli.

The resulting experiment tested for the separate effects of both liberal and conservative policies generated by the Republican-controlled 108th Congress. Both ideological conditions used real stories regarding federal spending on the Medicaid program of health care assistance to

TABLE 2.1. Experimental Condition Questions

CONDITION	STIMULUS
Liberal policy condition	"This past year, the current Congress passed an omnibus bill that included an additional ten BILLION dollars in spending for Medicaid, thereby increasing health care assistance for low-income Americans, but also increasing government spending."
Conservative policy condition	"In the current Congress, both the House and Senate have passed budget bills for 2005 that plan to cut as much as eleven BILLION dollars from Medicaid, thereby decreasing government spending, but also decreasing health care assistance for low-income Americans."

the poor. In the liberal condition, we used Congress's action in 2003 to increase Medicaid spending by ten billion dollars (in temporary relief) to aid states that were having difficulties funding the program. In the conservative condition, we used the congressional budget bills in 2004 that proposed Medicaid cuts of approximately eleven billion dollars. Each condition mentioned both the fiscal impact of the action (increasing versus decreasing government spending) and the social impact (increasing versus decreasing federal aid to health care for the poor), in an effort to avoid having only one of these two dimensions dominating. In other words, to respond positively to the liberal message, one must not only approve of increasing aid to the poor but also accept increased federal spending to get it—a consistently liberal stance.

The survey measured attitudes toward Congress using a typical question on job performance: "Do you approve or disapprove of the way the U.S. Congress is handling its job?" In addition, the survey included standard demographic variables and other variables that have been shown to impact perceptions of Congress, including ideology, party identification, and approval of one's own member of Congress.

Our general argument is that when a citizen hears information that Congress is taking actions consistent with her or his own policy preferences, this information will make that citizen more likely to approve of Congress's job performance. Conversely, when a citizen hears information that Congress is taking actions divergent from her or his own policy preferences, this information will make that citizen less likely to approve of Congress's job performance. Based on this general argument, we can derive some specific predictions about what we expect to see in the data.

First, since we asked respondents about an actual Congress, not a hypothetical one, we can expect that they already had a baseline evaluation of that Congress from real-world information they heard in advance of our survey. In particular, many of the actions of the Republican-controlled 108th Congress that received significant attention in the news media were decidedly conservative. Two of the most prominent congressional actions of 2003 were a bill cutting taxes by 350 billion dollars and enactment of the Partial Birth Abortion Ban Act, which outlawed the late-term abortion procedure of intact dilation and extraction. In 2004, Congress enacted another 143 billion dollars in tax cuts for businesses and passed the Unborn Victims of Violence Act ("Laci and Conner's Law"), making it a crime to harm a fetus during commission of one of a number of violent federal crimes. Because the real-world 108th Congress generally took more conservative actions than liberal ones, we expect that independent of our intervention, conservatives would already be somewhat more approving of Congress and liberals somewhat less approving. We will be able to test this expectation by looking at congressional evaluations within the control group. The control group received no new information during the survey, so its evaluations are based only on preexisting, real-world information.

These baseline views must be taken into account when making predictions about our experimental results. In a perfectly controlled experiment, we could deny subjects any information about Congress except our own stimuli. The resulting neutral baseline would lead to the expectation that the liberal experimental condition should display the same magnitude of an effect as the conservative experimental condition, but in the opposite direction. If, however, baseline views are not neutral—as we suggest they are not—we would not expect the liberal condition to have the same type of observable effect as the conservative condition. If citizens already view the Republican Congress as conservative, a story about that Congress taking a conservative action would not necessarily change people's views very much. Instead, the intervention's main effect would be to reinforce subjects' preexisting views. Unfortunately, such a reinforcement effect, though it may be very important, is essentially unobservable in the context of this experiment. The most we could hope to observe is that liberals, who already tend to disapprove of Congress, may be a bit more disapproving if they hear the conservative policy story, while conservatives, who already tend to approve of Congress, may be a bit more approving if they hear the story. In other words, while we may see marginal effects, we do not expect them, because attitude reinforcement, rather than change, is the most likely scenario.

In contrast, a story about a liberal action by this Congress does not simply reinforce preexisting information. The liberal experimental condition thus provides a more readily interpretable test of the effect that new information has on citizens' evaluations of Congress. We expect to find that liberals who hear about the liberal policy action are significantly more approving of Congress than liberals in the control group, while conservatives who hear about the liberal policy action are significantly less approving than conservatives in the control group.

While we do not necessarily expect to see a significant effect from our conservative condition, it still plays an important role in confirming that policy representation matters. For example, if we find that both the liberal and the conservative conditions reduce approval among conservatives, we could not claim that respondents were reacting to the ideological aspect of the story. Instead, we have to consider the possibility that conservatives dislike all government actions—both liberal actions and conservative ones—and thus that respondents react more to the very act of legislating than to its ideological content.

Finally, it is worth noting one aspect of this experiment that makes it an especially stringent test of our argument. Existing studies show that while evaluations of Congress do change, the most significant predictor of approval of Congress at a given point in time is previous approval of Congress (e.g., Durr, Gilmour, and Wolbrecht 1997). This suggests that preexisting opinions of Congress tend to remain very stable, and stable opinions are unlikely to be easily changed by a single piece of information provided by a stranger over the telephone. Given this backdrop, any experimental effects we find will provide sound evidence for our hypothesis that people care about and respond to policy information about Congress.

FINDINGS

Table 2.2 presents a simple overview of our survey experiment data. The first data column reports the baseline evaluations of congressional performance—those held by the control group. As expected, we see a preexisting difference in evaluations depending on a respondent's ideological views. Only 34 percent of liberals approve of Congress, 57 percent of moderates approve, and 66 percent of conservatives approve, as one would expect in reaction to a Republican-controlled Congress with a relatively conservative policy agenda.[6]

Our main interest is in comparing these baseline opinions to the opinions in our experimental conditions, to analyze how subjects are affected by each of the ideological stories we provided as stimuli. We predicted that in the liberal condition, when citizens are given information that Congress is taking a liberal policy action, this new information will produce opinion patterns different from those we would normally expect based on the control group. Specifically, liberals who would normally be extremely unsupportive of Congress should be more supportive than usual after hearing about a liberal policy action, and conservatives who would normally be very supportive should be less supportive than usual. However, we do not necessarily expect this single piece of new information to override all other information citizens have already absorbed about Congress, ideological or otherwise.

The results in the second data column of table 2.2 provide some initial empirical support for our theory. Given the story of a liberal congressional policy action—that Congress increased Medicaid spending (and thereby both health care spending for the poor and federal expenditures) by ten billion dollars—both moderates and conservatives became more negative in their opinions of Congress, with conservatives reacting the most. Moderate subjects' approval of Congress registered nine points lower in the liberal scenario than in the control condition, and conservatives' approval registered ten points lower. Both of these differences from the control group are statistically significant and relatively sizable.[7]

The liberal experimental condition does not appear to have a significant effect on the attitudes of liberal respondents in this test, but this may be due to aggregation. If we exclude respondents who merely "lean" liberal from inclusion in the liberal category, we do see higher levels of approval among liberals exposed to the liberal policy condition.

TABLE 2.2. Evaluations of Congress by Experimental Condition and Respondent Ideology

RESPONDENT IDEOLOGY	CONGRESSIONAL EVALUATION	EXPERIMENTAL CONDITION		
		CONTROL	LIBERAL	CONSERVATIVE
Liberal	Approve	34%	33%	41%
	Disapprove	66%	67%	59%
	γ		.00	.09
			($p = 1.00$)	($p = .50$)
Moderate	Approve	57%	48%	46%
	Disapprove	43%	52%	54%
	γ		−.26	−.27
			($p = .08$)	($p = .06$)
Conservative	Approve	66%	56%	66%
	Disapprove	34%	44%	34%
	γ		−.26	−.04
			($p = .02$)	($p = .73$)
Total N		206	194	216

Source: Experimental data collected for the authors by Time-sharing Experiments for the Social Sciences, National Science Foundation grant no. 0094964, Diana C. Mutz and Arthur Lupia, principal investigators.

Note: Gammas and corresponding *p*-values are based on each experimental condition compared to the control group, using the four-category approval variable including categories of "somewhat" and "strongly" approve/disapprove. Categories are collapsed (and "don't know" responses omitted) for presentation.

Unfortunately, the relatively small number of respondents in the "strong liberal" and "liberal" categories (thirty combined) prevents us from drawing confident conclusions here about this potential effect.

We predicted that the conservative experimental condition would work differently than the liberal one. Because citizens already appeared to view Congress as conservative based on real-world information (as observed in the control group), we expected that our own story of a conservative action by Congress would not produce much of an observable effect, if any. Table 2.2 demonstrates that this is indeed the case. The results for the conservative condition (reported in the last column of table 2.2) do not display effects comparable to those in the liberal condition. The control group's pattern of opinions in column 1 suggests that most citizens already viewed Congress as conservative independent of any intervention on our part. Not surprisingly, hearing our story about Congress taking a conservative policy action does not appear to have changed this prevailing impression much at all: overall, opinions of Congress do not display any systematic differences compared to the control group.

Taken together, the results of the liberal condition and the conservative condition allow us to draw two conclusions. First, the ideological direction of congressional policy action matters. It is clear that respondents were not simply reacting to the fact that *something* was done—if they had been, both the liberal and the conservative conditions would have elicited a similar response. Instead, some people appear to actually consider the ideological content of congressional actions, reacting differently to a policy action in one ideological direction than they do to a policy action in another direction. Second, new information that differs from prevailing views regarding congressional policy actions has a different impact on citizens than information that merely coincides with their preexisting impressions. In the latter case, the only effect we necessarily expect is the reinforcement of existing evaluations of Congress—an important yet subtle effect that is difficult to document empirically. In comparison, new information that differs from preexisting impressions of Congress has the potential to actually change evaluations of Congress.

As a check on the significant effects we found in table 2.2 using bivariate analysis, we also conducted a more detailed analysis through multiple regression. In particular, we wanted to be sure that the observed differences between the liberal condition and the control condition were not artificially enhanced or muted by the simplified nature of that analysis. To this end, our regression analysis offers a few key improvements. First, whereas some level of aggregation was necessary in the bivariate analysis due to a relatively small sample size, our regression analysis took into account the full range of every variable, including seven categories of respondent ideology—ranging from strong liberal to strong conservative—and five categories of congressional approval—ranging from strong disapproval to strong approval.[8] Second, our analysis controlled for other factors that can affect public evaluations of Congress.[9] Specifically, we controlled for party identification, approval of one's own member of Congress, and demographic characteristics often found to influence political opinions, including education, gender, age, income, and race. Details on the coding of all variables are contained in the appendix.[10]

We estimated the model among respondents in either the control or the liberal policy condition. A dummy variable represented the presence of the liberal policy condition, with the control condition included in the constant term. The key variable in the model, however, was the interaction between a respondent's personal ideology—higher values representing more conservatism and less liberalism—and exposure to the liberal policy condition. According to our theory, we expected to find that the interaction between a respondent's ideology and the liberal policy condition was negative and significant. Such a finding would indicate that the more conservative a person is, the more likely hearing about a liberal congressional action should reduce that person's approval of Congress compared to the control group. Conversely, the more liberal a person is, the more likely hearing about a liberal action should increase approval of Congress, relative to the control group.

The results of this test are presented in table 2.3. Consistent with our argument, the coefficient for the key interaction is negative and significant. Hearing about a liberal policy action matters, but its effect depends on one's personal ideology. Relative to the control group, a liberal action is more likely to harm evaluations of Congress among conservatives and more likely to improve evaluations of Congress among liberals. Identifying the precise effect of the liberal condition among each ideological grouping requires that we plug specific values into the model.[11]

Figure 2.1 graphs the relationship between one's location on the seven-point ideological scale and one's predicted approval of Congress, from model estimates, in both the liberal experimental condition and the control condition. Similar to the bivariate analysis, in the control condition, conservatives are much more approving of Congress than liberals. Very liberal respondents have only a 23 percent probability of approving of congressional performance, while the probability that very conservative respondents will approve is better than 50 percent. But in the liberal experimental condition, ideology displays a very different relationship with attitudes toward Congress. The additional precision afforded by the model estimates reveals that strong liberals are slightly (ten points) more likely to approve of Congress when they hear about a liberal policy action by Congress than they are in the control group. But an even bigger difference is found, as it was in the bivariate analysis, among conservatives. Strong conservatives are a dramatic twenty-nine points less likely to approve of Congress when told of a liberal congressional action than they are in the control condition, having received no such information. Hearing of a single liberal action in the Republican Congress appears to be

TABLE 2.3. Effects of Ideology and the Liberal Policy Condition on Congressional Approval

INDEPENDENT VARIABLES	CONGRESSIONAL APPROVAL
Ideology	.22°
	(.09)
Liberal condition	.76
	(.52)
Ideology × liberal condition	−.29°
	(.11)
Party identification	.21°
	(.05)
Member approval	.62°
	(.09)
Education	−.30°
	(.13)
Income	.05
	(.07)
Gender	.25
	(.20)
Age	−.02°
	(.01)
White	−.26
	(.24)
Pseudo R^2	.27
Number of cases	395

Source: Experimental data collected for the authors by Time-sharing Experiments for the Social Sciences, National Science Foundation grant no. 0094964, Diana C. Mutz and Arthur Lupia, principal investigators.
Note: Table entries are ordered logistic regression estimates (standard errors in parentheses).
°$p \leq .05$ (two-tailed)

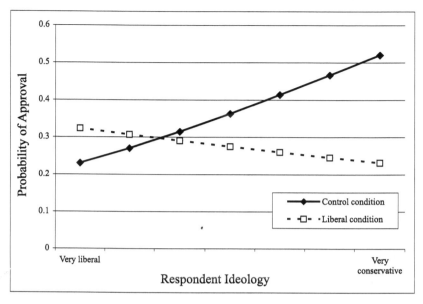

Fig. 2.1. Respondent ideology and probability of congressional approval by experimental condition. Lines represent probability transformations of the estimates in table 2.3.

enough to turn conservatives against it, presumably because they learn from that action that the legislature may not agree with their preferences after all. Yet liberals become a bit more willing to give a Republican Congress the benefit of the doubt when they hear that it at least once passes legislation that agrees with their own preferences.

CONCLUSION

In this chapter, we momentarily put aside potential concerns about the information levels and processing capabilities of Americans and focused exclusively on the question of whether Americans care about policy representation from Congress. Our review of existing studies found that despite a general tenor of skepticism among scholars, the empirical evidence has actually been relatively supportive of the proposition that Americans partly base their evaluations of Congress on policy compatibility with Congress. This was true across a variety of alternative specifications and even in studies that have chosen to emphasize other important explanatory factors.

Our review also noted these studies' exclusive reliance on standard survey data. Because standard attitude surveys do not provide adequate control over information, they cannot definitively demonstrate causal relationships in and of themselves. For this reason, we used a different methodological approach designed to address this gap in the empirical literature. Specifically, we designed a survey experiment to test whether Americans who are given information about policy actions by Congress will actually use that information to help form their public judgments of Congress. Despite the fact that our intervention was minimal—a single story, lasting an average of seventeen seconds and read by a stranger over the telephone—we found significant effects of policy information on respondents' evaluations of Congress.

Consistent with our argument, we discovered that when exposed to information about Congress taking an unexpected policy action, individuals on both sides of the ideological divide altered their opinions. Conservatives who normally approved of the Republican Congress were likely to shift from positive to negative judgments upon hearing about a liberal action that ran counter to their own preferences. At the same time, liberals became somewhat more likely to approve of Congress when hearing that it passed legislation agreeing with their policy preferences. Also as predicted, we found that when citizens heard about Congress taking actions consistent with those it had taken in the past, these individuals did not alter their evaluations.

We do not claim that our experimental findings alone should be viewed as definitive on this subject. Rather, we view them as providing important corroborating evidence for the results from some of the nonexperimental analyses that we reviewed earlier in this chapter. Taken together, these findings and results present solid empirical evidence in support of our specific claim in this chapter: Americans do appear to care about policy representation by Congress.

Of course, it may matter little that Americans care about policy representation by Congress if they are not capable of actually discerning the policy direction of Congress. In the experiment presented here, we provided citizens with policy information. While it is significant to find that Americans are able to both process and use information in this controlled test, we need to know more about whether and how people obtain similar information in the noisy and distracting environment of the real world. Specifically, can the politically inattentive and unknowledgeable public described in the public opinion literature actually absorb and understand enough information about government to divine a sense of the policy direction of Congress? In the next chapter, we delve into this second aspect of our overall hypothesis. Specifically, we address the question of Americans' capacity for collecting and processing political information in the real world.

CHAPTER 3

Failing Pop Quizzes but Passing the Test

A focus on what voters don't know and can't do misses much of what they do know and can do.
—Samuel Popkin (2006, 235)

We demonstrated in the previous chapter that Americans care about the policy orientation of Congress. What we could not tell from the preceding test, however, is whether citizens operating in the noisy environment of the real world have the ability to receive and process the information necessary to evaluate Congress in line with their personal policy preferences. While it may be relatively straightforward in an experimental survey situation, performing such a task in the confusing world of politics is another matter altogether. In fact, extensive scholarly work on American public opinion argues that the average American is incapable of such information reception and processing.

Research into the political abilities of the American public frequently argues that citizens do not have the knowledge to gauge even the general ideological direction (liberal versus conservative) of congressional policy action. If this pessimistic view on Americans' informational capacities is correct, most citizens do not have the information necessary to compare the policies emerging from Congress with their own political preferences, and most citizens would therefore not have the ability to make the policy-based performance evaluations of Congress that we hypothesize they do.

In this chapter, we have two goals. Our first, overall goal is to demonstrate that, in general, Americans do receive and use information related to the policy direction of Congress when forming and updating their evaluations of congressional job performance. Second, we specifically want to show that this ability is not restricted to a slim stratum of elite citizens but instead extends to a broad swath of Americans—even among some of those who are often viewed as thoroughly incapable of such actions.

We do not by any means argue that the American public consists of political experts. Rather, we assert that the public has ways of dealing with their information shortages. Much like the literature describing information shortcuts used by voters, in which voters rely on familiar cues to guide them (e.g., Popkin 1991), we argue that individuals are able to judge their elected leaders—specifically Congress—through mental methods (heuristics) that may not match the classic democratic ideal of full information and consideration but that do help mitigate, in practice, against their relatively low levels of political sophistication.

One of the simple yet important cues citizens could use to gauge Congress's general policy direction is knowing which party is in control of Congress. If citizens understand there are general policy differences between the two major parties and if they understand that congressional policy direction will generally follow the majority party's preferences, knowledge of party control can serve as a valuable information shortcut. It should allow anyone who has some awareness of which party controls Congress to form a reasonable sense (see, e.g., Rahn 1993) of Congress's policy leanings.

The main focus of the analyses in this chapter is an examination of whether information regarding party control of Congress can be used to help citizens evaluate congressional performance in reference to their own policy preferences. If Americans cannot ascertain and process relatively simple party cues, there is even less hope that other information will matter. Party cues are not the only information that citizens can use to gauge the policy direction of Congress, however. There may also be specific political events that become salient to citizens at certain points in time—even if only through passive contact with information. These bits of information may also be incorporated into citizens' sense of the policy direction of Congress, and we address this possibility at the end of this chapter.

While we have portrayed knowledge of congressional party control as a relatively common piece of information, many feel it is anything but common. Scholars of public opinion argue that a large segment of the American population does not know who the majority party in Congress is. Even if such politically unaware Americans could distinguish the parties from one another ideologically, they could not use these distinctions to help them judge congressional performance. The claim that Americans do not know who controls Congress stems from dismal public performance on survey tests of political knowledge. We argue, however, that factual questions on political surveys do not accurately reflect individuals' informational abilities to evaluate Congress.

We begin this chapter by reviewing the existing literature's findings on citizen competence and knowledge, as well as some alternative interpretations of these findings. Then, building on existing theories and findings in the field of political psychology, we present an argument explaining how citizens might be able to judge Congress even while failing to consistently provide correct answers to survey quizzes regarding party control. We then test the predictions of our argument using a variety of survey data—including an ANES panel survey, two original surveys of our design implemented by the Center for Survey Research and Analysis at the University of Connecticut, and several news media polls. In support of our argument, we find evidence that the general public has a sense of party control of Congress, judging Congress in a manner consistent with the ideological cue provided by this information. Furthermore, the public is aware of changes in party control of Congress, and when change occurs, they update their judgments of Congress accordingly, regardless of whether they correctly answer knowledge tests in surveys. Finally, at the end of the chapter, we present evidence that additional information besides simple party control can also affect citizens' opinions of Congress.

POLITICAL KNOWLEDGE

Classic democratic theory expects citizens in a democracy to be conscientious and engaged in order for the system to work. Over fifty years ago, Berelson, Lazarsfeld, and McPhee (1954) described the kind of information citizens need to have to contribute responsibly to a democratic system.

> The democratic citizen is expected to be well-informed about political affairs. He is supposed to know what the issues are, what their history is, what the relevant facts are, what alternatives are proposed, what the party stands for, what the likely consequences are. (308)

Not surprisingly, researchers have focused on exactly these types of information when gauging whether or not American citizens are democratically "competent." This research takes on a distinctly normative flavor by measuring what Americans do or do not know and taking them to task for any shortcomings found. Most frequently, citizens are found lacking in their levels of political information. The end result, according to many researchers, is a populace that makes low-quality decisions because its citizens are deficient in the knowledge that would help them do otherwise.

Public opinion and knowledge experts find that a lack of political knowledge limits one's ability to form "instrumentally rational" opinions (Delli Carpini and Keeter 1996; Neuman 1986; Zaller 1992). For example, Delli Carpini and Keeter (1996) find that those citizens who are the least politically knowledgeable do not connect their own ideological preferences with their stated opinions on presidential performance. These and other authors argue that individuals who do not have adequate levels of political knowledge not only do not but cannot make such connections between their personal preferences or underlying beliefs and their political judgments, opinions, or decisions.

Select research into social cognition has reached similar conclusions, finding that the politically sophisticated have a much easier time using abstract political ideas and thereby making political connections between similar issues (e.g., Judd and Downing 1990). Nonexperts, in comparison, are far less able to connect their choices on political issues in a way that would indicate political beliefs that are cohesive (as per Converse 1964). Researchers also find that people with more political knowledge are much more capable of absorbing new information into their existing political belief system. Fiske, Lau, and Smith (1990) and, more recently, Gilens (2001) demonstrate experimentally that politically knowledgeable subjects are better able to process new political information and subsequently use it in opinions or judgments than are those with little or no political knowledge.

The general conclusion from decades of this research is that the American public largely lacks the political information necessary to form opinions, judgments, or decisions based on their underlying beliefs. This conclusion has become the conventional wisdom within the field of public opinion, as well as in the discipline of political science more generally. But there is, to our eyes at least, one major flaw in the existing research in this field and its resultant conclusion.

Most of the studies of political information we have mentioned, as well as many others, measure political knowledge or sophistication in a similar way, by correct or incorrect answers to questions regarding political facts (Gilens 2001 is a notable exception). As a result, their findings are dependent on an individual's ability to answer such questions at any given point in time. The literature leads us to believe that without factual political knowledge available to an individual at the time of a survey, individuals are incapable of making decisions or judgments consistent with their own preferences, as the classic democratic model suggests they should. There is little doubt that factual survey questions about government are expeditious and seemingly logical as measures of political knowledge. We argue, however, that they are not always accurate measures of it.

We take issue with the prevailing literature for its faith in these measures as accurate gauges of knowledge. We do not challenge the normative argument that American citizens should be able to make quality political choices. Nor do we challenge the basic idea underlying this research: that political information is important to forming quality attitudes and making political decisions that are in one's own interest.[1] We do not, however, believe that factual survey questions are the best or only yardstick for measuring this ability. We posit that individuals can often make connections between their own preferences and the actions of government even without being able to correctly answer such questions when asked by survey researchers to do so.

We are not entirely alone in this contention. Other political scientists have similarly argued that democratic competence should not be defined by one's ability to answer factual questions about government. For example, in discussing tests of factual knowledge, such as Delli Carpini and Keeter's (1996), Doris Graber argues, "If citizens score poorly on such tests, it is wrong to infer that they will make unwise political decisions" (2006, 170). She finds fault, as do we, with the assumption that an inability to answer a question on factual knowledge automatically indicates political ignorance.

Such critiques as Graber's stem from two main observations. First, qualitative analyses of individuals' knowledge of politics produce results at odds with those of survey tests. For example, through focus groups on political reasoning and information, Gamson (1992) finds that citizens are far more politically savvy than typically given credit. When they are given the chance to discuss politics with others—rather than merely answer questions in a quick, one-shot survey—they demonstrate both knowledge about how politics works and the ability to make the kinds of cognitive connections between their beliefs and choices that political scientists frequently seek but fail to find among all but the most sophisticated.

A second observation underlying critiques of the assumption of citizen ignorance is that factual survey questions have many shortcomings when it comes to accurately gauging public knowledge. There has been a long-running debate in the field of political information about how exactly to measure political knowledge. This debate points out some serious problems with scholars drawing definitive conclusions in this area. Kuklinski and Quirk (2001) explicitly take the field of research to task for its lack of a conceptual framework by which to measure political knowledge. Most researchers tend to forge their own way in this regard, choosing their own particular set of questions and indices to measure political knowledge. While they may do so in ways that are logical, the end result remains that their studies are not comparable to others, and they can therefore only draw conclusions that are particular to their own technique. Kuklinski and Quirk explain, "Different studies or approaches will reach conflicting conclusions for reasons that are neither debated nor even recognized. In an important sense, such conclusions are essentially arbitrary" (289).

Scholars have also raised questions about how citizens answer the type of factual survey questions traditionally used to measure knowledge and about the subsequent validity of such questions. For example, it is well known in survey research that asking respondents factual questions about themselves and their past behavior is problematic. Given adequate time to do so, survey respondents might be able to calculate, say, how many times they have visited the doctor over the past five years, but in the immediate situation of a survey, they frequently cannot (e.g., Schwarz 1999). Asking respondents about facts that they have not directly experienced becomes even more problematic. Nadeau and Niemi (1995, 340) demonstrate that "relatively skilled, motivated" respondents are more likely to rely on contextual cues when they are not completely secure with their answer, with the result that they can sometimes answer a question wrong when they know the information but are not completely confident in its correctness. Such tendencies highlight serious caveats in the interpretation of factual questions as measures of actual knowledge.

Further undermining the reliability of factual questions, Mondak and Davis (2001) examine the role that "don't know" responses play in measuring knowledge through the use of factual survey questions. The authors find troubling evidence that "don't know" responses are not necessarily synonymous with not knowing. They argue that a respondent who knows the correct answer to a question but is less than 100 percent certain may choose not to answer the question. In many studies, such a person's "don't know" response would be considered an incorrect answer for analysis purposes. In their research, the authors find that a survey's attempts to either encourage or discourage "don't know" responses significantly affects resulting levels of "knowledge" as measured by factual questions—by as much as eighteen percentage points. Such substantial differences in results caused by one simple difference in a survey should certainly cast doubt on the wisdom of drawing strong conclusions about the public on the basis of such tests. Mondak and Davis's finding is especially significant for questions on party control of Congress, because the second most common answer to the question—the correct one being the first—is not the incorrect answer but, rather, "don't know" or no answer given. For example, in the 2004 ANES survey, when asked which party had the most members in the House prior to the election, 49 percent of respondents correctly stated the Republicans, 13 percent incorrectly said the Democrats, and 26 percent did not provide an answer.[2]

Additionally, even aspects of a survey that are completely unrelated to the questions used can impact the answers given by respondents. The survey interviewers themselves have been shown to affect whether or not people provide an answer to factual questions at all. Billiet and Loosveldt (1988) find that as interviewer training increases, so do response rates for factual questions. Given that the bulk of the answers coded as "wrong" in survey knowledge tests are effectively nonanswers ("don't know"), such minor factors as interviewer training can greatly skew our assumptions about public knowledge levels as long as we measure knowledge in this way.

The sum total of this research lends support to the idea that these factual questions do not accurately capture how much an individual citizen does or does not know about government and politics. As a result, we take a different approach to assessing whether or not citizens know enough to hold their government accountable. We believe that most citizens have a general sense of who is in control of Congress, at least at some point in time, and that this helps them update their opinions of Congress. We do not, however, expect citizens to keep this specific fact about party control foremost in their minds and quickly accessible.

HOW POLITICAL KNOWLEDGE IS USED TO FORM POLITICAL JUDGMENTS

We now turn to the question of how citizens form their judgments of political actors. In this section, we contend that by processing information as they receive it, citizens do not always need to retain factual political information—such as who controls Congress—to have attitudes consistent with their own preferences.

Research by Lodge and Stroh (1993) demonstrates how individual political attitudes can be informed without retaining corresponding factual knowledge in memory. They find that while citizens may not be able to produce political facts on demand, they can nevertheless hold impressions based on these facts. Their argument is one of "online" or "impression-driven" processing (see also Lodge, McGraw, and Stroh 1989; McGraw, Lodge, and Stroh 1990). According to their model, citizens update their attitudes as they encounter new facts, continually reacting to environmental stimuli and adjusting their attitudes and judgments accordingly. Once they have updated their judgments, they no longer have need of the specific fact or information that caused them to adjust their views. As a result, they are likely to subsequently "discard" (forget or bury) the information. Their attitudes, however, are still based on that information with which they once came into contact. This model provides an explanation for why tests of political knowledge appear to find that citizens possess limited political information: the information may have already been used to update opinions and then discarded. More important, this model supports the idea that citizens are able to make quality judgments. Lodge and Stroh explain,

> We see impression-driven processing as a reasonable and generally effective method for informing one's judgments because the summary tally is based on all of the information that the individual attends to and infers from prior experience, not the information one can recollect at some later point. (1993, 262)

In addition to its use by citizens in forming attitudes, the online method of information processing is used by voters in making political decisions. Gant and Davis (1984) argue that voters do not need to retain specific information about electoral candidates to make reasonable choices between (or among) them. Rather, voters use online processing (which Gant and Davis call "mental economy"), updating their impressions of candidates as they encounter information, then letting the original piece of information go. As a result, when survey respondents give vague or general answers to questions about candidates, the responses are enlightening (rather than being meaningless) because they are based on the respondent's actual previous knowledge about the candidate.

This argument requires, of course, that citizens occasionally come into contact with useful political information—something many researchers also doubt occurs. One of the central tenets of politics is that the public has little time, ability, or motivation to inform themselves. After all, the cost to citizens of collecting political information—specifically issue information—is thought to be quite high, because the information is not readily available and because citizens need to pay substantial time costs in collecting it and cognitive costs in processing it (Downs 1957). These information costs are frequently used to explain the woeful levels of political knowledge that researchers find among American citizens.

Information collection does not always involve high costs, however. As Fiorina (1990) points out, for example, citizens have multiple avenues of cost-free contact with political information. One example is incidental contact, such as viewing trailers for the evening news during entertainment shows or reading about current affairs in magazines in a doctor's office when no better option is available. Research also demonstrates that individuals who seek entertainment through soft news programs, such as *Oprah* or *Entertainment Tonight,* accidentally absorb political information because such programs increasingly blend political issues with entertainment (Baum 2002). Last but not least, individuals regularly acquire political information through their social networks—friends, family, and coworkers (Huckfeldt and Sprague 1995).

In a rather recent phenomenon, the public also now has access to shows that provide real, hard news under the guise of comedic entertainment. Known popularly as "fake" news shows, these comedy shows extensively and factually cover current events by mocking them. Examples of this are *The Daily Show with Jon Stewart* and *The Colbert Report* with Stephen Colbert, both of which closely followed the 2006 battle for control of Congress and regularly discuss events in Congress as part of their shows. This brings an exposure to politics that, even if a viewer is not intentionally seeking information, can affect political opinions and judgments. In an April 2006 survey by the Pew Research Center for the People and the Press, 32 percent of Americans reported having seen *The Daily Show,* and 21 percent said they watch it at least "sometimes."[3]

In these and multiple other ways, people often gather information without being aware of it. More important, they can gather information by these methods without expending any effort in collecting it. According to the model of online processing, as people gather facts in these and other ways, they can automatically update their political impressions or preferences accordingly, before discarding or possibly forgetting the information.

The model of online processing contrasts with memory-based models of judgment formation. Memory-based models require individuals to store political information in order to be able to form judgments at the time they are requested, as in a survey (see, e.g., Zaller 1992). When asked for their attitude or judgment on an issue, citizens search their memory for relevant concepts and information. They then form their opinion on the spot, based on an average of the considerations that come most easily and quickly to mind. The concepts that come to mind are usually the most recent or the most salient—making expressed opinions heavily dependent on context, as well as only valid at any one given point in time (Zaller and Feldman 1992). In this model, opinions can "change" quickly from one time point to another, because they are based not on true, underlying values but, rather, on whatever concepts are most accessible in memory at the time an individual needs to form an opinion.

If memory-based models were the only way citizens operated, it would be fair to equate poor performance on a test of political knowledge with political ignorance and inability to form politically consistent judgments. Fortunately, there is no need to decide which model is correct and which is incorrect. While the two models do offer different cognitive paths to judgment formation, they are nevertheless very compatible. Druckman and Lupia (2000) point out that these two methods can coexist and may simply be used at different times for different purposes (see also McGraw 2000). They contend that individuals are likely to use online processing when they believe they might need an impression down the road, whereas memory-based processing may suffice for targets that are less important or less permanent. This reasoning comports with the evidence that has been presented in support of each theory. Empirical evidence in support of online processing has largely come from studies regarding evaluations of political actors—targets for whom citizens would want to have existing impressions for later use (e.g., in an election). Memory-based models have more frequently been used to explain people's evaluations of less salient objects, such as attitudes toward specific or, occasionally, obscure government policies on which voters might not feel the need to run an ongoing opinion tally (Delli Carpini and Keeter 1996).

PARTY CONTROL OF CONGRESS AND
POLITICAL JUDGMENTS

Our argument in this chapter is that Americans have the ability to gauge the general policy direction of Congress even if they do not score well on specific surveys of political knowledge. Given the literature presented in the last section, we can now articulate a logical explanation as to how this could be true. We believe that citizens are often passively exposed to political information that provides important cues regarding the policy direction of Congress. Consistent with theories of online processing, citizens update their opinions of Congress using this information as it is received, then often forget the specific original information after it has been incorporated into their opinions.

Online processing has specific relevance to evaluations of Congress. As we already noted, Druckman and Lupia (2000) find that online processing is used when citizens see a future use for an impression. In previous research (e.g., Jones and McDermott 2004) and in chapter 5 of this book, we show that voters do use these evaluations in making their voting decisions in congressional elections. Thus, just as citizens have been found to use online processing to evaluate other political actors that face election (see, e.g., Gant and Davis 1984; Lodge, McGraw, and Stroh 1989), it is consistent with the literature to believe that citizens would also use online processing when evaluating Congress.

If Americans do form their impressions of Congress using online processing, an influential piece of information for them to encounter is party control of Congress. Even voters with very low information levels may be able to judge Congress in a manner consistent with their policy preferences if they use political party control as an information shortcut. We know empirically that party control of Congress is an excellent indicator of the overall policy direction of Congress. Research demonstrates that Congresses with a Republican majority take consistently and distinctly conservative policy actions, while Congresses with a Democratic majority take consistently and distinctly liberal policy actions (e.g., Poole and Rosenthal 1997). If citizens understand that there are general policy differences between the two major parties and that congressional policy

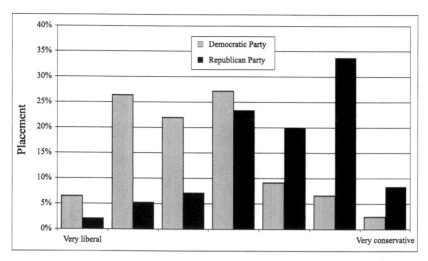

Fig. 3.1. Respondents' ideological placement of the two parties, 1980–2004. (Data from ANES 2005.)

action will generally follow the majority party's preference, knowledge of party control can serve as a valuable information shortcut, allowing anyone who has been aware of party control to obtain a reasonable sense of Congress's policy leanings. As long as citizens come into contact with this information at some point and update their attitudes toward Congress accordingly, they can judge Congress based on policy direction.

Empirical evidence suggests that citizens do understand there are general policy differences between the two major parties. Figure 3.1 provides citizens' ratings of the two major political parties on the ANES seven-point ideological scale, from 1980 through 2004. As the figure clearly shows, Americans have a reasonable sense of where the parties stand. There is a definite distinction between their ratings of Democrats and their ratings of Republicans: citizens rate Democrats as predominantly in the moderate to very liberal range, Republicans as moderate to very conservative.[4]

It also seems reasonable that the public would associate the majority party with congressional performance in general. The majority party in Congress is the most public representation of Congress and its actions in the media and, as such, is likely to be the most salient representation of the institution to Americans. Every major leadership position in Congress is given to members of the majority party, from Speaker of the

House and Senate Majority Leader down to each and every committee chair and subcommittee chair. These are the members of Congress that are most likely to show up on television and in the print media as spokespersons for Congress, defining for the public what Congress thinks and what it plans to do.

That being said, survey evidence from the ANES—discussed shortly— suggests that Americans may not actually have a very good sense of which party is in the majority in Congress. As our discussion of online processing indicates, however, such surveys may not always be the best indicators of citizen knowledge. Consistent with these theories, we believe that most Americans know, at some point, which party is in the majority and that they use this information to update their evaluations of Congress. They may not retain this original information about party control and have it available when quizzed by a survey researcher, but the evaluations of Congress shaped by that information remain.

If we are correct, we should find that citizens make evaluations of Congress that are consistent with their own preferences even if they do not always correctly answer questions about who controls Congress in a given survey. Additionally, we should find that citizens update their congressional evaluations in response to real-world changes. But before testing these empirical predictions, we first need to establish that while the results of the typical knowledge tests may seem poor, most citizens know, at some point, which party controls Congress. If so, it is possible that they have used this information to help form their judgments.

KNOWLEDGE OF CONGRESSIONAL CONTROL

The public has a decidedly mixed performance when answering the ANES question, "Do you happen to know which party had the most members in the House of Representatives in Washington before the election this/last month?" Figure 3.2 contains the percentage of correct answers given by survey respondents in most election years from 1958 to 2004. Correct answers range from a high of 73 percent (in 1996, after Republicans' historic takeover of power in Congress) to a dismally low 28 percent (in 2002, with a Republican House but a Democratic Senate), with an overall average of 57 percent correct.

These results, while not impressive, should not be taken to indicate broad ignorance on the part of the American public when it comes to congressional party control. As discussed earlier, question wording, in-

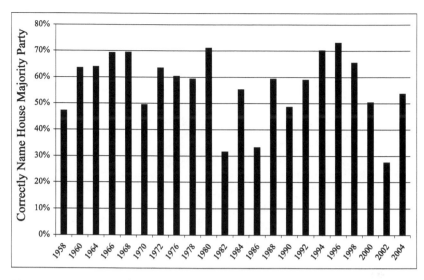

Fig. 3.2. Percentage of Americans correctly naming the House majority party, 1958–2004. (Data from ANES 2005.)

terviewer training, and other factors have a dramatic effect on respondents' ability to answer questions on factual knowledge. In the case of the ANES, a primary issue is the timing and subject of the question. The ANES asks this question after the election but asks which party controlled the House before the election. Such a retrospective fact question is a particularly challenging test for respondents.

The memory-based model states that when asked to recall facts from memory, as in this case, individuals pull up a sampling of what they have learned over time. However, it is not a random sample. Rather, it is a sample of what is most recent and/or salient (Zaller 1992; Zaller and Feldman 1992). For this reason, the postelection period should be among the hardest times for an individual to remember preelection party control. Even if control did not change, the electoral victory of one side over the other should serve to wipe clean citizens' retrospective memories of party control, according to the models of both memory-based processing (the old information is unlikely to be asked again, so discard it) and online processing (the impression has already been updated by new electoral results, so discard the previous information).

For the same reason, postelection should be a good time to ask citizens about prospective congressional control—which party is going to run Congress in the next session. The information is salient, having been amply covered in the media (Jerit, Barabas, and Bolsen 2006), as well as very recent, and should therefore still be readily available to citizens. If individuals are likely to come into contact with party control information, postelection provides a good chance. As a result, we would expect public knowledge of upcoming party control (asked directly after an election) to be much higher than public knowledge of retrospective or even current party control.

Table 3.1 contains the results of three separate postelection surveys conducted after three different elections, each measuring whether the public knew the party outcome of the general election for Congress. Unfortunately, no survey organization asks this question on a regular basis, so we must deal with limited time points: the 1994, 1996, and 2002 elections. These surveys paint a more promising picture than the ANES figures.

In each of these years, approximately four-fifths of the public was able to correctly answer which party was going to have the majority of seats come the following January, and the proportion that answered incorrectly is never greater than 9 percent. Given the usual dismal portrayals of Americans' political knowledge, these numbers are a change of pace, especially given their breadth—covering three separate elections, one in which control changed and two in which it did not, with one being a presidential-year election in which the party that won the presidency did not win Congress. Not surprisingly, the 1994 elections are followed

TABLE 3.1. Answers to Prospective Congressional Party Control Questions, Postelection

CONTROL OF NEW CONGRESS IN JANUARY	CBS NEWS 11/94[a]	WASHINGTON POST 11/96[b]	CBS NEWS/ NEW YORK TIMES 11/02[c]
Republicans (correct)	85%	80%	78%
Democrats (incorrect)	8%	9%	8%
Don't know/no answer	7%	12%	14%
Number of cases	1,120	1,205	996

[a]"When the new Congress begins in January (1995), which party will have more seats—the Republicans or the Democrats?" (poll conducted November 27–28, 1994).

[b]"Can you tell me which party, the Democrats or the Republicans, has the most members in . . . the U.S. (United States) House of Representatives . . . after the election yesterday/this past week?" (poll conducted November 6–10, 1996).

[c]"When the new Congress begins in January (2003), which party will have more seats—the Republicans or the Democrats?" (poll conducted November 20–24, 2002).

by the highest proportion answering correctly—naming the Republicans as the winning party. This is somewhat comforting. If citizens are updating their impression of Congress as information comes to them, a change in party control is the type of information necessary to maintaining a reasonably accurate impression.

These numbers demonstrate that at given points in time, very high proportions of Americans have known who was in control (or about to be in control) of Congress. These numbers do not, however, demonstrate that individuals retain this specific knowledge. Multiple studies and the ANES questions discussed earlier show that these information levels regarding party control of Congress are not sustained. In fact, in a *Washington Post* survey in November 1995, one year after the CBS News survey producing the extremely high percentage of correct responses reported in column 1 of table 3.1, those who could name the Republicans as the party in power had dropped to 61 percent.[5] For online processing to work, however, it is not necessary for the information to be retained—all that is required is initial exposure to the information so that a judgment can be formed (or updated). These figures show, at the very least, that the American public does have exposure to party control information and that, at certain points in time, as much as 85 percent can vocalize it. If online processing works, at least these 85 percent of Americans should subsequently retain impressions of Congress that are at least partly based on knowledge of party control.

TESTING THE EFFECT OF KNOWLEDGE LEVELS
ON JUDGMENTS OF CONGRESS

This section presents a simple, initial test of our argument that Americans form and update their evaluations of Congress in accord with political information such as party control, and that this is true even among those who do not retain this information in memory. More specifically, we investigate whether individuals' answers to the traditional ANES survey question regarding House party control—those who answer correctly versus those who do not—make any difference in whether their individual policy preferences predict, and presumably help determine, their judgments of Congress.

Throughout all of our tests, our general expectation is that liberals should be relatively more approving of a Democratic Congress than conservatives are (because Democratic Congresses tend to pursue a more liberal policy direction) and that conservatives should be relatively more approving of a Republican Congress than liberals are (because Republican Congresses tend to pursue a more conservative policy course).[6] While we expect these general differences between liberals and conservatives, the fact that other influences, such as the economy and congressional processes, have also been shown to affect evaluations of Congress means that we do not expect a perfect 100 percent correspondence between ideological preferences and congressional evaluations.

We conduct our first test using the 2004 ANES data, the most recent available at the time of this writing. The survey was conducted when the Republicans had a majority of seats in both the House and the Senate. If our hypothesis is correct, those who answer the question regarding House control incorrectly or who volunteer that they do not know which party is in the majority (the existing literature's standard classification for not knowing) should react to Congress in a similar fashion as those who provide the correct answer to the factual question. Specifically, in both cases, we expect liberal respondents to give the Republican Congress low marks, while conservatives give it relatively high ones.

Table 3.2 contains the results from the survey.[7] The results show that respondents who did not answer the ANES question about House control show precisely the same expected ideological difference in evaluations as those who answered correctly. Specifically, a 59 percent majority of liberals who did not answer the House majority question correctly—and who would traditionally be judged as having no sense of congressional control—nevertheless disapproved of the job Congress was doing

TABLE 3.2. Congressional Approval among Liberals and Conservatives by House Majority Question, 2004

EVALUATION OF CONGRESS	2004—REPUBLICAN CONTROL					
	CORRECT ANSWER			NOT CORRECT ANSWER		
	LIBERALS	CONSER-VATIVES	OPINION DIFFERENCE BY IDEOLOGY	LIBERALS	CONSER-VATIVES	OPINION DIFFERENCE BY IDEOLOGY
Approve	29%	62%	−33 points°	41%	64%	−23 points°
Disapprove	71%	38%		59%	36%	
Number of cases	139	191		68	112	

Source: Data from ANES 2005.
°$p \leq .01$ (two-tailed)

at the time. Conversely, conservatives in this same group expressed majority approval, at 64 percent. These results indicate a significant and substantive division of opinions in the predicted direction. Among those who answered the control question correctly, 71 percent of liberals disapproved of congressional performance, while 62 percent of conservatives approved. While the resulting division in opinions is slightly larger among those answering the factual question correctly, the results in each group follow the same pattern.

These results provide promising evidence in support of the hypothesis that citizens use online processing in forming judgments about Congress. They also support the general argument that factual survey questions are not necessarily an accurate gauge of whether or not individuals can make appropriate political judgments. Those who could not correctly recall the answer to the question about House party control in 2004 nevertheless made judgments of Congress that reflect an underlying sense of party control, as hypothesized by the online model.

TESTING THE EFFECTS OF NEW INFORMATION: HOUSE MAJORITY PARTY SWITCH

We next turn to a test of whether, in the real political world (rather than in an experimental setting), Americans update their evaluations of Congress in accord with new political information. Our experimental results in chapter 2 found that when presented with information that Congress was perhaps more liberal than most would have thought, many respondents reacted to this information as we hypothesized. In particular, conservative subjects became significantly more disapproving of Congress, and liberals became marginally more approving.

We now test whether respondents who lived through the actual shift in the direction of congressional policy following the 1994 elections—from a Democratic Congress that pursued mostly liberal policy actions to a Republican Congress that pursued mostly conservative policy actions—display a reaction consistent with our theory. We expect to find two changes. First, we predict that when control of Congress changes from a liberal party to a conservative party, citizens will update their impressions such that liberal citizens will become less approving of Congress than they were before the change, while conservatives will become more approving. Second, we again predict that this overall effect will not be driven only by changes among citizens who are "knowledgeable" (as measured by the party control question) but will also be found among those who do not answer the control question correctly.

The 1992–97 ANES panel study provides a unique opportunity to examine change in public opinion during this period. Because it is a panel study, we are able to follow the same respondents both before and after the 1995 change in congressional control, rather than being restricted to examining aggregate effects. The panel survey thus provides an appropriate and stringent test of this chapter's hypothesis, as it measures individual change in direct response to change in congressional control.

To analyze the ideological effects of the congressional power shift, we look at the change in opinions of liberals and conservatives between a time of Democratic control, 1994, and a time of Republican control, 1996. We define liberals and conservatives as those panel members who maintained a consistent ideological self-identification over the period in question.[8] Table 3.3 shows individual change in opinion among liberals and conservatives from 1994 to 1996.

The results reported in the table are consistent with our expectations. Liberals who already disapproved of Congress in 1994 remained relatively stable in their evaluations of Congress after Republicans took over: 78 percent continued to disapprove, while only 22 percent shifted to approval. But conservatives who disapproved of the Democratic Congress in 1994 exhibited a substantial shift once Republicans came to power. Only 40 percent of conservatives who had negative views of the Democratic Congress retained those views for the Republican Congress in

TABLE 3.3. Individual Change in Congressional Approval from 1994 to 1996 among Liberals and Conservatives

DEMOCRATIC (1994) TO REPUBLICAN (1996) CONTROL	LIBERALS	CONSERVATIVES
Disapprove to disapprove	78%	40%
Disapprove to approve	22%	60%
Number of cases	124	294
Approve to approve	50%	83%
Approve to disapprove	50%	17%
Number of cases	68	64
Net change in approval (d/a–a/d)	−28 points°	+43 points°

Source: Data from ANES 2005; data weighted by 1996 panel weights.
°$p \leq .01$ (two-tailed)

1996, while 60 percent changed to approval. When we look at respondents who were initially approving of Congress in 1994, we again see a difference in the behavior of liberals compared to conservatives. Among liberals who approved of congressional performance during Democratic control in 1994, 50 percent switched to disapproval after the Republicans took control. Among conservatives who approved in 1994, only 17 percent changed to disapproval in 1996.

Overall, the direction of effects is as we predicted given the type of change that occurred in Congress. Among liberals, the change from a liberal Democratic Congress in 1994 to a conservative Republican Congress in 1996 produced a net twenty-eight-point reduction in congressional approval. Among conservatives, the same change in party control led to a net forty-three-point increase in congressional approval.[9]

We have argued that these effects are not limited to a narrow segment of the population. The alternative hypothesis, suggested by the bulk of the existing literature on public opinion, is that the results in table 3.3 were primarily driven by citizens who explicitly knew who controlled Congress—those who answered the House majority question correctly. If this alternative hypothesis is correct, those who did not answer the question correctly should not show changes in opinion consistent with the change in party control: "uninformed" liberals should not become more disapproving overall after a change to Republican control, and "uninformed" conservatives should not become more approving overall. To test this possibility, we again divided respondents into two groups: those who answered the House majority question correctly and those who answered either "don't know" or incorrectly. Because we are dealing with two separate years of differing party control, one group consists of respondents who did not answer correctly in either or both years, and the other consists of respondents who gave the correct answer both times.[10]

As we hypothesized—and contrary to the alternative hypothesis—the ideological shifts in individual opinion are nearly identical between the two groups, demonstrating that the expected pattern of opinions shown in table 3.3 was not caused by the behavior of an elite few. Table 3.4 shows individual opinion change by respondent ideology among those who consistently answered the party control questions correctly and among those who did not. For liberals who answered the party control question correctly in both years, the change from Democratic to Republican control of Congress produced a net twenty-seven-point decrease in approval of Congress—similar to the overall result in table 3.3. More interesting, however, are the effects of the change in House party control on the opinions of those who did not answer the control questions correctly—the "uninformed" group. The net shift among liberals who did not answer the House majority question correctly was a thirty-three-point decrease in approval—in the same direction and with roughly the same magnitude as the net shift among those who correctly answered the party control question.

For conservatives, we predicted positive shifts in opinion toward Congress regardless of whether a respondent answered the party control question correctly. According to table 3.4, conservatives correctly answering the majority party questions had a net forty-eight-point increase in approval. Among those who did not give the correct answer, we see a similarly substantial and significant thirty-three-point net increase in approval.

Consistent with table 3.2, these data demonstrate that even those respondents who have traditionally been classified as ignorant of party control—those who cannot answer the ANES question correctly—demonstrate the ideological shifts in opinion we expect citizens to have in reaction to a switch in party control. In fact, the "unknowledgeable" group's behavior closely mimics that of the "knowledgeable" group, raising at least the possibility that those who do not correctly answer the fac-

TABLE 3.4. Individual Change in Congressional Approval from 1994 to 1996 among Liberals and Conservatives by House Majority Question

DEMOCRATIC (1994) TO REPUBLICAN (1996) CONTROL	LIBERALS	CONSERVATIVES
Correct majority answer		
Disapprove to approve	23%	63%
Approve to disapprove	50%	15%
Net change in approval	−27 points°	+48 points°
Number of cases	131	271
Incorrect majority answer		
Disapprove to approve	19%	50%
Approve to disapprove	52%	17%
Net change in approval	−33 points°	+33 points°
Number of cases	62	87

Source: Data from ANES 2005; data weighted by 1996 panel weights.
°$p \le .01$ (two-tailed)

tual question on party control nevertheless either really do know or have at one point known who controls Congress.

TESTING THE EFFECTS OF NEW INFORMATION: SENATE MAJORITY PARTY SWITCH

The change in party control of Congress as a result of the 1994 elections was an extremely salient event. As such, some might argue (although we are not among them) that it offers only a moderate test of the public's ability to recognize changes in congressional control and react to them. To address this potential criticism, we conduct one further test of the public's ability to maintain and update their judgments of Congress when changes occur, this time surrounding a relatively obscure and short-lived shift in control: the change in party control of the Senate alone from Republican to Democratic in mid-2001, followed by the switch back to Republican control after the 2002 elections. These changes provide an exceptionally rigorous test of the public's awareness and use of congressional control in evaluating Congress, because the period of Democratic control was caused by a nonelectoral partisan change of only one single Senate seat (that of Senator James Jeffords) and only lasted for nineteen months, less than one full congressional term.

On May 23, 2001, Senator James Jeffords of Vermont, a moderate Republican, changed his partisan allegiance from Republican to independent. At the time of Jeffords's switch, the Senate was evenly divided, with fifty Republican Senators and fifty Democrats. The Republicans were in the majority by virtue of Republican vice president Dick Cheney's tie-breaking vote as president of the Senate. Jeffords's switch upset the balance of power in the Senate and gave Democrats a slim majority of fifty to forty-nine. In the 2002 elections, however, the Republicans regained Senate majority status by a slim margin, having increased their seat number to fifty-one.

Unlike all other modern changes of partisan control in Congress, the 2001 Senate shift was not the result of a well-publicized electoral outcome. Rather, it was a relatively inside-baseball type of action—the kind of news the media love, but for which the public typically has little time or attention. Jeffords's switch involved marginal control of only one chamber of Congress. Not surprisingly, shortly following the switch, a survey conducted by the Pew Research Center for the People and the Press reported only 21 percent of Americans saying they were following the story very closely in the news. In contrast, 56 percent were very closely following news reports on the price of gasoline.[11] Jeffords's switch was clearly not an event that dominated the public's agenda.

Because of the narrow margin of control for each party at each point—Republicans by one seat before the switch, the Democrats by one seat after the switch, and the Republicans by three seats after the election—this situation presents a tough challenge for public awareness and processing of change in congressional control. Expectations based on the traditional literature would be that the public would have minimal, if any, knowledge of these majority party shifts and would thus be unable or unlikely to react to them. We predict, however, that the public did have at least enough knowledge of the brief period of Democratic control to alter their judgments of congressional action and performance as a result of the shifts.

To test this hypothesis here, we use two original surveys, one conducted during Democratic control of the Senate in 2002 (after the Jeffords switch) and the other conducted in 2003, after Republicans had retaken control of the Senate as a result of the 2002 election. Both surveys were conducted by the Center for Survey Research and Analysis at the University of Connecticut. The first was conducted from October 9 to 14, 2002, among 1,006 adults nationwide. The second took place in March 2003, among 994 adult respondents nationally.

Each of these surveys contained questions gauging attitudes toward the Senate and the House separately. Specifically, the surveys included questions that asked citizens their opinions of the job performance of the Senate, as well as the job performance of the House, in addition to the usual question measuring attitudes toward Congress as a whole. (Full wording for all questions is located in the appendix.) This design allows us to compare the pattern of change in approval of the House, where party control did not shift, to the pattern of change in approval of the Senate, where party control did shift.

If our hypothesis of individuals' ability to perceive the ideological implications of partisan changes in Congress proves correct in this more stringent test, we expect a shift in opinions of a chamber's performance when party control—and thus policy direction—of that chamber shifts. Specifically, liberals should be more approving of the Senate in 2002, when policy is being driven by the Democratic Party, than in 2003, when Republican control shifted policy in a more conservative direction. At the same time, conservatives' views of the Senate should move from relatively disapproving to relatively approving.

In the House, while the Republican Party did gain seven seats after the 2002 elections, this gain did not shift party control or the ideological direction of policy activity in this chamber. Since our hypothesis rests on directional change in party and policy outlook, not on the margin of party control or electoral success per se, we do not expect that the pattern of change in House approval among liberals will be very different than the pattern of change among conservatives from before to after the election.

Table 3.5 contains the public's judgments of both the Senate and the House before and after the 2002 elections. As expected, liberals and conservatives differ markedly in how their evaluations of Senate job performance changed after the election. While Senate approval among liberals dropped nearly imperceptibly, conservatives' opinions shifted significantly from disapproval to approval by a net change of twenty-two points. In contrast, while opinions of the House also changed some, the change is not statistically significant among either liberals or conservatives. In other words, when the shift of only a few seats in the Senate gave control over the agenda to the more conservative party, conservatives became Senate approvers. In contrast, when the shift of only a few seats in the House essentially maintained the ideological status quo in that chamber, there was no real change in House approval.

TABLE 3.5. Aggregate Change in Senate and House Approval from 2002 to 2003 among Liberals and Conservatives

	LIBERALS			CONSERVATIVES		
	2002	2003	CHANGE IN APPROVAL	2002	2003	CHANGE IN APPROVAL
Senate						
Democratic to Republican control						
Approve	53%	51%	−2 points	40%	62%	+22 points°
Disapprove	47%	49%		60%	38%	
Number of cases	51	78		45	175	
House						
No change in control						
Approve	55%	59%	+4 points	67%	78%	+11 points
Disapprove	45%	41%		33%	22%	
Number of cases	50	77		45	175	

Source: Authors' survey data collected by the Center for Survey Research and Analysis at the University of Connecticut.
°$p \leq .05$ (two-tailed)

Even under rare and obscure circumstances—a mere nineteen-month and three-seat shift in party control of one chamber in Congress—the public demonstrates some ability to keep up with the implications of these changes and to update their impressions of Congress accordingly. While scholars have often downplayed the public's awareness and use of information about Congress, the positive results in this test suggest that the public may have more ability than is traditionally assumed, even if not at perfect or ideal levels.

We again face the possibility that the results in table 3.5 could simply be driven by the most knowledgeable citizens, reflected in aggregate. After all, with a situation like this brief and marginal shift, it seems highly unlikely that the unaware American voter portrayed in the literature could make the connections necessary to behave as predicted by our hypothesis. Nevertheless, we maintain that even those citizens who fail the factual question on party control of an institution may still have some ability to connect their preferences to congressional performance and to judge Congress accordingly. We can again test this claim by comparing the opinion patterns of those who answer a party control question correctly and those who do not.

The 2003 survey—conducted four months after the seating of the new Republican Senate—contained a factual question on party control regarding the U.S. Senate.[12] Our theory predicts that regardless of whether respondents answered the party control question correctly, conservatives should be more likely than liberals to support a Senate controlled by a conservative Republican Party. Table 3.6 contains cross-tabulations of

TABLE 3.6. Senate Approval among Liberals and Conservatives by Senate Majority Question, 2003

	2003—REPUBLICAN SENATE CONTROL					
	CORRECT ANSWER			INCORRECT ANSWER		
EVALUATION OF SENATE	LIBERALS	CONSER-VATIVES	OPINION DIFFERENCE BY IDEOLOGY	LIBERALS	CONSER-VATIVES	OPINION DIFFERENCE BY IDEOLOGY
Approve	47%	54%	+7 points	59%	79%	+20 points
Disapprove	53%	46%		41%	21%	
Number of cases	52	123		26	52	

Source: Authors' survey data collected by the Center for Survey Research and Analysis at the University of Connecticut.

Senate approval and ideology among those who answered the Senate control question correctly and those who did not.

Among those who reported correctly that Republicans controlled the Senate in 2003, conservatives were seven points more approving of Senate performance. In addition, as predicted, those who did not correctly answer the Senate control question also displayed a distinct ideological difference. While both liberals and conservatives approved of the Senate's performance, demonstrating other evaluative factors at work besides ideology, conservatives were a full twenty points more likely than liberals to approve of the relatively new Republican Congress. In other words, as with the preceding tests in this chapter, we find that Americans are generally capable of making connections between their own preferences and the policy direction of Congress, even if they cannot answer a factual question that would seem important and relevant to doing so.

TESTING THE EFFECTS OF NEW INFORMATION: THE FIRST HUNDRED DAYS

We saw in table 3.1 that immediately following an election, an overwhelming majority of Americans have a good idea of which party has a majority in Congress, and we have explained how this knowledge alone could account for the strong correlation between ideology and congressional approval in our empirical tests. It is furthermore possible that additional information, encountered when coverage of Congress is abnormally high, could also contribute to the expected patterns we have found. Unfortunately, in most situations, it would be almost impossible to detect whether or not citizens' opinions of Congress were affected by such information. As explained in chapter 2, once citizens already possess some information leading them to view Congress as, say, conservative, subsequent actions by Congress that are consistent with this view (conservative actions) will usually only serve to reinforce their view of Congress, not to change it. This reinforcement would be an important effect of information, but one that would be mostly invisible to a researcher. Empirical research suggests that such situations are generally the norm because Republican Congresses tend to take consistently conservative actions, while Democratic Congresses tend to take consistently liberal actions (Poole and Rosenthal 1997).

There is, however, at least one situation in which we might be able to observe the effects of a Congress pursuing its natural policy direction: the beginning of a new congressional regime. When a new party takes control of Congress after having been out of power for many years, citizens will have some idea of what to expect policy-wise simply on the basis of party, but it is also possible that their views of the new Congress will be somewhat tentative. Put simply, citizens' impressions of a new congressional majority may not solidify completely until they encounter some information about what Congress is actually doing in the policy arena.

For opinions of Congress to evolve early in a new regime based on new policy information, the average American citizen must come into contact with and to some extent process this kind of information. This is a tall order that demands even more from the public than the impressions of Congress based on partisan control that we have examined to this point. As we cited earlier, however, some existing research suggests that such information can be—and in fact is—often picked up incidentally by the public (e.g., Fiorina 1990; Huckfeldt and Sprague 1995). In this case, even citizens who do not seek out political or policy information may nevertheless acquire it and, as a result, adjust their opinions appropriately in response.

In this section, we consider two real-life situations that allow us to test this possibility: the beginning of the new Republican Congress in 1995 and the beginning of the new Democratic Congress in 2007. Prior to 1995, Republicans had not been in control of both chambers of Congress for four decades. Following their electoral landslide in the 1994 elections, Republicans swept into office with a bold conservative policy agenda planned for the first hundred days. They were, as the *New York Times* described them, a "restless new class of conservatives clamoring for rapid-fire action on Speaker Newt Gingrich's Contract With America" (Berke 1995). Their priorities included tax cuts; cuts in the government's cultural funding to the humanities, the arts, and public television (a fight characterized as an attempt to kill Sesame Street's Big Bird, a childhood icon for generations of Americans); and reforming social welfare programs—all decidedly conservative positions. They also publicly promised to work hand in hand with the religious Right, specifically the Christian Coalition, as reported in the *Washington Post*.

> House Speaker Newt Gingrich (R-Ga.) yesterday pledged that the House will vote on restricting abortion and on a constitutional amendment to allow prayer in schools and other public places as Republican leaders hailed the Christian Coalition's new 10-point "blueprint" for moral and social reform. (Goodstein 1995)

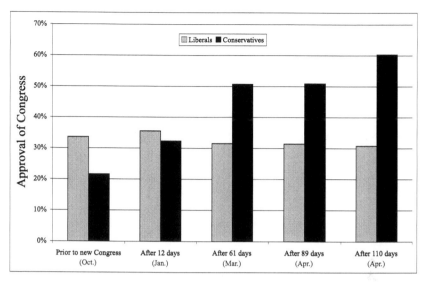

Fig. 3.3. Congressional approval among liberals and conservatives, October 1994–
April 1995. (Data from polls conducted by NBC News/*Wall Street Journal*, October 14–18, 1994 [N = 1,509], January 14–17, 1995 [N = 1,003], March 4–7, 1995
[N = 1,011], April 3–4, 1995 [N = 803], and April 21–25, 1995 [N = 1,504].)

In general, the Republicans made clear that Congress was making a dramatic switch to conservatism under their leadership. For those who might
not have been sure what to expect from the new Congress, almost every
day seemed to offer additional evidence—in both word and deed—of this
shift to the right.

To test whether Americans were paying any attention to the policy
shift and updating their impressions according to this new information, we
here analyze whether opinions among liberals and conservatives changed
during the first hundred days of the Republican Congress. Figure 3.3
presents data from NBC News polls suggesting that Americans were not
only receiving but also processing information on Congress's actions.[13]

In the last poll prior to the 1994 election, liberals were twelve points
more likely to approve of Congress than conservatives were. In the first
poll of January, taken twelve days after the election, we see that opinions
had already changed; namely, conservatives' level of approval increased
to the same level as liberals' approval (which did not change in that period). Seven weeks later, in a March survey, the patterns we saw earlier in

this chapter began to emerge: conservatives were nineteen points more likely to approve of Congress than liberals were. This gap persisted into early April. Finally, in the first poll taken after extensive media coverage summarizing the first hundred days of the new Republican Congress, we see a nearly thirty-point difference between conservatives and liberals—a difference roughly consistent with the size of the difference in evaluations between liberals and conservatives found in our tests of change in party control discussed earlier in this chapter.

Interestingly, it appears that the growth in the difference between liberals and conservatives from January to April came mainly from citizens who would appear to be ideologically compatible with the new Congress (in this case, conservatives), not from its natural ideological opponents (in this case, liberals). Liberals remained relatively constant in their lack of approval of the Congress from day one, dropping only about five points from January to mid-April. In contrast, conservatives appear to have been cautious in their approval at first, only eventually becoming more approving of the new Congress as pieces of evidence emerged. By mid-April, conservatives had increased their approval by a total of twenty-eight points compared to January. Together, this amounts to a thirty-three-point swing in the difference between liberals and conservatives from the first poll asking respondents about the new Congress to a poll measuring opinions after the first hundred days. Overall, this evidence suggests that events occurring in Congress and in the media, even well after the election, do have some impact on the public and their evaluations of Congress.

While the findings in figure 3.3 are important in and of themselves, we can have even more confidence in the results and conclusions if we can find the same pattern of effects for a situation that is essentially the reverse: the return to power by Democrats in 2007 after twelve years in the minority in one or both chambers. Like Republicans in 1995, these Democrats spent their early days in power trumpeting their ideologically based policy efforts in areas that had previously received either little attention or had been subject to opposite policy actions under Republican leadership. In the House, Democrats elected the first woman Speaker, Nancy Pelosi, a strong liberal from liberalism's mecca—San Francisco, California. She spent most of her time in the limelight promoting the Democrats' policy agenda for the 110th Congress's "first hundred hours" (which turned out to actually mean "legislative hours"). Among the policy items addressed by Democrats during the start of their new reign were raising the minimum wage, allowing the federal government to negotiate lower drug prices for Medicare recipients, rolling back tax breaks for oil companies and increasing their royalty payments, and cutting interest rates on federal student loans—all in stark contrast to Republicans' economic prescriptions. The Democrats also increased federal funding for stem cell research—an area where social conservatives had sought federal funding bans. Then, during the second week in March, Democratic leaders announced that they would introduce a bill calling for the complete withdrawal of U.S. combat soldiers from Iraq by September 2008—a clear shift in congressional policy direction in the public's primary area of concern at the time.[14]

Once again, for anyone who was not already sure, the series of actions and rhetoric by the new majority party once it came into office set a new (in this case, distinctly liberal) policy tone. As a result, we would expect that Americans' attitudes toward Congress evolved over the early part of the Democrats' control, similar in scope to the changes in 1995, but in the opposite direction. Although few complete polls are publicly available from 2007 at the time of this writing, we were able to obtain cross-tabulations of ideological and approval data from the CBS News Election and Survey Unit.[15] The results are presented in figure 3.4.

In the last poll prior to the 2006 election, liberals were sixteen points less likely to approve of the Republican Congress than conservatives were. In the first poll in January after the new Democratic Congress convened, liberals were no longer less likely to approve of Congress—but neither were they significantly more likely to approve. Liberals became only a bit more likely than conservatives to approve of Congress in February (six points), and this difference continued almost unchanged into early March. However, after Congress shifted its focus to the issue of Iraq—the issue dominating Americans' national concerns—we finally see a large disparity emerge between liberals' and conservatives' congressional evaluations. By mid-April, liberals were seventeen points more likely to approve of Congress than conservatives were—almost exactly the same spread, in reverse, seen at the end of the Republican Congress in 2006.

As was the case in 1995, the growth in the difference between liberals and conservatives in congressional approval from January to April 2007 came mainly from citizens who would appear to be ideologically compatible with the new Congress (in this case, liberals), not from its natural ideological opponents (in this case, conservatives). Conservatives were already quite disapproving in January 2007 and dropped only another three points by mid-April. This time, it was liberals who started the

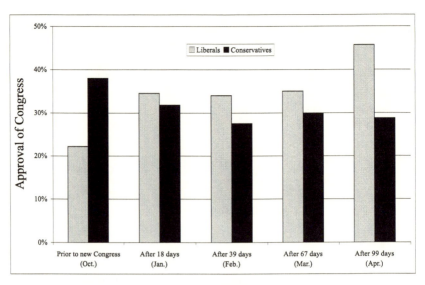

Fig. 3.4. Congressional approval among liberals and conservatives, October 2006–April 2007. (Data from polls conducted by CBS News/*New York Times*, October 27–31, 2006 [$N = 1,084$], January 18–21, 2007 [$N = 1,168$], February 8–11, 2007 [$N = 1,142$], March 7–9, 2007 [$N = 1,362$], and April 9–12, 2007 [$N = 994$].)

new year withholding approval of the new Congress, eventually increasing their approval by eleven points only after seeing Congress take steps to try to end the war in Iraq. In sum, we observe a fourteen-point increase in the difference between liberals and conservatives from the first poll in January to the April survey marking ninety-nine days of the Democrats in power.

We cannot and do not use these results to claim that Americans pay attention to every (or even to most) policy actions or pronouncements of Congress. After all, unique circumstances and press attention surround a new party coming into power. While not typical political occurrences, these examples are nevertheless quite useful, because they provide a window into the evolution of public opinion in response to congressional policy change. Specifically, they help inform us how citizens process new information about Congress that is not merely based on partisan election results. Here we see that the election of a new Congress in some ways acts as a "reset" button, equalizing much of the previous difference in congressional evaluations between liberals and conservatives. Then, as citizens get bits of information that perhaps confirm some of their suspicions based on party cues alone, this ideological divide in congressional evaluations reemerges.

These results strongly suggest that real-world policy actions typical of a given Congress can and do have an impact on the public when evaluating Congress. Party cues are necessarily of crucial importance in helping citizens form their opinions of congressional policy direction, but policy actions can also matter. In truth, the two are likely to be closely related. After all, people's impressions of what a party stands for in the first place are likely based at least partly on what that party typically does when it is in power.

CONCLUSION

This chapter demonstrates, in multiple ways and with regard to diverse situations, that Americans are capable of receiving and using real-world information related to the policy direction of Congress when they form and update their evaluations of congressional job performance. Furthermore, this ability is not restricted to a slim stratum of elite citizens but instead extends to a broad swath of Americans—even to some of those who are often viewed as incapable of performing such tasks. Consistent with some previous research, we find further support for the claim that individuals do not need to be able to answer factual questions about the government to be able to form judgments of the government that are at least partly based on their underlying preferences. Citizens who do not answer correctly when asked who controls Congress nevertheless make judgments of Congress that align with the judgments they would be likely to make if they did in fact know who was in control. More to the point, they make the same judgments, relative to their own preferences, as those citizens who do answer such a question correctly.

The literature on political knowledge argues that American democracy suffers when its citizens do not possess enough information to make decisions that are consistent with their core values. It further argues that citizens lack exactly this kind of knowledge. As a result, our democracy is in a seemingly woeful state—populated predominantly by citizens who are incapable of making what are typically considered to be responsible democratic decisions. We feel this chapter's findings provide at least a ray of hope for American democracy, by demonstrating that many citizens do seem to have the knowledge and reasoning ability necessary to judge their government based on their policy preferences. The field of political science's prevailing belief that Americans cannot do so has been fueled by almost uniform reliance on factual survey questions as gauges of citizen knowledge. Our results help to demonstrate that the trust researchers have in such measures may be misplaced. While individuals may not be able to recall information at a given point in time well enough to correctly answer a survey question about it, large numbers of them nevertheless behave as we would want responsible citizens to do.

Our evidence in chapter 2 and this chapter provides support for our first two hypotheses: first, that Americans care about policy representativeness on the part of Congress; second, that they manage to acquire and process at least some of the information needed to compare their own policy preferences to Congress's policy orientation and to form a related judgment of congressional performance. These two findings are important to our argument. However, there is another step in our story of opinion formation. To this point, we have used a simplistic view of policy orientation, looking only at the dichotomous distinction of liberal versus conservative. We now need to provide more detail on precisely how citizens compare their own ideological views with those of Congress and how this comparison affects their evaluations of the institution.

CHAPTER 4

Evaluating Congress Ideologically

In the spring of 2007, Americans witnessed a classic game of chicken between the president, George W. Bush, and the newly elected and installed Democratic Congress. In early spring, the president asked Congress to pass a supplemental defense appropriation to continue funding for the wars in Iraq and Afghanistan. To the delight of those who saw the Iraq War as immoral and to the consternation of those who viewed it as vital to the War on Terror, Democrats sent the president a funding bill on April 26 that required troop withdrawal from Iraq to begin by the end of 2007 and that set a target date of March 2008 for a complete pullout. Bush vetoed the bill, insisting that Congress send him a bill with no restrictions.

Unable to override the veto, congressional Democrats were faced with a difficult choice. On the one hand, they could hold their ground by continuing to send Bush bills calling for withdrawal. This would appease liberal hard-line antiwar activists but would risk upsetting citizens concerned that U.S. soldiers stuck in Iraq might run out of needed supplies. On the other hand, they could send Bush a bill he would sign, then they could simply claim they had tried to stop the war. This might be understood as the more responsible action by some Americans but would surely alienate those who had hoped the new Congress would end the war. On May 24, the Democratic Congress swerved first, sending the president a supplemental defense appropriations bill with no requirements for troop withdrawal.

Media coverage of public opinion surveys taken shortly after the showdown focused on the low aggregate approval ratings of Congress that the incident left in its wake (e.g., Cook 2007). From our perspective, however, what is more interesting is how the actions of Congress affected evaluations across different ideological groups within the public. Congress's actions—first facing off with Bush over the war and then backing down—had clear ideological implications, but not strictly linear ones. The moderated policy the Democratic leadership settled on was almost sure to disappoint their most liberal constituents but appeal to moderate and moderately liberal portions of the public.

A national NBC News/*Wall Street Journal* poll from June 2007 asked respondents, among other things, to rate their own ideological outlook and to state whether they approved of Congress's job performance. Figure 4.1 illustrates the differences in approval levels among the 96 percent who rated themselves ideologically. The figure shows that Americans' evaluations of congressional job performance were indeed related to their ideological outlook, but not in a simply dichotomous fashion (e.g., not with liberals uniformly approving and conservatives uniformly disapproving). On the left side of the figure, we see that in the aftermath of the showdown over war funding, those who described themselves as very liberal were in fact less approving of Congress than those who described themselves as somewhat liberal.[1] On the right side of the figure, we also see that not all conservatives rated Congress the same. Those who were very conservative were the least approving, giving significantly lower ratings than those who were somewhat conservative. Overall, it seems fair to speculate that this pattern of approval reflects a public that generally viewed Congress as slightly left of center: those on the far right, whose ideological preferences were the most divergent from the stance of Congress, disapproved most; moderates were more favorably disposed but did not like everything they had been hearing; mainstream liberals seemed most comfortable with Congress; and extreme liberals appeared to be disappointed at the lack of ideological purity.

This anecdote helps to illustrate several points that are central to our argument in this study. First, consistent with chapter 3, it suggests once again that Congress is not just a black box to Americans. Rather, citizens are able to pick up and use simple information to make reasonable judgments of where Congress stands. Second, the fact that 96 percent of the public placed themselves on this survey's ideological scale suggests that most Americans are willing to think of themselves in ideological terms. This is encouraging for our argument, and we will explore the ideological abilities of Americans in more detail later in this chapter. Third, this example helps illustrate that the simplified liberal/conservative dichotomy we employed in chapters 2 and 3, while appropriate for test-

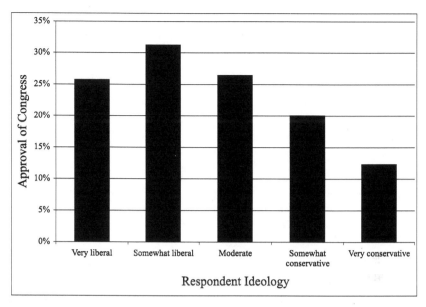

Fig. 4.1. Congressional approval by respondent ideology, June 2007. (Data from NBC News/*Wall Street Journal* poll conducted by Hart and Newhouse Research Companies, June 8–11, 2007 [N = 1,114].)

ing the basic ideas in those chapters, now needs expanding to capture the more nuanced effects that may exist along the ideological continuum.

Incorporating all of these elements, our central argument in this chapter is that when evaluating congressional job performance, Americans take into account their relative ideological or policy difference from the majority party in Congress. Those who perceive a greater difference between their own policy views and those of the Congress, as run by the majority party, will be less approving. Those who perceive less difference will be more approving, all else being equal.

We again find ourselves swimming upstream with this argument, challenging some long-held scholarly notions about the ideological capacity of American citizens. Prominent research analyzing how Americans organize their political beliefs, if they do at all, holds that citizens do not structure their beliefs in an ideological manner (i.e., according to how ideology is traditionally conceived in political science). As a result, the argument goes, individuals are unable to make ideological comparisons between themselves and government or to judge governmental performance based on ideological criteria. While the previous chapter focused on challenging the notion that citizens do not have the knowledge necessary to form logical impressions of Congress's policy orientation, this one focuses on whether individuals have the ability to judge Congress's performance based on ideological comparisons, once they hold the general impression of Congress that would allow them to do so.

We begin the rest of this chapter by reviewing the literature on ideology in the American public. We discuss well-known works that view ideology as something only used by a relatively small group of Americans, if any. But we also review a body of empirical research that has challenged whether this image of Americans is still—or ever was—entirely accurate. While almost none of this research on Americans' ideological capabilities has directly addressed the collective institution of Congress, we argue that it does apply. We then derive and test predictions in two areas: at the level of the individual citizen and at the aggregate level.

THE ROLE OF IDEOLOGY IN ATTITUDE FORMATION

A broad examination of survey evidence reveals that the vast majority of Americans are, at a minimum, willing and able to rate themselves on a liberal to conservative scale. The average rate of self-placement across surveys conducted by major commercial survey organizations over the past quarter century is approximately 95 percent.[2] The proportion of those willing to rate themselves in the standard academic ANES survey is similar, although differences in question wording can obscure this fact.

Unlike in major media surveys, which use a volunteered "don't know" category, the initial ideological self-placement question in the ANES survey offers respondents an explicit "out" category with the phrase "or haven't you thought much about this?" Extensive research on question wording in surveys demonstrates that offering respondents an explicit category allowing them to not choose a substantive answer significantly increases the proportion who will do so, even when they actually have substantive answers they would otherwise give (e.g., Mondak and Davis 2001; Schuman and Presser 1996). Consistent with this literature, after the ANES follow-up question pressing those in the "haven't thought much about" category to choose among liberal, moderate, and conservative categories, the total proportion who classify themselves ideologically is virtually identical to those in the major media surveys—93 percent.[3] In other words, both types of surveys demonstrate that nearly all respondents can and do choose an ideological profile for themselves.

Just because most Americans are willing to use these ideological terms to describe themselves and the other political actors, however, does not necessarily indicate that Americans use ideology in a meaningful way when forming political attitudes. In the following section, we review the debate in existing research on this latter concern.

Ideology as an Elite Outlook

The idea that the public's judgments of government actors are driven by the relative ideological compatibility between the public and these actors is long-standing. In 1957, Downs hypothesized that voters evaluate political actors (both those in government and those running to be) based on where the actors are located on a one-dimensional liberal-conservative continuum relative to where the voter is located. In an electoral situation, Downs argued, voters will choose the candidate who is closest to them on this ideological spectrum.

Empirically, however, there has been some doubt and considerable debate about the extent to which the American public can and does use ideology in its political reasoning and judgment. Looking at the 1956 ANES, the authors of *The American Voter* (A. Campbell et al. 1960) found that only a small proportion (12 percent) of the electorate provided any ideologically related reason for their choice of one political party over another. Converse's (1964) seminal work on citizens' ideological conceptions and constraint argued that few Americans even had belief systems that could qualify as ideologies, let alone be compared to the belief systems of political actors.

More recent research paints a similar picture. Bennett (1995) finds that many Americans lack a real sense of the standard ideological continuum and, as a result, cannot link their own ideology to political referents. Measuring ideological knowledge based on four separate components— placement of political parties, placement of presidential candidates, identification of the more conservative party, and volunteered definitions of the terms *liberal* and *conservative*—he classifies Americans' ideological knowledge as "dismal" (266).

Researchers have also found that citizens' use of ideology varies based on their level of political sophistication. Among others, Jacoby (1986) has found that individuals with lower levels of political conceptualization, or understanding, are less likely to use ideological approaches to candidate evaluation. Stimson (1975) has similar findings. His analysis of different ways of conceptualizing constraint shows that the higher an individual's level of ideological constraint is, the more ideologically consistent that individual's evaluations and voting decisions are. Zinni, Mattei, and Rhodebeck (1997) also find differences among the decision-making strategies of the sophisticated and the unsophisticated. They argue that while sophisticated Americans use ideology as a guide to their political thinking, the less sophisticated are more likely to rely on emotions.

A last set of evidence against citizens' use of ideology also concerns levels of sophistication, but with a specific eye toward the role of ideology versus the role of party affiliation. Party is the five-hundred-pound gorilla of Americans' political attitudes (see, e.g., Bartels 2002) and electoral choices (see, e.g., W. Miller 1991) and, as such, leaves little room for other influences. Both Kam (2005) and Knight (1985) find that this is especially true for the least politically sophisticated, who are found to rely primarily on party cues in forming opinions and making choices. While both studies also find that, in contrast, the politically sophisticated rely on ideological reasoning when making decisions, other authors argue that ideology itself may be merely a reflection of party preferences. Jacoby (1988) suggests that party affiliations actually cause ideological views, and Sharp and Lodge (1985) find that partisan reasoning and ideological reasoning are highly correlated, to the point of being "interchangeable" (156).

Ideology as a Matter of Course

The claim that Americans are relatively incapable of understanding—let alone using—ideology in making political judgments has been internalized by many scholars, but for others, the story is quite different. Despite the repeated criticisms of the probability—or even possibility—of ideological use by the American public, it remains a central factor in numerous studies of attitude formation and voting. Public ideology seems to be the uninvited party guest who will not leave, even after the festivities are long over.

Part of ideology's staying power stems from multiple subfields of research that challenge the conclusions previously described. These challenges include research suggesting that political conditions in recent decades have made the use of ideology more likely than in the past (e.g., Abramowitz and Saunders 1998; Hetherington 2001; Jacobson 2000), findings that the organization of Americans' ideological thinking is more constrained than previously thought (e.g., Green 1988), evidence that political sophistication may not be a requirement for actual ideological thinking (e.g., Goren 2004; Luttbeg and Gant 1985; MacDonald, Rabinowitz, and Listhaug 1995), research into organizational schema that finds that Americans regularly use ideological thinking when making political decisions (e.g., Conover and Feldman 1984; 1986), and related findings that citizens' use of ideological reasoning is distinct from their use of partisanship (e.g., Huckfeldt et al. 2002).

Many studies have looked at the political conditions under which citizens are more likely to use ideology. A main finding of this research is that Americans can and do use ideology to evaluate candidates and officeholders when there is a clear ideological distinction between candidates. Nie, Verba, and Petrocik (1980) argue that when ideological differences between the candidates are salient, citizens use ideology as a factor in deciding between or among them. Abramowitz (1981) demonstrates that the further apart the candidates in Senate elections in 1978 were ideologically, the more likely it was that voters would base their choices on ideology. Wright and Berkman (1986) find similar results in the 1982 Senate elections. Additionally, Stimson (1975) finds that linkages between individuals' ideologies and evaluations of McGovern in 1972 were uniform across different levels of ideological constraint. This was presumably because McGovern was widely considered an extreme left-wing candidate and thus provided a clear ideological choice for citizens.

Lawrence's (1994) research extends this argument to include political parties as well. His analysis of presidential election outcomes from 1968 through 1980 finds that perceptions of the Democratic Party as far to the ideological left hurt the party's chances in presidential elections during this period, as self-described moderate voters were susceptible to more moderate Republican messages. Voters' own ideological and issue preferences, combined with their ideological perceptions of the parties, determined electoral behavior. As Lawrence puts it, choices during this period were made on a "substantial ideological basis" (415).

This repeated finding that ideological clarity helps voters make decisions based on their own ideological preferences is of increasing importance to American politics. Recent work demonstrates that beginning with Reagan's election in 1980 (or perhaps even earlier—see Holm and Robinson 1978; Taylor 1996), the American political landscape has changed, with increasing ideological polarization between the two major political parties. Stone, Rapoport, and Abramowitz (1992) demonstrate that party activists on both sides of the aisle became more ideologically extreme throughout the 1980s, a trend that continued into the 1990s. This elite ideological shift has subsequently increased both the public's awareness of ideology and ideology's importance to the public, as would be expected (Abramowitz and Saunders 1998; Hetherington 2001; Jacobson 2000). Because ideological choices are so much more distinct now, voters are more likely than ever to use ideology and ideological distance when making party choices and voting decisions (Abramowitz and Saunders 1998).

The traditional literature argues that Americans are confused or ambivalent when it comes to their ideological thinking (e.g., Converse 1964). Green (1988) challenges this argument by examining the dimensionality of ideological thinking among Americans. He demonstrates that many of the studies finding that Americans lack ideological bipolarity or constraint are the result of statistical artifact—measurement error in the survey questions typically used. Controlling for such error, Green finds a distinctly bipolar dimension to Americans' ideological attitudes. Also in contrast to Converse's characterization of a lack of ideological constraint within the American public, Goren (2004) finds that individuals do have relatively constrained beliefs—at least within such policy domains as social welfare and foreign policy—that look quite like ideology (see also Feldman 1988; Hurwitz and Peffley 1987). Equally important, Goren also finds that individuals use their core beliefs to make political decisions at all levels of political sophistication: "Simply put, all citizens hold genuine core beliefs and values and rely more or less equally on these when taking positions on many specific issues" (2004, 462).

Luttbeg and Gant (1985) also present findings that call into question conventional scholarly wisdom on ideology and sophistication, but from the explicit angle of ideological understanding. Scoring (as correct or incorrect) respondents' definitions of what the terms *liberal* and *conservative* mean, Luttbeg and Gant find that the results "portray a fairly sophisticated electorate" on average (82). They also find, similar to Goren, that one's level of sophistication does not necessarily determine one's ability to vote based on issues or ideology. Citizens who did not venture definitions for ideological labels were equally as likely to vote based on issues as were those who defined both *liberal* and *conservative* correctly. According to their findings, the public generally does understand ideology, and even those who cannot explicate it are still capable of making use of it. MacDonald, Rabinowitz, and Listhaug (1995) also find that both politically sophisticated voters and politically unsophisticated voters use the same criterion of ideological proximity—although to different degrees—when evaluating parties and candidates.

In another, related field of research, an extensive literature has built up around the notion of ideology as a decision-making schema—a way in which the public simplifies the confusing world of politics (see, e.g., Conover and Feldman 1984, 1986). This research argues that the terms *liberal* and *conservative* can be meaningful constructs that citizens use to form judgments of political actors based on inferred issue positions, characteristics, or affect. According to this literature, Americans effectively and regularly use ideology in the political process.

Traditionally, party identification has been accepted as the most powerful political schema, but there is a good deal of evidence that ideology plays an important and distinct role as well. Feldman and Conover's (1983) examination of political inference makes this clear. They examine the role that both partisan and ideological schema play in providing voters with inferential information about candidates' issue stands. They find that both have substantial impacts on ANES respondents' perceptions of candidates' positions and that the impact of each is much stronger than the effect of any potential projection. They conclude, "Our analysis clearly revealed that when voters attempt to determine where candidates stand on various issues they rely to a great extent on their prior experiences with the issue positions of members of that party or ideological group" (836; see also Hamill, Lodge, and Blake 1985).

Working in the same field, Lau and Redlawsk (2001) use a unique computerized method of simulating a political campaign to test five potential decision-making sources of information—party, ideology, endorsements, viability, and appearance. More than 90 percent of subjects made use of each one, including 93 percent who used the ideological schema. Further, 63 percent of the unique pieces of information within the ideological domain were accessed by subjects at some point. In other words, rather than shy away from ideological information as too confusing, individuals actively seek it and use it in a campaign environment.

Similar to these studies, Huckfeldt and his colleagues (2002) test both partisan and ideological schemas in candidate evaluation and preference. By combining party and ideological descriptions of candidates into congruent and noncongruent pairings (e.g., conservative Republican for the former and liberal Republican for the latter), they examine which schema dominates individual decision making. The authors find that the two reinforce each other in congruent cases but that only ideology has a significant effect on judgments in noncongruent scenarios.

Further studies also take on the debate regarding ideology versus party. Levitin and Miller (1979) find that ideology is a much better predictor of how close individuals feel to the Democratic and Republican parties and their candidates—both in general and on a host of issues— than is party identification. For example, when ideology and party were seemingly conflicting (e.g., liberal Republican), ideology appeared to win out, having the more determinative effect on resulting attitudes and judgments. Robinson and Fleishman (1988, 137) reach a similar conclusion in their analysis of ideology in presidential elections: "While party identification remains the major predictor of vote in American presidential elections, self-identified liberals and conservatives differ more meaningfully and significantly on political issues than do self-identified Democrats and Republicans." These studies indicate that ideology's influence on individuals' political preferences and choices seems to be not only independent from but occasionally as powerful as party affiliation.

Abramowitz and Saunders (2006) argue that ideology and party preference are not distinct but, rather, that ideology actually determines party affiliation. Conducting an analysis of party affiliation and ideological self-identification over time, they conclude that increases in Republican Party affiliation since the early 1990s have been the result of party affiliations falling in line with stable ideological preferences.

> Based on our evidence, . . . it appears that the questions most voters ask themselves in deciding which party to support are actually: "What do Democrats and Republicans stand for?" and "Which party's positions are closer to mine?" (186)

At a minimum, the sum total of this research raises serious questions about the traditional wisdom that citizens have little or no capacity for ideological reasoning. There is ample evidence that Americans do think ideologically, organizing political information in accord with the left-right construct and using that construct to judge candidates and make political choices. Additionally, there is evidence that this use of ideology is not limited to the most politically sophisticated among us and that it is not merely a reflection of the powerful force of individual partisan affiliation.

We do not believe or here attempt to convince the reader that Americans are ideological sophisticates. Again, our contention is simply that

Americans have more of an ideological capacity than they are traditionally given credit for and that they use this capacity to judge political
actors based on their policy behavior. Given the extensive supporting
research we have just discussed regarding the ideological capacities of
citizens, we hope readers will at least allow for this possibility as we proceed with a specific discussion of judgments of Congress and our empirical tests.

Ideology and Evaluations of Congress

To this point, we have spoken about the use of ideology in general terms.
We now focus our attention on Congress specifically. Many of the studies
previously cited looked at the use of ideology in evaluating hypothetical or
real electoral candidates, and there is indeed an extensive literature supporting the specific idea that congressional candidates' issue positions or
ideological stances significantly affect voting in these elections (for a review, see Canes-Wrone, Brady, and Cogan 2002). Additional research
finds that the degree of ideological congruence between citizens and their
member of Congress affects the performance rating the public gives that
member (Binder, Maltzman, and Sigelman 1998).

The public's ability to make these kinds of evaluations may not, however, transfer directly to institutions, particularly to one as large and complex as Congress. Scholars have argued that evaluating an institution is
different for citizens than evaluating individual political actors (e.g.,
Hager and Sullivan 1994; Mutz and Flemming 1999). Put simply, citizens may not want or be able to think about the collective Congress in
ideological terms.

To make meaningful ideological comparisons between themselves
and Congress, the public must have the capacity to judge the ideological
position of Congress reasonably accurately. In chapter 3, we presented
indirect evidence that Americans have some sense of the true policy direction of Congress—even those individuals who are typically classified
as less knowledgeable. Specifically, Americans alter their judgments of
Congress when there is a change in party control of Congress (and presumably then in the institution's policy direction). Direct evidence for individuals' ability to gauge Congress's policy behavior, or general ideological position, is more difficult to find, since almost no surveys ask the
public to place Congress on an ideological scale. An exception is the 1997
ANES pilot study, which asked a question about the ideological orientation of Congress. Using this question, Wlezien and Carman (2001) find

that respondents' placements of Congress on an ideological scale make sense both objectively and in relation to their placement of other political actors. They find this to be true for both the less educated and the more educated. Taken together with the evidence reviewed earlier in this chapter that citizens have a sense of where they themselves stand ideologically (or at least to which camp they belong), it would appear that Americans should be able to judge the comparative ideological distance between themselves and Congress.

Given Americans' desire for policy representation from Congress (as found in chap. 2), along with their reasonable informational and ideological abilities (as noted in chap. 3 and the immediately preceding discussion), we believe that just as research has shown that citizens evaluate other political actors on the basis of ideological compatibility, so, too, will they use such considerations to evaluate the entire Congress. Our general argument is that Americans partly base their evaluation of Congress's job performance on their perceived ideological distance from Congress as run by the majority party, with greater distance leading to less approval. In the following sections, we present specific predictions and tests of those predictions for individual citizens' evaluations of Congress and then for aggregate congressional approval ratings over time.

EFFECTS OF IDEOLOGICAL DISTANCE
ON INDIVIDUAL CITIZENS

We believe that individual citizens have a sense of not only where their own policy preferences are located on an ideological continuum but also where Congress's general policy stance is located on that same continuum, a sense largely defined by their ideological impressions of the majority party running Congress. In evaluating congressional performance, citizens take into account the relative proximity or distance between their own location and that of Congress on this continuum. Since Americans prefer a Congress whose policy actions more closely reflect their own policy preferences, we hypothesize that those who perceive a greater absolute distance between their own policy views and those of the congressional majority party will be less approving and that those who perceive relatively smaller differences will be more approving.

Our measure focuses on absolute ideological distance, rather than distance distinguished by ideological direction or strength, because we have in mind situations like the one presented in figure 4.1. While strong conservatives were the least approving of the Democratic Congress, strong liberals were not the most approving, indicating a nonlinear relationship between ideology and congressional approval. Consistent with this example, we believe that even if they are on the same side of the ideological spectrum as Congress, some ideologues (though these may well be few) could perceive Congress as being too moderate for their tastes. Those who feel this way should behave similarly to those who view the party as too liberal or too conservative: all should be more likely to disapprove of congressional job performance than those who feel more ideologically compatible with the majority party, and their likelihood of disapproval should be in proportion to their degree of ideological distance.

We test our hypothesis among individuals by employing data from the ANES from 1980, the first year the ANES asked the standard question on congressional job approval, to 2004, the year of the most recent available ANES survey.[4] Previous cross-sectional studies have generally been limited to a single Congress. The broad range of data employed here allows for analysis of our hypothesis across various configurations of partisan congressional control and ideological policy stances: strict Democratic control in 1980 and 1988–94; split control from 1982 through 1986; and strict Republican control in 1996, 1998, 2000, and 2004.[5]

The dependent variable in this study is approval of Congress's job performance. ANES asks respondents, "Do you approve or disapprove of the way the U.S. Congress has been handling its job?" We employ a trichotomous variable ranging from -1 to 1, placing those without a definitive opinion in between those who approve (1) and those who disapprove (-1).[6]

The key independent variable representing our hypothesis of ideological proximity is citizens' perceived distance from the majority party in Congress.[7] We measure this variable as the absolute value of respondents' self-placement on the ANES seven-point liberal-to-conservative ideological scale minus their placement of the party that holds a majority in Congress on the same ideological scale.[8] This variable ranges from 0 to 6, with higher values indicating a larger perceived distance from the party controlling Congress.

Ideally, this distance measure would use respondents' ideological ratings of the majority party's contingent in Congress specifically, rather than the party in general (e.g., "the Republican Party in Congress" instead of "the Republican Party"). Unfortunately, the biennial ANES surveys do not include ideological measures of the majority party in Congress per se. As a result, we use ideological placement of that party in general.

We conducted several tests to ensure that views of a party in general are reasonable surrogates for views of that same party "in Congress." First, one possible complication of using this measure is that views of a party could be influenced by referents other than the party's congressional delegation—in particular, the president. In practice, however, this does not turn out to be a significant concern. McCarty and Poole (1995) find that most presidents are ideologically located near the median of their party's congressional delegation, thus creating no particular discrepancy. As a check, we ran a version of our model controlling for perceived ideological distance from the president, but this variable never displayed a statistically significant effect in any of the twelve years and did not alter the basic results of our key variable. Second, we found that the average ideological location of the membership of the House majority party based on members' actual votes in Congress is a significant predictor of individuals' ANES ideological ratings of that party generally.[9] Finally, we were able to locate a Gallup survey from 1998 that asked respondents to state their ideological compatibility with the parties in Congress specifically rather than with the parties generally. While the range of control variables is more limited than in the ANES surveys, a streamlined replication of our analysis using this more specific measure of the congressional party's ideology produces the same basic result as our analysis using the ANES party measure (see the appendix for this analysis).

Figure 4.2 presents an initial bivariate test of the relationship between distance from the majority party and evaluations of Congress. The mean approval rating for Congress—measured with the trichotomous approval variable—is located on the y-axis, with individuals' perceived ideological distance on the x-axis. The chart includes all available years between 1980 and 2004 in which a single party controlled both chambers of Congress. In general, the figure skews strongly to the negative, as congressional ratings have been consistently on the negative side over time.

The figure demonstrates a clear pattern in support of our hypothesis that citizens' perceived ideological distance from Congress influences their judgments of congressional performance. As perceived ideological distance from the majority party increases, positive attitudes toward Congress decrease. For example, those who see no difference between their ideological position and that of the majority party have a 0.04 average approval rating of Congress. In contrast, those who see the furthest

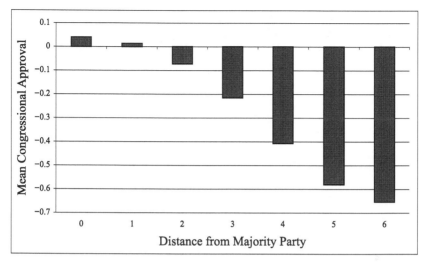

Fig. 4.2. Ideological distance from the majority party and congressional approval—years of single-party control, 1980–2004. (Data from ANES 2005.)

possible ideological distance rate congressional job performance at an average of -0.65 on the three-point scale, in solid disapproval territory. The overall effect of ideological distance is -0.69, more than one-third of the entire congressional evaluations scale.

While consistent with our expectations, these results are not definitive. If our hypothesis is correct, the results should be replicable in a test that controls for other possible influences on congressional approval. First, to control for the possibility that distance from the majority party is no better a predictor of congressional approval than distance from the minority party, the model includes measures of an individual's perceived ideological distance from both parties in each year. However, since we argue that citizens see the majority party as primarily responsible for the ideological direction of the institution, we do not expect the minority party variables to be significant. In the special cases of split control in the data (1982, 1984, 1986), we are unsure what to expect, given that each party has a majority in one of the two chambers.

The model also controls for variables that previous research has found (in some studies at least) to influence approval of Congress.[10] In chapter 2, we briefly discussed two main causal theories regarding public approval of Congress. First, several longitudinal studies find that economic concerns affect congressional approval (Durr, Gilmour, and Wolbrecht 1997; Parker 1977; Patterson and Caldeira 1990). Second, Hibbing and Theiss-Morse (1995) argue that evaluations of Congress are affected by citizens' process concerns: specifically, concerns about both efficiency and fairness in the legislative process. We control for the process concerns of efficiency and fairness, respectively, using questions asking citizens to what degree they believe government spending is efficient and whether they think the government is run for the benefit of all people. For economic concerns, we include a measure of whether respondents think the economy has gotten better or worse over the previous year.

Certain personal attributes of individuals also contribute to their opinions. While evidence has been mixed, some studies find that congressional approval is higher among individuals with a high level of "external efficacy," or perceived personal influence on government (Hibbing and Theiss-Morse 1995; Patterson, Ripley, and Quinlan 1992); lower among those who are more interested in politics (Patterson, Ripley, and Quinlan 1992); and lower among those in higher income brackets (Hibbing and Theiss-Morse 1995). Accordingly, we include controls for all of these personal characteristics.

Citizens' attitudes toward other political actors may also be related to their evaluations of Congress. Patterson, Ripley, and Quinlan hypothesize that "favorability toward [a citizen's] own representative might be transferred to the legislature of which they are a part" (1992, 322; see also Hibbing and Theiss-Morse 1995; Kimball and Patterson 1997). Other studies find that approval of the sitting president may increase approval of Congress (Kimball and Patterson 1997). Variables measuring the job performance of each of these actors are included in the model.

Finally, party identification has been found to affect congressional approval. People who align themselves with the congressional majority party are more likely to approve of the job Congress is doing, while members of the minority party are more likely to disapprove (Hibbing and Theiss-Morse 1995; Kimball and Patterson 1997; Patterson, Ripley, and Quinlan 1992). Accordingly, our model includes variables that capture whether a respondent is a Democrat or a Republican (independents are included in the constant term).[11]

Controlling for all of these other possible influences on congressional approval, we test our hypothesis by conducting a separate ordinal regression analysis for each year.[12] Table 4.1 presents the results. The table is organized according to party control of Congress. The first five columns

TABLE 4.1. Effects of Ideological Distance from the Majority Party on Congressional Approval, 1980–2004

INDEPENDENT VARIABLES	DEMOCRATIC CONGRESSES					REPUBLICAN CONGRESSES				DEMOCRATIC HOUSE/ REPUBLICAN SENATE		
	1980	1988	1990	1992	1994	1996	1998	2000	2004	1982	1984	1986
Ideological distance from Democratic Party	-.17** (.07)	-.32** (.05)	-.17** (.05)	-.28** (.05)	-.18** (.05)	.11* (.05)	.15** (.05)	.05 (.05)	-.02 (.05)	-.25** (.07)	-.17** (.05)	-.09* (.04)
Ideological distance from Republican Party	-.00 (.06)	.08 (.05)	.09 (.05)	.03 (.04)	.04 (.05)	-.17** (.05)	-.17** (.05)	-.10* (.05)	-.17** (.06)	.17** (.06)	.10* (.05)	.05 (.04)
Economy	.01 (.11)	.14* (.07)	.09 (.07)	.05 (.07)	.01 (.07)	.02 (.07)	-.01 (.07)	.06 (.05)	.20** (.08)	.05 (.08)	.05 (.06)	.22** (.05)
Government efficiency	.71** (.19)	.33** (.12)	.44** (.12)	.55** (.12)	.55** (.13)	.36** (.12)	.45** (.12)	.54** (.12)	.24 (.14)	.64** (.16)	.26* (.11)	
Government fairness	.28 (.20)	.63** (.14)	.64** (.14)	1.00** (.14)	.93** (.16)	.59** (.14)	.83** (.15)	.42** (.13)	.66** (.17)	.41* (.19)	.60** (.13)	
Efficacy	.10 (.06)	.12** (.04)	.03 (.04)	.10** (.04)	-.03 (.05)	.07 (.04)	-.01 (.04)	.09* (.04)	.09 (.05)	.18** (.05)	.11** (.04)	
Interest in politics	-.28** (.09)	-.20** (.07)	-.25** (.06)	-.41** (.07)	-.37** (.07)	-.24** (.07)	-.34** (.07)	-.20** (.07)	-.21** (.08)	-.29** (.09)	-.22** (.06)	-.24** (.05)
Income	.05 (.07)	.08 (.06)	-.13** (.05)	-.08 (.05)	-.10 (.06)	.01 (.06)	-.03 (.06)	.06 (.06)	-.00 (.06)	-.01 (.07)	.04 (.06)	.00 (.04)
Member approval	.09 (.05)	.21** (.06)	.09** (.05)	.13** (.05)	.13** (.06)	.13** (.04)	.07 (.06)	.09* (.04)	.07 (.06)	.13** (.05)	.14** (.04)	.14** (.04)
Presidential approval	.28** (.09)	.15* (.07)	.31** (.07)	.29** (.07)	.42** (.07)	-.00 (.08)	-.02 (.08)	.17* (.07)	.30** (.10)	.56** (.11)	.24** (.08)	.23** (.03)
Democrat	.13 (.19)	.43** (.15)	.19 (.14)	.51** (.14)	-.08 (.15)	.18 (.15)	.14 (.15)	-.22 (.14)	.08 (.18)	.41* (.20)	.48** (.14)	.50** (.12)
Republican	-.18 (.21)	-.19 (.15)	-.21 (.15)	-.28 (.17)	-.08 (.17)	.54** (.17)	.44** (.17)	.32 (.17)	-.35 (.20)	-.20 (.22)	.06 (.15)	.24 (.13)
Pseudo R^2	.15	.17	.13	.21	.23	.11	.14	.10	.17	.19	.12	.06
N	699	1,293	1,443	1,598	1,349	1,236	1,090	1,154	878	715	1,378	1,735

Source: Data from ANES 2005.

Note: Table entries are ordered logistic regression estimates (standard errors in parentheses).

*p ≤ .05   **p ≤ .01 (two-tailed)

contain the results for the Democratically controlled Congresses of 1980, 1988, 1990, 1992, and 1994. The next four columns contain the results for the Republican-controlled Congresses of 1996 through 2004. Finally, the last three columns contain the results for the split Congresses of 1982, 1984, and 1986.

In every single year we analyze, the results support our hypothesis. Not only does perceived ideological distance have a significant impact on judgments of congressional performance, it also has a consistently significant effect in the predicted direction. In each year, respondents' perceived ideological distance from the majority party has a negative impact on their performance rating of Congress. In other words, the greater the perceived ideological discrepancy between a citizen and the majority party is, the lower that individual's probability of approving of congressional performance is.

Specifically, for Congresses controlled by Democrats (in 1980, 1988, 1990, 1992, and 1994), ideological distance from the Democratic Party displays a consistently negative and significant effect. In these years, the farther citizens perceive the Democratic Party to be from themselves ideologically, the less likely they are to approve of the Democratic-controlled Congress's job performance. In contrast, the effect of one's distance from the Republican Party—the minority party in Congress in these years—appears relatively small and statistically insignificant in each year.

During Republican Congresses (from 1996 to 2004), the effects of these two variables measuring ideological distance reverses, as expected. In each year, ideological distance from the Republican Party has a significantly negative effect: the farther a citizen feels from the Republican Party ideologically, the less likely that citizen is to approve of Congress's job performance. At the same time, an individual's distance from the minority Democratic Party has far less substantive effect than distance from the majority party does, although the effect of the former is occasionally significant.

During Congresses in which Democrats held a majority in the House while Republicans held a majority in the Senate (in 1982, 1984, and 1986), the majority party in the House appears to hold more sway over public opinion of the collective Congress than does the majority party in the Senate. In each of these years, an individual's distance from the Democratic Party has a consistently negative and significant effect: the farther respondents see themselves from the House majority party, as opposed to the Senate majority party, the less they approve of Congress's performance. Distance from the Republican Party does not display a negative effect on approval and in fact appears to have a positive effect in 1982 and 1984—albeit an effect smaller than the negative effect of distance from the Democratic Party. These findings suggest that under divided congressional control, the public may primarily consider their distance from the House majority, rather than the Senate majority, when incorporating ideological opinions into their evaluation of Congress.

Importantly, the results in table 4.1 show that the overall pattern of support for our hypothesis is found even while controlling for other significant influences on congressional approval. The effects of most of these other factors are generally similar to those found in existing studies. Process concerns (efficiency and fairness), interest in politics, member approval, and presidential approval are all generally significant and in the expected direction. Efficacy is in the correct direction in all but one year and significant in five. As in other individual-level analyses, both national economic concerns and personal income display little effect (Patterson, Ripley, and Quinlan 1992).

One somewhat surprising finding is that party affiliation has only a sporadic effect on congressional evaluations in these models. The signs of the variables for party affiliation are generally in the expected direction, but they are significant in only seven of the twelve years.[13] While somewhat surprising at first, this finding is actually consistent with some existing literature. Wlezien and Carman (2001) find that party identification does not have an independent effect on individuals' affective evaluations of Congress when the model includes ideological distance from Congress. Hibbing and Larimer (2005) find similarly insignificant effects of party in a model that includes policy concerns. In contrast, studies that have found strong effects of party identification have generally not controlled for policy compatibility. Thus, in our model, it appears that the strength and consistency of our ideological distance variable may be explaining much of the variance traditionally attributed to party affiliation.

To further clarify the effects of ideological distance on congressional judgments, we translate the results in table 4.1 into estimated probabilities and present them graphically for both Democratic and Republican Congresses. Figure 4.3 displays the effect of ideological distance in years of Democratic control. Specifically, in each year and for each level of perceived ideological distance from the majority party, the figure

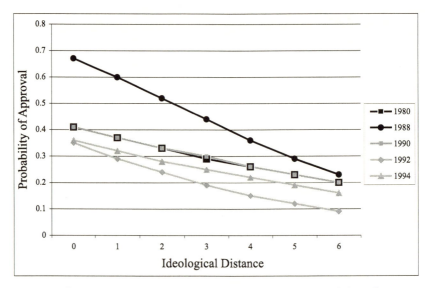

Fig. 4.3. Ideological distance from the majority party and probability of approving of Congress—years of Democratic control, 1980–94. Lines represent probability transformations of the estimates in table 4.1.

plots the probability that an otherwise average individual would approve of Congress.[14]

In these Democratic Congresses, the effect of the difference between maximum ideological distance compared to perfect ideological compatibility for this hypothetical citizen ranges from a twenty-point difference in the probability of approval in 1994 to a forty-four-point difference in 1988. For example, in 1988, an otherwise average individual who saw no distance between his or her own ideological preferences and the preferences of the Democratic Party had a 67 percent probability of approving of Congress and was therefore a likely approver. If that same person instead saw a large ideological distance (e.g., a four-point difference), his or her probability of approving of congressional performance would drop to 36 percent, making that person a likely disapprover. If that individual perceived complete incompatibility between his or her own ideology and that of Congress, he or she would have only a 23 percent probability of approving of Congress. In this way, the perceived ideological position of the majority party relative to one's own ideology helps determine whether one evaluates Congress's job performance positively or negatively.

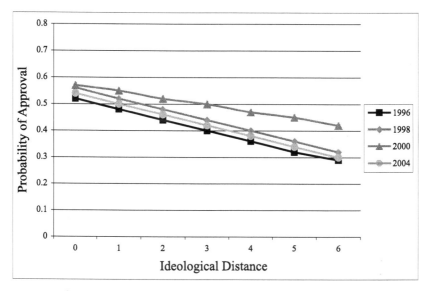

Fig. 4.4. Ideological distance from the majority party and probability of approving of Congress—years of Republican control, 1996–2004. Lines represent probability transformations of the estimates in table 4.1.

The results for Republican Congresses are virtually identical to those for Democratically controlled Congresses. Figure 4.4 contains the predicted probabilities for Republican Congresses. The maximum predicted effect of perceived ideological distance is twenty-four points in both 2004 and 1998 and twenty-three points in 1996. In 2004, the most recent year available, an otherwise neutral respondent who felt as ideologically distant as possible from the Republican Party had only a 30 percent chance of approving of Congress. In contrast, a citizen who saw no difference between his or her own ideology and that of Republicans had a 54 percent chance of approving of Congress—a twenty-four-point difference.

Overall during this period, regardless of whether Republicans or Democrats controlled Congress, Americans who rated themselves as ideologically similar to the majority party had an even chance of approving of Congress (50 percent probability), while those who rated themselves as ideologically distant were very unlikely to approve (25 percent probability)—an average effect of twenty-five points. This generally negative tendency in public evaluations of Congress even among those perceiving no ideological difference serves as a reminder that policy discrepancy is only one among multiple concerns that individuals regularly have regarding Congress. When we compare the effects of our variable of ideological distance to the effects of the traditional explanatory variables in the model, we see that they are of roughly the same magnitude. For example, in 1994, a year in which ideological distance had a below average total effect of twenty points on the probability of approval, the process variables of government efficiency and fairness had total effects of twenty-five points and twenty-one points, respectively. That same year, presidential approval had a seventeen-point effect on the probability of approval. These comparisons help demonstrate the relative importance of ideological distance in explaining individuals' evaluations of Congress.

AGGREGATE EFFECTS OF IDEOLOGICAL DISTANCE

We have shown that individuals rate Congress based partly on how distant its policy preferences seem from their own preferences. Our final task in this chapter is to test whether these individual-level effects have an impact on aggregate approval of Congress. Aggregate congressional approval ratings vary over time and across different Congresses, indicating that dynamic processes are at work influencing them. If our general argument about ideological distance is correct, temporal variation in the public's aggregate ideological compatibility with Congress should have an influence on the variation in aggregate ratings of the institution's job performance. Like the scholarly literature on individual evaluations of Congress, the literature explaining aggregate congressional approval ratings has largely ignored policy considerations as a possible explanatory factor (Durr, Gilmour, and Wolbrecht 1997; Parker 1977; Patterson and Caldiera 1990; Rudolph 2002). Our expectation, however, consistent with our argument and evidence regarding individual behavior, is that in the aggregate, the greater the degree of ideological distance between the public and Congress is, the lower the percentage of Americans who approve of Congress's job performance will be.

There are two ways in which aggregate ideological compatibility of Congress and the public can differ from one time period to another. First, the relative liberalism or conservatism of the public can vary. While the American public is basically moderate, the balance of public sentiment sometimes shifts to a relatively more liberal point of view or a relatively more conservative point of view within this moderate range (Stimson 1999). At the same time, we know that Democratic Congresses tend to pursue distinctly liberal policies and that Republican Congresses tend to pursue distinctly conservative ones (Poole and Rosenthal 1997). As a result, we can assume that the more liberal the policy preferences of the public are, the smaller the overall ideological distance between the public and a Democratically controlled Congress will be. Conversely, the more liberal the policy preferences of the public are, the greater their distance from a Republican controlled Congress will be.[15] Therefore, based on our theory of ideological proximity, our first hypothesis is that greater public liberalism (lower conservatism) will increase the percentage of Americans who approve of a Democratic Congress but will lower the percentage of Americans who approve of a Republican Congress, all else being equal.

The second source of changes in ideological proximity is variance in the ideological thrust of the policies pursued by Congress. One type of ideological variation in congressional policy activity is the dramatic difference in policy that occurs when a new party wins control of Congress, as discussed in chapter 3. Changes in party control are rare, however, and thus cannot explain most of the continual variation in congressional approval ratings over time. For this reason, we do not dwell on these differences here.[16]

A more common—albeit more slight—type of ideological variation in congressional policy activity is the relative ideological differences across Congresses controlled by the same party. Some Democratic Congresses are more liberal than other Democratic Congresses. Some Republican Congresses are more conservative than other Republican Congresses. Since Americans' aggregated views are relatively moderate, the greater the ideological extremism of the policies pursued by Congress is, the greater the overall ideological distance will be between the public and Congress, both during Democratic Congresses and during Republican Congresses. As a result, our theory of ideological proximity leads to a second hypothesis: greater ideological extremism (either liberal or conservative) by Congress will decrease the percentage of Americans who approve of Congress's job performance, all else being equal, while ideological moderation by Congress will lead to higher approval ratings.

Testing our expectations regarding collective approval ratings is not as simple as merely aggregating the ANES data from the last section. The ANES surveys comprise only thirteen points in time and would preclude any effort to explain variation in congressional approval within each two-year Congress. Instead, following the lead of other studies in

Fig. 4.5. Quarterly approval of congressional job performance, 1974–2006. (Data from archive at the Roper Center for Public Opinion Research at the University of Connecticut.)

this area (Durr, Gilmour, and Wolbrecht 1997; Rudolph 2002), we begin by creating a quarterly measure of congressional approval.

Survey questions on congressional job performance have only been asked irregularly, in a variety of nonstandard forms, and hardly ever before 1974. James Stimson (1999) has, however, created an algorithm allowing a researcher to combine irregular, nonidentical marginal survey results into one coherent time series. Using this technique, we combine the results from 689 available survey questions to create a single quarterly measure of public approval of Congress's job performance, from 1974 through 2006—the longest longitudinal measure of congressional approval that has been published to date.[17] Figure 4.5 displays our time series of quarterly congressional approval.

To measure the ideological leanings of the American public in each quarter during this time period, we use the commonly employed "policy mood" series created by Stimson (1999). Based on hundreds of policy-related survey questions, the measure captures the underlying level of liberal policy sentiment (nonconservative sentiment) in the public. As discussed earlier, we expect this variable representing public liberalism to have a positive effect on congressional approval ratings during Democratic Congresses and a negative effect during Republican Congresses.

To measure the ideology of the policies pursued by Congress, we employ the first dimension of Keith Poole and Howard Rosenthal's DW-NOMINATE roll call coordinate data. For each chamber in each Congress, these scholars calculate a measure of the average winning policy location on a policy space that has a primary liberal-to-conservative dimension and is comparable over time. Because the two chambers' scores are highly correlated over time ($r = .95$), we use a weighted average of the two. Consistent with our assumption that the parties pursue significantly different policies when in control of Congress, these scores demonstrate that the average winning policy locations during Republican Congresses never come close to approaching the average winning policy locations during Democratic Congresses.[18] Since our hypothesis regarding congressional ideology is stated in terms of extremism versus moderation, not liberalism versus conservatism (like the hypothesis regarding public ideology), we transform the scores so that for both Democratic Congresses and Republican Congresses, higher values always represent Congresses that are more distant from the moderate center of the scale—Democratic Congresses that are highly liberal or Republican Congresses that are highly conservative. As a result, the variable we include in our analysis measures ideological extremism by Congress, not ideological direction, and we expect it to have a consistently negative effect on congressional approval ratings, as previously discussed.

Since the variables of public ideology and congressional ideology are measured on fundamentally different scales, with no clear means of mapping one onto the other,[19] we cannot calculate the relative distance between these two referents as we did for the individual-level analysis in the previous section. Nevertheless, the logic of statistically controlled regression analysis means that we can effectively accomplish the same thing by including each of the two components of ideological distance as separate variables within the same model. By doing so, we are able to test the effect of differences in public ideology while holding constant the ideology of Congress, and we can simultaneously test the effect of differences in congressional ideology while holding constant the ideology of the public.

To fairly test our hypotheses, we also need to control for other possible influences on aggregate congressional approval, as suggested by the literature. First, we must ensure we are explaining evaluations reflecting contemporary events rather than carryover attitudes from times prior. To do so, we include the lagged value of congressional approval from the prior quarter as one explanatory factor.

Earlier studies have found evidence that both the economic environment and presidential evaluations affect aggregate levels of congressional approval (e.g., Parker 1977; Patterson and Caldiera 1990). Following Durr, Gilmour, and Wolbrecht (1997), we control for economic factors by including a variable that is a composite of several standard economic indicators. To account for effects of presidential approval, we include a measure of the average presidential approval rating from Gallup polls in each quarter.

There are also various institutional processes and events that can influence levels of congressional approval at any given time. Durr, Gilmour, and Wolbrecht (1997) argue that several process variables negatively influence approval of Congress: major legislative action, intrabranch conflict, and interbranch conflict in the form of vetoes and veto overrides (but see Rudolph 2002). We include measures of all of these variables in our model. We also control for the possible negative effect of congressional scandals, including a set of variables each representing a particular scandal. Finally, because Congress and the president often compete with each other in the public arena, with some presidents getting the better of Congress and others serving as a useful foil for it (Groeling and Kernell 2000; Peters 2005), we test whether each presidency has its own unique effect on congressional approval.[20] Given the sizable number of presidency and scandal variables, we drop insignificant ones from the final model, for parsimony.

The aggregate-level hypotheses we have laid out distinguish, of necessity, between Congresses controlled by a Democratic majority and those controlled by a Republican majority. Therefore, we conduct separate tests for each type of Congress.[21]

Table 4.2 presents the results of a robust linear regression analysis testing our hypotheses. The control variables generally behave as expected,[22] and the overall model provides a good fit to the data. Most important for our story, even after accounting for the traditional predictors, the results show that both the public's ideological sentiments and congressional ideological output have their own significant impact on aggregate congressional approval.

The first row of data displays the effects of public liberalism on congressional approval during Democratic Congresses and during Republican Congresses. In the former case, we predicted that greater liberalism in public attitudes would decrease the public's ideological distance from a Democratic Congress and therefore increase its approval of Congress. Consistent with this prediction, the results in the first column show that public liberalism significantly increases congressional approval ratings during Democratic control. Conversely, we predicted that greater liberalism in the public would increase its ideological distance from Republican Congresses, thereby decreasing aggregate approval. The results in

TABLE 4.2. Effects of Public Liberalism and Congressional Extremism on Aggregate Congressional Approval, 1974–2006

INDEPENDENT VARIABLES	APPROVAL OF CONGRESS DURING DEMOCRATIC CONGRESSES	APPROVAL OF CONGRESS DURING REPUBLICAN CONGRESSES
Public liberalism	.22°	−.29°°
	(.15)	(.11)
Congressional policy extremism	−.34°°	−.21°°
	(.16)	(.11)
Prior quarter approval of Congress	.41°°	.53°°
	(.12)	(.14)
National economic conditions	.03	.24°°
	(.04)	(.09)
Presidential approval	.15°°	.23°°
	(.04)	(.08)
Presidential vetoes	.07	−.09
	(.09)	(.54)
Veto overrides	−.64	−.91
	(.79)	(4.22)
Intra-Congress conflict	.06	−.03
	(.17)	(.07)
Major bills	−.43	−.07
	(.41)	(.19)
House Bank scandal	−6.48°°	
	(2.02)	
Reagan presidency	6.15°°	
	(1.70)	
Clinton presidency		−4.37°°
		(1.95)
Constant	−.62	6.41
	(8.41)	(10.54)
Adjusted R^2	.86	.90
Number of cases	59	42

Note: Table entries are regression coefficients (robust standard errors in parentheses).
°$p \leq .10$ °°$p \leq .05$ (one-tailed)

the second column support this hypothesis as well, showing that the more liberal the public is, the lower its approval of Congress during Republican control is.

The second row of data displays the effects of congressional policy extremism, testing our second hypothesis. In this case, holding public ideology constant, we predicted that greater ideological extremism on the part of Congress (extreme liberalism on the part of Democratic Congresses, extreme conservatism from Republican Congresses) would increase its ideological distance from the public and, in so doing, decrease congressional approval. The statistically significant negative coefficients in each model demonstrate that as either type of Congress increases the ideological extremism of its policy activity, the public's approval of congressional job performance drops. In other words, as Democratic Congresses behave more liberally, a relatively moderate public evaluates their performance more negatively, and as Republican Congresses act more conservatively, the same public responds by judging them more harshly as well.

We illustrate the magnitude of these effects by comparing the levels of approval predicted by the model under specific conditions. During Democratic Congresses, the model estimates that, all else being equal, an increase in public liberalism of one standard deviation will produce an increase of 0.9 points in the percentage of Americans who approve of Congress. Concomitantly, an increase in congressional policy extremism (liberalism) of one standard deviation will produce a decrease of 1.4 points in approval of Democratic Congresses. During Republican Congresses, the model estimates that an increase in public liberalism of one standard deviation will lead to a decrease of 1.3 points in congressional approval and that an increase in congressional policy extremism (conservatism) of one standard deviation will lead to a decrease of 1.0 points in approval.

CONCLUSION

The results from both the individual-level and aggregate-level tests carry several important implications. First, Americans are capable of using ideology even when evaluating such a complex, collective body as Congress. Individuals are able to place themselves and those controlling Congress on a standard ideological scale and to consider the relative difference in these placements when making judgments about institutional performance. Furthermore, it appears they have been able to do so for several decades now. These findings demonstrate capacities and actions that scholars have traditionally discounted over the past half century.

It is similarly encouraging (from the perspective of Americans' democratic capabilities) to find that in the aggregate analysis, Americans respond to the actual ideological direction of congressional policymaking when forming evaluations of Congress. While this does not by any means prove perfect awareness on the part of all citizens, it does suggest—albeit indirectly—that Americans' ideological perceptions overall are closely related to real congressional policy activity. Even across different Congresses controlled by the same party, the American public has been generally aware of and has frowned on Congresses whose legislative actions were relatively extreme ideologically.

Not only are Americans capable of making ideological comparisons, but they actively do so, and the effects of these ideological comparisons are substantively important to their evaluations of Congress. For individuals, greater or lesser ideological distance from the party controlling Congress can often make the difference between approval and disapproval of Congress. Those who perceive greater ideological compatibility between themselves and the majority party in Congress are more likely to approve of congressional performance, and those who perceive greater distance are more likely to disapprove.

These individual effects also cumulate to display significant effects on overall levels of congressional approval. In terms of congressional ideology, the generally moderate American public disapproves of Congresses that pursue highly ideological agendas, whether liberal or conservative. Within the public's narrow range of ideological variation, when the public is more liberal, it is more approving of Democratic Congresses but less approving of those controlled by Republicans. When it is more conservative, the opposite pattern holds. In sum, both individual and aggregate findings show a public that actually cares about the ideological nature and actions of those who control Congress. All things being equal, Americans prefer a Congress that is more in tune with their own ideological outlook.

It is particularly noteworthy that individuals' use of ideology in evaluating congressional performance occurs above and beyond any influences of party identification alone. Citizens are not blind party loyalists when it comes to Congress. Some Republicans may feel that the policies pursued by a Republican Congress are too conservative, while others may see them as not conservative enough. Similarly, many Democrats may wish that the actions of a Democratic Congress were not so liberal, while others may view them as too moderate. More important, ideological moderates from either party could be satisfied with a Congress run by the opposing party, if its actions were ideologically moderate.

Finally, this research carries potential implications regarding congressional elections. Given that individuals' opinions toward Congress are significantly shaped by their attitudes regarding the policy direction of Congress, it is certainly conceivable that the members of the party seen as responsible for that policy direction—the majority party—may suffer disproportionately on election day when voters disapprove of Congress. The next chapter begins to address these electoral implications and their wider significance for democratic responsiveness.

CHAPTER 5

Voting the Bums Out

One of the most famous puzzles in the study of Congress is that while a majority of Americans frequently disapprove of Congress as a whole, Americans by and large continue to vote to keep their individual member of Congress in office. According to the time series data we compiled in chapter 4, public approval of Congress's job performance averaged only 37 percent from 1974 through 2006, but during the same period, an average of two-thirds of Americans cast ballots to reelect their own House member.[1] This seeming disconnect between attitudes toward legislator and legislature is so well known that is has acquired its own label, Fenno's Paradox—so named for the classic exposition of the trend by political scientist Richard Fenno in the 1970s (Fenno 1975, 1978). This phenomenon, along with political science's conventional wisdom that Americans do not know or think much about Congress, has led scholars to assume that Americans do not consider the performance of the collective Congress when casting their votes in congressional elections (Fenno 1978; Mayhew 1974; Stokes and Miller 1962). As a result, scholarly explanations of how Americans cast their votes in congressional elections normally do not consider views of Congress as a relevant factor (e.g., Jacobson 2004).

We nevertheless believe that there are sufficient grounds to revisit the standard academic view that members of Congress are electorally insulated from performance evaluations of the institution. First, Americans do have meaningful opinions about the collective performance of Congress, as we have demonstrated in previous chapters. We know these opinions are not "nonattitudes" (Converse 1964), because they are empirically correlated with logically relevant events, circumstances, and other opinions.[2] Second, a relationship between approval of Congress and congressional elections is not ruled out merely because a majority of Americans usually disapprove of Congress while most incumbents are easily reelected. The true test is whether variation in these evaluations of job performance can explain variations in voting in congressional elections.

Certainly, both congressional approval and congressional voting exhibit significant variation, despite the aggregate trends. We have seen that within the aggregate figure of congressional disapproval, precisely which Americans approve and which disapprove changes according to various circumstances, including the policy direction of the majority party. Even in the aggregate, there are some elections during which—contrary to the usual pattern—more Americans approve of Congress than disapprove, including the elections of 1998, 2000, and 2002.

Additionally, there is considerable variation in voting in congressional elections. While two-thirds of voters cast ballots for their House incumbent in the seventeen elections from 1974 through 2006, this means that one-third of voters cast ballots against their incumbent and for the challenger. Aggregate vote returns for incumbents ranged between 35 percent in some districts to 100 percent in others. Furthermore, 11 percent of House races in this time span had no incumbent running. In these elections, 42 percent of voters cast ballots against the candidate from the departing incumbent's party, and 58 percent cast ballots for the departing incumbent's party. Aggregate vote returns for these seats ranged from 16 to 96 percent for the departing incumbent's party.[3] It seems possible that differences in evaluations of Congress could help explain these differences in voting.

RETROSPECTIVE VOTING THEORY AND CONGRESSIONAL EVALUATIONS

V. O. Key was among the first political scientists to articulate a theory of how Americans' perceptions of past government performance can affect their vote choice on election day. Key writes,

> Governments must act or not act, and action or inaction may convert supporters into opponents or opponents into supporters. Events, over which government may, or more likely may not, have control, shape the attitudes of voters to the advantage or the disadvantage of the party in power. (1966, 9)

In other words, voters observe government actions and events in the period preceding the election, use these observations to evaluate the performance of government, consider which party is in power, then use the evaluations as a guide in determining that party's relative suitability for governing. If voters' observations lead them to feel more positively than negatively about a party's ability to govern, they will be more likely to vote for candidates from that party. If voters' assessments are more negative, they will be less likely to vote for that party's candidates. Though Key himself did not use the label, this general process he described is now known as "retrospective voting."

It is worth emphasizing the important role parties play in retrospective voting theory. In retrospective voting, the public holds government accountable not by rewarding or punishing incumbents per se but, rather, by giving credit or blame to any candidate from the party in power. Voters judge the party in power based on its performance and then decide whether to replace or return that party on election day. This means that voters use this lens in judging not only the ruling party's incumbents but also that party's candidates who are challenging incumbents or running for open seats. Such behavior may not seem intuitive, as these candidates are not actually in office at election time. Anthony Downs (1957, 40) writes, however, that it is more rational for voters to use a party's previous track record as a guide to the future performance of its members than to simply trust the promises candidates make about what they would do if elected. After all, actions speak louder than words.

The literature on retrospective voting in presidential elections finds that several kinds of retrospective evaluations, including evaluations of the nation's economy and relative peace, affect voting for president. However, the strongest effects come from evaluations of presidential job performance, which is considered to be a summary judgment of the president's job performance across all policy areas (Fiorina 1981, 80). In particular, when Americans approve of the president's job performance, more of them cast votes for the presidential candidate of the party currently holding the White House—even if that candidate is not the incumbent. When Americans disapprove of the president's job performance, more of them cast votes for the presidential candidate from the party not in the White House.

Scholars have also applied retrospective voting theory to congressional elections, but not in a manner parallel to presidential elections. The prevailing view of retrospective voting in congressional elections is that these elections are also a referendum on the performance of the president, rather than on the performance of the Congress. As David Mayhew has written, "national swings in the congressional vote are normally judgments on what the president is doing (or is thought to be doing) rather than on what Congress is doing" (1974, 28). In other words, when citizens disapprove of the president's performance, they are less supportive of congressional candidates from the president's party, and when they approve of the president's performance, they are more supportive of congressional candidates from the president's party. This view that voters only take the performance of the executive branch, not the legislative branch, into account when casting votes for Congress dominates both the literature on aggregate congressional election outcomes (e.g., J. Campbell 1986; Jacobson 2004; Lewis-Beck and Rice 1992; Marra and Ostrom 1989; Tufte 1975) and that on individual vote choice (e.g., Abramowitz 1985; Abramson, Aldrich, and Rohde 2007; Fiorina 1981; Jacobson 2004).

We find this prevailing view to be an incomplete explanation of retrospective voting in congressional elections. Our concerns are based on both logical and normative grounds. From a logical perspective, it seems unlikely that voters charged with selecting candidates best suited to serve in the legislative branch would base their decision on executive performance but not on legislative performance. After all, the winner will presumably have more impact on legislative actions than on any executive actions. Put simply, when voting for Congress, congressional performance would appear to be a more relevant criterion for voters than presidential performance.

One logical reason voters might treat congressional elections as a referendum on the president's performance but not on Congress's performance is if they believe that the president and his administration are solely or at least primarily responsible for national events and conditions and that congressional actions have virtually no impact. Given Fiorina's observation that "most analysts have viewed the presidency as stronger than the Congress at least since the time of FDR" (1992, 79), it might not be too surprising if ordinary citizens also shared this view. Trends in public opinion data seem to dismiss this possibility, however.

We searched the University of Connecticut's Roper Center iPOLL database for every survey question from 1974 through 2006 that asked respondents to identify who was "most responsible" for a specific national condition or event. From the fifty-six questions our search turned up, we selected only closed-end questions whose options included the president and Congress (sometimes among other options). The results from these questions are summarized in table 5.1. The table shows that

Americans are usually just as likely—in fact, in most cases, more likely—to say that Congress is responsible for national conditions and events than they are to say the president is responsible.[4] This is true not only for events about which the public felt negatively but also for events that were publicly popular, such as the passage of the 1997 Balanced Budget Act and the 1996 Welfare Reform Act. It seems clear from these survey results that a substantial number of Americans believe that Congress bears significant responsibility for national conditions and events.[5]

In addition, normative theories of representation would seem to argue that congressional performance evaluations should affect congressional elections. If members of Congress are not held accountable for the performance of their institution, they have little or no incentive to act in ways that are collectively responsible. Members may have some incentive to try to help burnish the image of a president from their own party, but during unified government, the majority party would have no

TABLE 5.1. Perceived Institutional Responsibility for National Conditions and Events, 1974–2006

ISSUE	SURVEY DATE(S)	AVERAGE % ATTRIBUTING TO		NUMBER OF TIMES ASKED
		PRESIDENT	CONGRESS	
National economy	1979–2003	27	33	17
Budget deficit	1982–90	21	44	7
Gridlock	1992–97	29	41	8
Gas prices	May 2005	17	3	1
Gun control failure	Apr. 2000	10	50	1
HMO reform failure	Dec.1999	12	34	1
Social Security reform failure	Jan. 1999	12	42	1
Budget agreement	May–Aug. 1997	36	45	4
Drug use increase	Sep. 1996	9	6	1
Welfare reform enactment	Aug. 1996	21	57	1
Government shutdown	Nov. 1995–Oct. 1996	31	49	3
National health care failure	Sep.–Oct. 1994	10	46	3
Economic stimulus plan failure	Apr.–Jul. 1993	18	57	2
Savings and loan crisis	Jul.–Aug. 1990	31	23	2
Tax reform enactment	Aug. 1986	33	44	1
Energy problems	Oct. 1979	23	42	1
U.S. influence in the world	Oct. 1979	43	26	1
Social Security tax hike	Jan. 1978	14	68	1
Total		25	39	56

Source: Roper Center's iPOLL database at the University of Connecticut (includes multiple polling firms).
Note: Figures do not include responses of "both."

incentive to perform its executive oversight duties diligently. Diligent oversight would be a hallmark of an effective Congress and would be a service to the nation. But if Congress is not judged on its own performance, the majority party's only concern would be protecting their president's image—something that strong oversight could harm. During divided government, in contrast, the majority party would have no incentive to facilitate positive political change—such as confirming appointments or enacting legislation—and might even have an incentive to obstruct such change. Doing so could harm the national welfare, but if voter anger only harms the president's party, it would be a rational electoral strategy.

For both logical and normative reasons, then, we believe that Americans do hold Congress responsible for its performance when they cast their votes on election day. Our specific expectations regarding the effect of congressional evaluations on voting in congressional elections flow from the general theory of retrospective voting. To review briefly, retrospective voting theory says that voters evaluate the performance of government in the period preceding the election, observe which party is in power, then use their retrospective assessments as a guide in determining that party's suitability for governing. If retrospective assessments lead them to feel more positively about a party's ability to govern, they will be more likely to vote for candidates from that party.

If we apply retrospective voting theory specifically to the legislative branch of government—in the same way it has already been applied to the executive branch—we arrive at the following narrative: Voters evaluate the performance of Congress in the period before the election. Consciously or unconsciously, voters also have a sense of which party is in control of Congress—as we have demonstrated earlier in this book.[6] Voters then use their own evaluation of congressional job performance in determining whether the majority party in control of Congress should be rewarded or punished. Voters who approve of the job Congress has been doing are more likely to vote for candidates from the majority party in the congressional election. Voters who disapprove of Congress's performance are less likely to vote for candidates from the majority party in the congressional election.

While the preceding narrative adheres the most closely to the standard, party-based retrospective voting model, there is an alternative, nonpartisan hypothesis that we also test in our analyses. Studies by Richard Born and by scholars at the Ohio State University have found that citizens' evaluations of Congress have a positive influence on their appraisals of their own incumbent member (Born 1990; Ripley et al. 1992). Since these studies were not restricted to districts with majority party members, this suggests the possibility that voters might use their evaluations of Congress to judge the suitability of all incumbents in Congress, not simply members of the majority party.[7] If this is the case, voters who approve of Congress's performance should be more likely to vote for incumbents (from either party), and those who disapprove of Congress should be less likely to vote for incumbents. Furthermore, unlike the partisan model, evaluations of Congress should not have any impact on open-seat races, since only the suitability of incumbents, not the suitability of an entire party, is at issue in this scenario.

There is also the possibility that Americans simply do not use retrospective evaluations of Congress when voting for Congress. This null hypothesis is the most consistent with the literature in political science. As we noted at the beginning of this chapter, work by Fenno and others suggests that incumbents are adept at inoculating themselves from public displeasure with the collective Congress. If this is the case, voters' evaluations of Congress's performance should not make them any more or less likely to vote for incumbent candidates or any more or less likely to vote for majority party candidates.

Scholars have generally not attempted to comprehensively distinguish among these alternative arguments.[8] However, a few recent studies contain evidence that is consistent with our partycentric theory of retrospective congressional evaluations affecting elections for Congress. First, Hibbing and Tiritilli (2000) find evidence suggesting that public disapproval of Congress significantly decreased voting for majority party incumbents in the 1994 House elections. However, their study does not control for effects of presidential approval, which many observers believe also played a large role in that election. In addition, Lipinski's (2004) study of congressional communications suggests that House members themselves believe that disapproval of Congress harms the majority party on election day. Lipinski finds that in their written communications with constituents, majority party members of Congress are significantly more likely to try to boost the image of Congress, while minority party members are significantly more likely to denigrate the performance of Congress.[9] Furthermore, among House members asked what effect low congressional approval ratings have on incumbents' reelection prospects, Lipinski's survey showed that 68 percent believed it hurt majority party prospects, while only 40 percent believed it hurt minority party prospects.

Are members of Congress correct in their beliefs about the role of congressional performance evaluations in elections? Should incumbents from both parties share the same concerns? Or are members free from the impact of these public evaluations? In the rest of this chapter, we present comprehensive empirical tests evaluating each of these hypotheses.

EFFECTS ON HOUSE VOTERS: INDIVIDUAL SURVEY DATA

Our analysis of how evaluations of Congress affect voting in congressional elections focuses on elections to the House of Representatives.[10] Our first approach to this empirical question employs the use of national survey data collected by ANES. The survey data cover the thirteen House elections between 1980, when ANES began asking the standard congressional approval question, and 2004, the year of the most recent available ANES survey.

A basic test of our hypothesis that those who approve of Congress are more likely to vote for majority party candidates than are those who disapprove is to pool the data and check the raw percentage who said they voted for the majority party candidate. Figure 5.1 presents the results of this simple test. The left-hand portion of the figure shows that among respondents who approved of Congress, 59 percent voted for the candidate from the majority party, while among respondents who disapproved, only 48 percent voted for the candidate from the majority party—a statistically significant difference of eleven points. This simple test provides some early evidence to refute the null hypothesis.

Distinguishing between our hypothesis and the incumbency-based hypothesis requires that we compare the difference that approval makes across each of the specific types of races. In particular, the incumbency-based hypothesis predicts that disapproval of Congress will decrease voting for majority party candidates when they are incumbents, increase voting for majority party candidates when they challenge incumbents, and have no effect in races without incumbents. In contrast, our party-based hypothesis predicts that disapproval of Congress will lower the percentage of votes for majority party candidates across all race types. Consistent with both arguments, figure 5.1 also shows that in races with majority party incumbents, 79 percent of approvers voted for the majority party candidate, but only 66 percent of disapprovers did so. However, in races with minority party incumbents and races with no incumbents, the results support our party-based hypothesis rather than the incum-

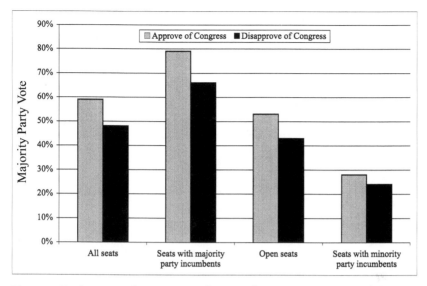

Fig. 5.1. Evaluations of Congress and voting for majority party candidates in House elections, 1980–2004. (Data from ANES 2005.)

bency hypothesis. With minority party incumbents, 28 percent of approvers voted for the majority party candidate (the challenger), compared to 24 percent of disapprovers who did so. In open-seat contests, 53 percent of approvers voted for the majority party candidate, while only 43 percent of disapprovers did so.[11]

While these simple tests support our argument, they do not take into account the many other factors that can affect voting in congressional elections. Therefore, we repeat the analysis with a regression model that takes into account these other factors.[12] Traditional predictors of congressional voting can be roughly grouped into national factors, local candidate-specific factors, and voter partisanship. National factors include retrospective assessments of the president's job performance and the nation's economy. Studies show that in both cases, positive evaluations increase the likelihood that a voter will support the president's party. As such, their effect on majority party voting should differ depending on whether the House majority party is also the president's party or not, and our model takes this interaction into account. Local candidate-specific factors include not only the incumbency status of the district but also the name recognition of each candidate—an indicator of candidate and campaign quality—and, for districts with incumbents, voters' evaluations of their own incumbent's job performance. Finally, whether a voter's partisanship matches or conflicts with that of the majority party candidate is also a strong predictor of one's congressional vote.[13]

The results of the full analysis, presented in table 5.2, confirm the pattern found in the preceding tests. Overall, approval of Congress has a significant, positive effect on voting for majority party candidates. Here again, this is not only true when the majority party candidate is an incumbent. We find a similarly significant, positive effect on voting for majority party candidates in open-seat races as well as in races with minority party incumbents. Across all race types, individual voters who approve of congressional performance are more likely to support the majority party's candidates, as hypothesized. In this case, because of the controls included in the model, we can be sure these effects are not merely a product of the other traditional forces thought to shape congressional voting, such as presidential evaluations, candidate characteristics, or partisanship.

We do not mean to suggest that evaluations of congressional performance are the driving force in citizens' voting decisions. As expected, traditional factors, such as party identification, play a much larger role than congressional approval. The relative magnitude of effects can be illustrated more clearly by translating our results into specific probabilities. Because additional tests reveal no significant difference in the size of effects across race types, we use the results of the pooled model, with all other predictors set at their typical values.[14]

For a voter who is from the same party as the majority party candidate—and has no other factors tipping her or him away from that candidate—that voter's particular evaluation of Congress will not be enough to overcome the influence of her or his partisan leanings. If that voter approves of Congress, her or his probability of supporting the majority party candidate is 81 percent; if that voter disapproves, this probability drops only six points, to 75 percent. Similarly, a voter from the minority party has an 18 percent chance of supporting a majority party candidate if she or he disapproves of Congress, a figure that rises only five points, to 23 percent, if she or he approves.

For voters who do not have a strong predisposition toward one candidate, however, the relatively modest effect of congressional approval can be decisive. For example, a typical independent voter has a 45 percent chance of voting for the majority party candidate if she or he disapproves of Congress, but the same voter has a 53 percent chance of voting for the majority party candidate if she or he approves—a shift from likely opposition to likely support.

In our analysis, we considered the possibility that the size of congressional approval's effect might differ depending on specific environmental factors, such as whether party control of the branches of government was

TABLE 5.2. Effects of Congressional Approval on Individual Vote for Majority Party Candidates in House Elections, 1980–2004

	ALL RACE TYPES	MAJORITY PARTY INCUMBENT	DISTRICTS WITH AN OPEN SEAT	MINORITY PARTY INCUMBENT
Congressional approval	.17°°	.16°°	.25°°	.12°
	(.03)	(.05)	(.08)	(.06)
Approval of majority party president	.53°°	.47°°	.46°°	.66°°
	(.07)	(.10)	(.15)	(.13)
Approval of minority party president	−.60°°	−.71°°	−.54°°	−.53°°
	(.05)	(.07)	(.10)	(.08)
Economy (majority party president)	.07	.16	−.13	.12
	(.09)	(.14)	(.19)	(.16)
Economy (minority party president)	−.29°°	−.27°°	−.49°°	−.23°
	(.06)	(.08)	(.14)	(.11)
Approval of majority party incumbent	1.77°°	1.81°°		
	(.07)	(.07)		
Approval of minority party incumbent	−1.80°°			−1.81°°
	(.09)			(.09)
Party identification	1.32°°	1.31°°	1.31°°	1.33°°
	(.05)	(.07)	(.11)	(.08)
Recognize majority party candidate name	1.15°°	.92°°	1.30°°	1.25°°
	(.09)	(.16)	(.20)	(.13)
Recognize minority party candidate name	−1.16°°	−1.06°°	−1.67°°	−1.01°°
	(.08)	(.10)	(.23)	(.21)
Majority party incumbent	−.04			
	(.10)			
Minority party incumbent	.19°			
	(.11)			
Majority party president	−.44°	−.16	−.74°	−.71°
	(.18)	(.28)	(.39)	(.30)
Constant	.22	.17	.74°	.37
	(.16)	(.21)	(.35)	(.27)
Pseudo R^2	.68	.61	.50	.61
Number of cases	9,891	5,221	1,246	3,424

Source: Data from ANES 2005.

Note: Table entries are logistic regression coefficients (standard errors in parentheses). Dummy variables for year are included in each model to capture any stationary effects, but most were insignificant and are suppressed from the results to conserve space.

°$p \leq .05$ °°$p \leq .005$ (one-tailed)

unified or divided and whether or not a presidential election was taking place. However, further statistical tests found no evidence that these factors made any significant difference in the effect of congressional approval.

This analysis of survey data provides support for our argument that voters use retrospective assessments of congressional performance in determining how they vote in House elections. However, there are some weaknesses inherent to the use of cross-sectional survey data when studying elections. First, on the basis of surveys alone, we cannot be sure that those who say they voted actually did (Silver, Anderson, and Abramson 1986). Consequently, our results may be biased by the responses of nonvoters. Likewise, surveys cannot confirm which candidate respondents actually supported. Some studies have found that self-reported vote choice in postelection surveys overstates actual voting for winning candidates (Atkeson 1999; Box-Steffensmeier, Jacobson, and Grant 2000; Wright 1993). Finally, cross-sectional surveys measure all variables at the same point in time. Without the certainty that evaluations of Congress preceded vote choice temporally, there remains some question about the proper inference regarding causal direction (Frankfort-Nachmias and Nachmias 2000). Fortunately, there is an alternative methodological strategy that is not subject to these particular weaknesses (although it has its own). In the following section, we analyze actual vote returns to see whether or not the results confirm those found in the survey data.

EFFECTS ON HOUSE VOTERS: ELECTION RETURNS

Analyzing vote returns means we are looking at actual votes rather than relying on the veracity of survey respondents regarding their voting patterns. If we can measure public evaluations of Congress in the period preceding each election, we can also gain confidence about our causal inferences. However, this method carries its own imperfections. In particular, use of the secret ballot prevents us from identifying which person cast which vote. Thus we cannot precisely match individual opinions with individual votes. As a result, the use of actual vote returns necessarily involves aggregation of data. A drawback with aggregation is that a relationship revealed at an aggregate level cannot automatically be assumed to exist at the individual level—it could merely be an artifact of aggregation. Fortunately, this potential concern is mitigated by the fact that we have already found evidence of significant effects at the individual level and are using aggregated data mainly as a secondary check on those results. We believe that using both methods together provides more analytic leverage than using either one alone.

In this analysis of vote returns, we investigate the effect of aggregate congressional approval ratings on the percentage of the actual two-party vote received by the majority party candidate in each district. To increase our confidence in the causal direction of this relationship, we need a measure of congressional approval in the period prior to the election. Drawing from the quarterly measure of congressional approval we created for the analysis in chapter 4, we here use the congressional approval rating from the third quarter of each election year—the measure most closely preceding the election.

To ensure that any effects of congressional approval we find are not attributable to other factors, our model controls for national and local variables that previous research has found to influence individual congressional elections.[15] Specifically, we control for presidential approval using the average percentage of citizens approving of the president's job performance in Gallup surveys conducted during the third quarter of the election year. Following other election studies (e.g., Jacobson 1989), we measure national economic conditions as the percentage change in real disposable per capita income over the year ending in the third quarter of the election year. We expect larger values of both of these variables to increase vote percentages for majority party candidates when the president is from the majority party, and we expect them to decrease vote percentages for majority party candidates when the president is from the opposing party. We take into account this expected differential by interacting each variable with presidential approval. The model captures local conditions by measuring the percentage of the two-party vote received by the majority party candidate in the last congressional election, the incumbency status of each seat, whether the incumbent is a freshman, whether the candidate from each party has prior political experience, and campaign spending by each candidate.

Our hypothesis in this aggregate analysis follows from the partisan hypothesis we tested in the individual analysis. In particular, we expect to find that higher levels of congressional approval will increase the percentage of votes cast for the majority candidate in each district. Such a finding would help confirm that the individual voter effects we found in the previous section are real and substantive, not artifactual or inconsequential.

The results in table 5.3 show that, consistent with our hypothesis and

TABLE 5.3. Effects of Aggregate Congressional Approval on Percentage Vote for Majority Party Candidates in House Elections, 1974–2006

	ALL RACE TYPES	DISTRICTS WITH A MAJORITY PARTY INCUMBENT	DISTRICTS WITH AN OPEN SEAT	DISTRICTS WITH A MINORITY PARTY INCUMBENT
Congressional approval	.29°°	.36°°	.12°	.20°°
	(.02)	(.03)	(.08)	(.03)
Approval of majority party president	.00	−.02	.09	.01
	(.02)	(.02)	(.08)	(.02)
Approval of minority party president	−.12°°	−.16°°	−.11°	−.08°°
	(.02)	(.02)	(.07)	(.02)
Economy (majority party president)	.02	−.02	.21	−.09
	(.13)	(.15)	(.48)	(.18)
Economy (minority party president)	−1.11°°	−.75°°	−.88°°	−1.58°°
	(.05)	(.07)	(.22)	(.07)
Previous vote percentage in district	.59°°	.58°°	.35°°	.60°°
	(.01)	(.01)	(.03)	(.02)
Experienced majority party candidate	3.82°°		3.36°°	2.69°°
	(.31)		(.81)	(.30)
Experienced minority party candidate	−3.28°°	−2.39°°	−4.04°°	
	(.30)	(.31)	(.81)	
Majority party incumbent	1.75°°			
	(.39)			
Minority party incumbent	−4.47°°			
	(.40)			
Majority party freshman incumbent	2.56°°	3.02°°		
	(.35)	(.33)		
Minority party freshman incumbent	−2.44°°			−3.74°°
	(.40)			(.35)
Majority party candidate spending	.68°°	−.14	3.20°°	6.90°°
	(.20)	(.23)	(.74)	(.41)
Minority party candidate spending	−2.01°°	−5.54°°	−4.06°°	−.07
	(.21)	(.32)	(.59)	(.31)
Majority party president	−10.62°°	−9.71°°	−14.32°°	−10.27°°
	(1.00)	(1.25)	(4.08)	(1.34)
Constant	20.40°°	26.46°°	38.26°°	12.67°°
	(1.00)	(1.39)	(3.12)	(1.17)
Adjusted R^2	.85	.59	.51	.66
Number of cases	5,495	2,749	576	2,170

Note: Table entries are regression coefficients (robust standard errors in parentheses).
°$p \leq .10$ °°$p \leq .005$ (one-tailed)

with the individual-level results, greater congressional approval significantly increases the percentage of votes received by majority party candidates (at the expense of minority party candidates). Also as in the individual-level results, we can be sure that this effect is partisan-based rather than incumbency-based (the alternative hypothesis), because the same basic relationship is found not only when the majority party candidate is the incumbent but also when the majority party candidate is the challenger or a contestant in an open-seat contest. In other words, greater congressional approval consistently increases voting for majority party candidates, regardless of candidate incumbency.[16]

The overall effect of congressional approval across all race types is approximately a three-point increase in a majority party candidate's aggregate vote percentage for every additional ten points of congressional approval. The standard deviation in congressional approval from election to election is just over eight points during this period. This means that a typical divergence from average congressional approval produces a change of about 2.3 points in the majority party's vote percentage across all races in an election. In terms of votes, this average change in congressional approval translates into an average of 1,556,716 changed votes nationally in an election, or an average of 4,196 changed votes in every contested House district in an election.[17]

CONCLUSION

This chapter has demonstrated that the public's evaluations of Congress's job performance do affect voting in House elections. Consistent with the expectations derived from previous chapters, these effects are based on the party membership of candidates, not their incumbency status. Put simply, the public holds the majority party responsible for the performance of Congress.

When voters approve of Congress, they are more likely to vote for majority party candidates, and when they disapprove, they are less likely to vote for majority party candidates. This effect is found not only on the marginal probabilities of individual votes but also on the aggregate percentage of actual votes cast. We find that Americans cast a higher percentage of votes for majority party candidates when approval ratings of Congress are high than when ratings of Congress are low.

These findings are significant for several reasons. Regarding voters, they show that public evaluations of Congress are not meaningless attitudes. Voters actually use these attitudes when making electoral decisions and casting votes on election day. In doing so, voters demonstrate that they would like to hold Congress accountable for its performance. This is important because if there were no evidence that voters attempt to hold Congress accountable through elections, there would be little reason to hope or expect that actual responsiveness on the part of Congress might be achieved.

A related reason for the findings' significance is that other political actors base their actions in part on expectations about voter behavior. In particular, potential candidates who are trying to decide whether or not to run for Congress try to anticipate whether or not such a run will be successful. If voter behavior did not depend on ratings of congressional job performance, political actors could safely ignore these ratings. But given our finding that vote margins do depend on congressional performance ratings, it is possible that potential candidates would take this factor into consideration as well. This possibility is the subject of the next chapter.

CHAPTER 6

Riding the Electoral Wave

The composition of Congress is determined not only by the decisions of voters but also by potential candidates' decisions on whether or not to run for office. Smart politicians will be strategic when making this decision. According to Jacobson and Kernell (1983), being strategic in this context involves taking into account how national political conditions prior to an election might affect one's prospects for success in that election. A strategic politician will be more likely to run when conditions are favorable and may choose to sit out when prospects for victory are grim. In chapter 5, we demonstrated that congressional approval ratings affect voting across all types of congressional elections and thereby affect the electoral fortunes of candidates who run in these elections. That congressional performance has an impact on electoral outcomes begs the question of whether savvy politicians, deciding whether or not to run for office, have some awareness of this relationship—if not consciously, then at least instinctually—and factor it into their decision-making calculus.

In this chapter, we analyze the possible connection between public evaluations of Congress and the strategic behavior of candidates. In particular, we are interested in two types of strategic behavior: that of incumbents and that of high-quality challengers to incumbents.[1] In each electoral cycle, congressional incumbents must decide whether to run for reelection—a safe bet much more often than not—or to retire. In addition, quality potential challengers must decide whether or not to take on an incumbent—a risky attempt under the best of circumstances. Existing research in each area suggests that such decisions are not random but are instead based on rational calculations made by the political actors involved. Incumbents occasionally retire rather than face potential defeat (e.g., Hall and Van Houweling 1995), and high-quality challengers sometimes take a chance and run against a current incumbent if they think they can win (e.g., Black 1972). Our purpose in this chapter is to determine what role, if any, public approval of Congress plays in influencing whether or not incumbents run and whether or not they face a quality challenger.

There is a distinct set of literature regarding the strategic behavior of quality challengers, there is another regarding strategic retirements by incumbents, and the factors known to affect each are not exactly the same.[2] Given this fact, it is entirely conceivable that congressional approval may not have the same effect in each situation. For this reason, we have chosen to treat each question separately—addressing strategic, high-quality challenges first and then strategic incumbent retirements. At the end of the chapter, we compare these findings and discuss what they say about the overall role congressional evaluations play in politicians' decisions of whether or not to run for Congress at any given time.

QUALITY CHALLENGES

It is well known that unseating a congressional incumbent is extremely difficult. From 1974 through 2006, only 4 percent of House incumbents who sought reelection were defeated on election day. Though defeat is rare, long-standing research has shown that a major factor that can lead to an incumbent's defeat is the quality of the challenger (e.g., Cox and Katz 1996; Jacobson 1989; Levitt and Wolfram 1997; Snowiss 1966).

What characteristics constitute quality when it comes to challenging a congressional incumbent? According to Maisel, Stone, and Maestas (2001), candidate quality involves both personal and political resources. Important personal resources include integrity, the ability to work effectively with others, and commitment to public service. Political resources include name recognition, fund-raising ability, and the ability to mobilize the support of other political actors and groups. In the most basic sense, a quality candidate is someone who is attractive to voters and who can run an effective campaign. As a result, those who have won other elective office before, thereby demonstrating these characteristics, are generally considered to be among the highest-quality challengers to congressional incumbents. Empirically, prior elective office has also proven to be a powerful predictor of challenger success. Over the period from 1974 through 2006, House incumbents facing such challengers were eleven points less likely to be reelected than incumbents facing inexperienced challengers.[3]

Because high-quality candidates are more likely to defeat congressional incumbents than low-quality candidates are—though even low-quality candidates have a better chance than none—there has been considerable interest in understanding how and when potential challengers decide whether or not to run. Central to theories of candidate emergence is the notion that these decisions are not determined by random chance but can instead be modeled as strategic behavior (Black 1972; Jacobson and Kernell 1983). In other words, potential candidates carefully weigh the perceived costs and benefits of running before making their decisions.

Surveys administered to potential House candidates by Maisel, Stone, and Maestas (2001) indicate that cost considerations include the unpleasant task of having to ask friends and strangers for campaign donations, the loss of personal and family privacy as a candidate for public office, the loss of time available for family and leisure activities, and the prospect of having to give up one's current job if the campaign is successful. Variation in these perceived costs depends largely on each individual's personal situation and values. The costs are clearly high. From 1974 through 2006, incumbents faced quality challenges only 18 percent of the time.

Balanced against these costs of running is the expected benefit of running. In his classic model of potential candidate behavior, Gordon Black (1972) notes that the expected benefit of running depends not only on the value of the new office but also on the probability of winning. All other things being equal, a potential candidate is more likely to take the plunge when conditions favor a promising outcome than when conditions suggest hopeless defeat. Variation in these perceived chances of success depends on both local and national factors. Local factors include whether or not an incumbent is running in the district and the past electoral performance of an incumbent. Because it has historically been easier to win an open seat than to defeat an incumbent, races with no incumbent at all regularly attract a higher percentage of quality candidates than races to challenge incumbents do. At the same time, incumbents who won their last election by a relatively large margin are often considered more or less invincible electorally. As a result, they are generally more successful than weaker incumbents at scaring off potential challengers, especially quality ones.

National factors can also affect the odds of success in individual congressional elections and can therefore similarly affect the strategic decision of potential candidates for Congress. National conditions often portend partisan tides. Just as the old adage says that a rising tide lifts all boats, a rising partisan tide raises the expected electoral viability of a party's candidates in districts all across the country. A race that a potential candidate might otherwise have perceived to be a long shot will seem more competitive when national short-term forces favor that candidate's political party. Jacobson and Kernell note, "National events and conditions shape the expectations of potential candidates and their supporters about their party's electoral prospects. Their expectations affect their strategies, and thus their behavior" (1983, 24).

Existing research on congressional elections has found effects of two particular national conditions on potential candidates' strategic decisions to run: the president's approval rating and the national economy (Jacobson 1989). The higher the nation's approval of the president's job performance is early in an election year, the less likely it is that incumbents from the president's party will face high-quality challengers, and the more likely it is that incumbents from the opposition party will. The same situation holds for perceived economic success or failure. Not coincidentally, these are also factors that affect congressional elections, as demonstrated in existing literature and in chapter 5. Challengers appear to understand these electoral effects, and they thus base their decision on whether to run or not partly on whether these national factors are favorable or unfavorable to their party.

While the evidence that national forces affect challenger decisions is strong, we once again question the scope of the national forces under consideration. We demonstrated in chapter 5 that public judgments of Congress are, similar to presidential approval and the economy, a national electoral force of their own. The literature shows that prospective quality challengers can be either scared off or encouraged to run based on the potential electoral effects of national factors. Therefore, public evaluations of Congress should affect these decisions as well.

Our specific hypothesis regarding the effect of congressional approval on quality challenges follows from our electoral findings in chapter 5. In particular, we have shown that greater public approval of Congress increases voting for majority party candidates and decreases voting for minority party candidates. Thus, when congressional approval is higher, potential challengers considering running against a majority party incumbent will be more inclined to sit out in a year that is even more favorable to that incumbent than usual, while those considering running against a minority party incumbent will be more likely to take advantage of an electoral season that weakens that incumbent. As a result, we predict that the greater the nation's approval rating of Congress is, the less likely it is that majority party incumbents will face a high-quality challenge, and the more likely it is that minority party incumbents will face a high-quality challenge, all else being equal. In contrast, potential challengers will perceive opposite electoral incentives when public approval of Congress is low. Consequently, poor congressional performance ratings will make majority party incumbents more likely to face high-quality challenges and will make minority party incumbents less so.

As was the case in our analysis in chapter 5, the literature suggests—indirectly—two alternative hypotheses in addition to our own. First, quality challengers may believe, as Fenno's (1978) research suggests, that neither party's incumbents necessarily become more vulnerable when Congress is unpopular. More generally, quality challengers may no longer view national forces as very important, compared to local conditions, when making their decisions to run. In either case, congressional approval would display no significant effect on quality challenges to any incumbent. A second possibility is that quality challengers may believe, consistent with the research of Born (1990), that high congressional approval ratings signify public support for all incumbents regardless of party. If this is the case, congressional approval should have the same negative effect on quality challenges to incumbents of both parties.

To date, no empirical research has examined the connection between congressional approval and quality challenges to incumbents. We test our hypothesis, as well as the null and incumbent-based alternative hypotheses, using data on incumbent reelection races in the seventeen elections from 1974 through 2006.[4] To do so, we first develop measures of our key variables as well as standard control variables.[5]

Our dependent variable is whether or not each running incumbent faced a high-quality challenge. Measuring the quality of challengers is an inexact science. While it is clear that some people have what it takes to win elections and others do not, differentiating among them is a highly speculative endeavor until they actually run for office. For this reason, researchers have generally used previous electoral success as a measure of candidate quality. Some candidates who have not yet won office may also possess the requisite personal and political resources, but we cannot be as confident of their potential as we are of candidates who have actually demonstrated these attributes. For this reason, we code the quality of House challengers using Gary Jacobson's data on challengers' prior elective experience. Specifically, we measure whether or not an incumbent faces a challenge from a major party candidate who has held prior elective office. Because our theory predicts that congressional approval will have the opposite effect on the quality of challenges to majority incumbents than on challenges to minority party incumbents, the analysis considers each group separately.

One possible explanation for the lack of research on how congressional approval affects challenger quality is problems of data availability. As we discussed previously, survey questions on congressional job performance have only been asked irregularly, in varying forms, and rarely before the mid-1970s. These problems make the creation of a longitudinal measure of congressional approval a challenging task. As a solution, we return to the longitudinal measure we created in chapter 4 using James Stimson's algorithm. In chapter 4, we were interested in the public's approval in the quarter immediately preceding the election (the third quarter). But challengers' decisions are made prior to this general election period. To be consistent with existing research on the timing of challenger decisions, we focus our analysis here on congressional approval in the second quarter of the election year.[6]

Other national conditions are measured in a similar fashion. Presidential approval is measured using the average percentage of citizens approving of the president's job performance in all Gallup surveys conducted during the second quarter of the election year. National economic conditions are measured as the percentage change in real disposable per capita income over the year ending in the second quarter of the election year. Larger values of these variables are expected to decrease quality challenges to incumbents from the president's party but to increase quality challenges to incumbents not in the president's party. Therefore, as in chapter 5, we first code whether or not the incumbent shares the president's party. We then interact this variable with the presidential approval and national economy variables, to capture the differential effects expected under each scenario. Local conditions are captured by measuring the partisan incumbency status of each seat and the percentage of the two-party vote received by the incumbent in the last election.

Table 6.1 displays our logistic regression analysis of the effect that congressional approval has on the likelihood that a quality challenger from the opposing party will run against an incumbent in the general election, controlling for the local and national forces discussed earlier. The two models show the separate effects for quality challenges to House incumbents from the majority and minority parties. We predicted that higher congressional approval would decrease quality challenges to a majority party incumbent because challengers will sense that majority party incumbents are harder to beat under such conditions. At the same time, we predicted that higher congressional approval would increase quality challenges to a minority party incumbent because challengers will sense that minority party incumbents are relatively more vulnerable under such conditions.

The empirical evidence provides solid support for our hypothesis. As expected, congressional approval displays a significant, negative effect on quality challenges to majority party incumbents (column 1) and a significant positive effect on quality challenges to minority party incumbents (column 2). We find these effects even after taking into account the potential impact of other national and local factors in the model, all of which, with the exception of the incumbent's past vote share, have either inconsistent effects or no effect on challenges to the two types of incumbents.

TABLE 6.1. Effects of Congressional Approval on Quality Challenger Emergence in House Elections, 1974–2006

	QUALITY CHALLENGE TO MAJORITY INCUMBENT	QUALITY CHALLENGE TO MINORITY INCUMBENT
Congressional approval	−.037°°	.021°
	(.010)	(.011)
Presidential approval (incumbent from president's party)	.006	−.032°°
	(.009)	(.007)
Presidential approval (incumbent not from president's party)	.003	−.012
	(.007)	(.010)
Economy (incumbent from president's party)	−.059	−.090°
	(.056)	(.035)
Economy (incumbent not from president's party)	.074°	.012
	(.033)	(.069)
Incumbent from president's party	−.099	1.534°°
	(.457)	(.484)
Previous vote percentage for incumbent	−.093°°	−.085°°
	(.006)	(.007)
Constant	5.489°°	3.670°°
	(.512)	(.543)
Pseudo R^2	.152	.159
Number of cases	3,114	2,431

Note: Table entries are logistic regression coefficients (standard errors in parentheses).
°$p \leq .05$ °°$p \leq .005$ (one-tailed)

Our results demonstrate that higher ratings of Congress by the public make it less likely that a quality candidate will decide to challenge a majority party incumbent but more likely that a quality candidate will decide to challenge a minority party incumbent. Conversely, lower ratings of Congress promote quality challenges to majority incumbents but deter quality challenges to minority party incumbents. The difference in effects between the two parties' incumbents supports our partisan hypothesis over the alternative incumbent-based hypothesis discussed previously.

To illustrate the meaning of these findings in more concrete terms, table 6.2 translates the results into probabilities. In particular, it shows the estimated probability that a quality candidate will challenge an incumbent when congressional approval is at either its lowest point or its highest point in the opinion data from the second quarter (20 percent approval versus 48 percent approval), controlling for all the other factors in the model.[7] When congressional approval is at its lowest, the chance that a House incumbent from the majority party will have to face a quality challenger is one in four. When congressional approval is at its highest, the odds that this same incumbent will face a quality challenger drop to only one in nine. The effect is reversed for a minority party incumbent, as expected: low congressional approval produces the lowest risk of a quality challenge (19 percent chance), while high congressional approval produces the highest risk of a quality challenge (30 percent).

Comparing across the two columns in table 6.2 provides another illustration of the fact that congressional approval affects each party differently. When congressional approval is low, a majority party incumbent is more likely to face a quality challenger than a minority party incumbent is. When congressional approval is high, the situation reverses: a minority incumbent is then almost three times more likely to face a quality challenger than a majority incumbent is. Overall, it appears as though congressional approval levels do influence the strategic calculi of quality

TABLE 6.2. Congressional Approval and Probability of a Quality Challenge

	QUALITY CHALLENGE TO MAJORITY INCUMBENT	QUALITY CHALLENGE TO MINORITY INCUMBENT
Low approval of Congress	.25	.19
High approval of Congress	.11	.30
Effect of higher approval	−.14	+.11

Note: Entries represent probability transformations of the estimates in table 6.1.

challengers—independent of economic and presidential considerations—and that they do so in the same partisan manner in which evaluations of Congress were found to affect voting in chapter 5.

INCUMBENT RETIREMENTS

An incumbent's decision to voluntarily retire from the House of Representatives is important not just for the individual member but also for the institution. We noted earlier that the decision of experienced candidates to challenge an incumbent is important because experienced challengers stand a better chance of defeating incumbents than do inexperienced challengers. Nevertheless, even quality challengers usually lose to incumbents. So while quality challenges create some uncertainty about who will be in the next Congress, retirement is a guarantee that there will be a turnover in membership. Retirement also makes it more likely that the next occupant of the office will be from the opposing political party. Open seats, which occur when an incumbent retires, are historically the seats most vulnerable to partisan change. Between 1974 and 2006, only 4 percent of incumbents who decided to run for reelection lost their seats to the opposing party in a general election, while 27 percent of open seats changed party hands after the departure of an incumbent.

Like the decision to challenge an incumbent, the decision to retire can be modeled as a strategic choice. Once again, the individual making the decision—in this case, the incumbent—is assumed to weigh the costs and benefits of each alternative. While the underlying choice is the same—to run or not to run—the different context that the incumbent faces leads to a decision-making calculus that is not entirely the same.

Since incumbents have already chosen to run for Congress at least once in the past, we can assume that they place a high value on the office itself. Indeed, a fundamental assumption of scholars who analyze incumbent behavior is that reelection is their primary motivating goal (Mayhew 1974). At the margin, other contextual factors may render the office slightly more or slightly less valuable. Partisan status is one such consideration. Being a member of the majority party appears to make incumbents less likely to retire than does being a member of the minority party (e.g., Brace 1985; Hibbing 1982a; Moore and Hibbing 1998; Kiewiet and Zeng 1993; Livingston and Friedman 1993).[8]

In general, the costs of running (benefits of retirement) are similar to those faced by challengers: time and effort. Again, the different context of being an incumbent changes the calculus somewhat. Fund-raising is still an unpleasant chore, but incumbents generally have an easier time with this than challengers (Jacobson 2004). The prospect of continuing to hold office means less privacy and family time than if one were out of office, but incumbents have presumably grown used to this aspect of the job. One significant difference is that while challengers may see running for Congress as an opportunity to move up the political ladder, incumbents may perceive remaining in Congress as forgoing an opportunity to win higher political office, such as in the Senate (Kiewiet and Zeng 1993).

Not all incumbents perceive these costs equally, however. As an incumbent gets older, time away from family, perhaps including grandchildren, may feel like a greater cost than it would to a younger person. The effort expended at fund-raising and campaigning may take more of a toll on an older body than on a young one. In other words, even when costs remain relatively stable, contextual factors like age may lead the costs to feel more burdensome. Another factor that can affect the perceived time and effort needed for a campaign is the expected competitiveness of the race. As we saw in the previous section, seats that incumbents have won by a large margin in the last election are less likely to draw a serious challenge, thus requiring less campaigning and less fund-raising, but seats won by a narrow margin are likely to be targets again, forcing incumbents to devote more time and effort to these tasks. Consistent with this logic, both age and electoral margin have been found to influence incumbent retirement in numerous studies (e.g., Hall and Van Houweling 1995; Hibbing 1982a; Jacobson and Dimock 1994; Livingston and Friedman 1993; Theriault 1998).

The literature is more divided on the question of whether short-term national forces affect the decision to retire. Jacobson and Kernell (1983) argue that traditional national forces, such as presidential approval and the national economy, do affect incumbent retirement. Jacobson states that "incumbents of the disadvantaged party are marginally more likely to retire when facing the prospect of a tougher-than-usual campaign" (2004, 165). However, the election data on which this claim is based end in 1970. Moore and Hibbing (1998) find no evidence that presidential approval or the national economy help to explain the difference in the parties' retirement rates. Livingston and Friedman (1993) reach a similarly negative conclusion based on data from the 1980s. But the tests conducted in each of these studies are based on aggregated data that do not control for the individual incumbent characteristics discussed earlier. While it is there-

fore difficult to conclude exactly what impact national forces have on retirement, it does appear that their impact is considerably less on the decisions of incumbents than on those of challengers.

Nevertheless, the fact that past election margin affects an incumbent's
retirement decision suggests that incumbents do take into account electoral considerations. In chapter 5, we found that congressional approval
affects the percentage of votes a House candidate receives. Therefore, it
seems plausible—even likely—that incumbents might take congressional
approval into account as another electoral consideration when deciding
whether to run for reelection or retire. Since approval of Congress improves the electoral prospects of majority party candidates and since disapproval harms them, we would expect that higher rates of congressional
approval would reduce the likelihood of retirement by majority party incumbents and would increase the likelihood of retirement by minority
party incumbents.

But there is another reason, aside from electoral effects, that an incumbent might take into account the public's evaluation of Congress. One
part of an occupation's perceived value may be the degree of esteem it
holds in the public consciousness. To the extent that an incumbent member of Congress prefers his profession to be held in high esteem, fluctua-
tions in public evaluations of Congress should affect the perceived benefits of the office to that incumbent (Hibbing 1982b; Parker 1996). A
retiring member of Congress once said, "We all like to be proud of the
work we do, but some people seem to think I should be ashamed to have
served in the U.S. Congress" (quoted in Hibbing 1982b, 63). After briefly
considering the possibility that public evaluations of Congress might affect
retirements, Moore and Hibbing (1998, 1090) dismiss it on the basis that
such evaluations do not vary dramatically enough from year to year to explain variation in retirements. Yet our quarterly time series data from
chapter 4 show that at least when it comes to job performance, the public's
ratings have spanned almost a forty-point range, from a low of around 19
percent to a high of over 57 percent. So it is possible that approval of Congress also affects retirement decisions via members' egos.[9]

This possibility complicates our expectations regarding the overall effect of congressional approval on retirement. If all incumbents devalue
the office when approval of Congress is low, then low approval will lead
incumbents from both parties to more seriously consider retirement. For
majority party incumbents, this is the same effect that low approval
would have on their electoral prospects, so our overall expectation is the

same as it was earlier. But minority party incumbents may face conflicting instincts. On the one hand, low approval may devalue the office; on
the other hand, low approval makes reelection a bit easier because the
public is less disposed to vote for majority party candidates. These conflicting instincts may mean that congressional approval has a minimal
overall effect on retirement decisions by minority party members.

Once again, no existing studies of retirement from Congress at the
individual level have actually performed empirical tests of the effect of
congressional approval.[10] To conduct such an analysis, we first need an
appropriate definition of retirement. Like other scholars, we restrict our
definition to include only individuals who voluntarily leave the House
and make no effort to seek other office (see Moore and Hibbing 1998).
Our model also includes the incumbent's previous vote percentage in the
district, presidential approval, national economic conditions, and congressional approval—all of which are measured the same way they were
in our analysis of quality challengers. We also add a variable for incumbent age, which is measured at the beginning of each member's current
term of office.[11]

Table 6.3 presents the results of a logistic regression analysis of the
effect congressional approval has on the likelihood that an incumbent
will decide to retire to private life rather than run for reelection, controlling for both incumbent-specific factors and other national forces. Consistent with our expectations, congressional approval has a significant,
negative effect on retirement among majority party incumbents. The
more the public approves of Congress, the less likely it is that majority
party incumbents decide to retire. Local factors of candidate age and
previous vote share also display significant effects in the model, but none
of the other national forces besides congressional approval appear to
have any significant impact.

Among minority party incumbents, public approval of Congress does
not appear to have any clear effect. While the coefficient for congressional approval is negative, its size does not approach standard levels of
statistical significance.[12] We cannot know for sure why congressional
approval plays no significant role in the decisions of minority party incumbents, but it may be that, as we suggested earlier, whatever effects
congressional approval had on these members' electoral calculations are
being canceled out by its effects on the "prestige value" they place on the
office. It is also worth noting that most of the model's other variables representing national forces are also insignificant and/or insubstantial. Part

of the explanation for the limited effects of congressional approval in this instance may be that local forces, such as age and previous vote share, largely dominate the decision-making calculi of incumbents considering retirement.

In table 6.4, we once again translate the central results of the regression into probabilistic terms for ease of interpretation. The table entries show the probability of retirement for incumbents of each party at the lowest and highest values of second-quarter congressional approval in the data, controlling for other factors.[13] Among majority party incumbents in the first data column, high congressional approval ratings decrease the odds of retirement by five points, from a 6 percent chance of retirement to a minimal 1 percent chance. Among minority party incumbents in the second column, high congressional approval has almost no effect, producing only a two-point drop in the chances that a minority

TABLE 6.3. Effects of Congressional Approval on Voluntary Retirement from the House, 1974–2006

	MAJORITY INCUMBENT RETIRES	MINORITY INCUMBENT RETIRES
Congressional approval	−.063°°	−.023
	(.016)	(.017)
Presidential approval (incumbent from president's party)	.020	−.004
	(.014)	(.012)
Presidential approval (incumbent not from president's party)	.013	−.017°
	(.014)	(.021)
Economy (incumbent from president's party)	.062	−.043
	(.086)	(.065)
Economy (incumbent not from president's party)	−.043	.044
	(.072)	(1.495)
Incumbent from president's party	.342	.401
	(.815)	(.942)
Previous vote percentage for incumbent	−.043°°	−.036°°
	(.010)	(.011)
Incumbent age	.091°°	.103°°
	(.008)	(.011)
Constant	−3.686°°	−3.615°°
	(.883)	(.989)
Pseudo R^2	.158	.151
Number of cases	3,305	2,586

Note: Table entries are logistic regression coefficients (standard errors in parentheses).
°$p \leq .05$ °°$p \leq .005$ (one-tailed)

TABLE 6.4. Congressional Approval and Probability of Incumbent Retirement

	MAJORITY INCUMBENT RETIRES	MINORITY INCUMBENT RETIRES
Low approval of Congress	.06	.05
High approval of Congress	.01	.03
Effect of higher approval	−.05	−.02

Note: Entries represent probability transformations of the estimates in table 6.3.

party incumbent will retire. Overall, while these effects are modest, a look back at table 6.3 reminds us that congressional approval still represents the main national force affecting incumbents' voluntary retirement decisions.

CONCLUSION

Public evaluations of Congress are a national force that affects congressional elections in multiple ways. The previous chapter demonstrated that public evaluations of Congress affect voting on election day, with approval boosting support for majority party candidates and with disapproval benefiting minority party candidates. Precisely this outcome leads to the effects we find in this chapter. Here we show that because public feelings toward Congress will impact the next election, aggregate approval ratings of Congress many months prior to the election affect the strategic choices made both by quality candidates considering a run against a sitting incumbent and by incumbents considering whether to retire or run for reelection. Rather than being separate, however, these two effects are related. Quality challengers are more likely to run when incumbents are vulnerable, and congressional approval affects incumbent vulnerability. Incumbents have reason to worry how congressional approval affects their vulnerability not only directly, through expected effects on voting, but also indirectly, via its effect on the likelihood of quality challenges.

We also find here, as in the last chapter, that evaluations of Congress do not affect all incumbents in the same manner. Instead, we again observe a partisan pattern of effects. Greater approval of Congress is good news for majority party incumbents, who will be less likely to face quality challenges and also less likely to feel electoral pressure to retire. The same cannot be said for minority party incumbents. Greater approval of

Congress actually increases quality challenges to incumbents from the minority party, as expected, and does nothing to reduce their electoral concerns when considering retirement. Finding these partisan differences in the real-world behavior of strategic challengers demonstrates that even though most scholars have been unaware of the importance of congressional approval, politicians themselves seem to intuit—or at least they behave as though they do—that the public holds the majority party responsible for the performance of Congress.

Another reason these findings are important is that both retirements and the number of quality challenges to incumbents should affect the eventual composition of Congress. In the next chapter, we determine whether the combined effect of these two avenues of electoral change—voters' electoral decisions and candidates' decisions whether or not to run for office—is enough to produce policy responsiveness in Congress.

CHAPTER 7

Responding to Public Evaluations

Conventional wisdom in political science suggests that Congress is not responsive to public evaluations of its performance, as discussed in chapter 1. This belief is largely based on two related lines of thinking. First, observers note that although Americans tend to disapprove of Congress, congressional incumbents tend to win reelection. In fact, from 1974 through 2006, 96 percent of running incumbents were reelected. Since incumbents appear to stay in office despite generally low congressional approval ratings, it is assumed that the overall composition of Congress is unaffected by these ratings. Second, that incumbents seem to have little reason to fear defeat in the face of public disapproval of Congress implies that they also have no electoral incentive to change their individual behavior in office from one term to the next. Consistent with this notion, incumbents usually do not exhibit dramatic changes in behavior over the course of their career (e.g., Poole and Rosenthal 1997). In combination, the image of generally low chances of incumbent defeat and generally stable behavior by incumbents leads many to conclude that Congress is not responsive to the traditionally high levels of public disapproval of Congress.

We do not dispute the much-noted aggregate tendencies of the public to disapprove of Congress, of incumbents to win reelection, and of incumbent behavior to be highly stable. However, in each of these areas, we see real temporal variation. Our aggregate analysis in chapter 4 demonstrated that public evaluations of Congress vary meaningfully over time. Regarding incumbent turnover, while incumbents rarely lose, they are not invincible. Sometimes they lose; sometimes they decide to retire rather than face reelection. Through a combination of both of these avenues of leaving office, turnover in each Congress actually averages a healthy 14 percent in each election.[1] Finally, while the voting behavior of individual members is relatively stable, it does change over the course of their careers (e.g., Stratmann 2000). The true test of congressional responsiveness to public evaluations, then, is whether or not the variation in public evaluations of Congress can consistently explain the changes that occur in the composition of Congress, the behavior of its individual members, and the actions of the institution overall.

Based on the evidence we have presented in the preceding chapters, we believe there is good reason to think that Congress is responsive to public evaluations of its performance. For example, while we have not yet analyzed how public evaluations affect the actual composition of Congress, we have demonstrated that they affect several variables related to congressional elections, including the public's voting behavior, quality challenger emergence, and incumbent retirement. This evidence suggests that public evaluations of Congress may also affect the overall composition of Congress following an election. It further indicates that if incumbents want to avoid reduced vote margins and strong challengers in future elections, they need to be concerned about congressional approval ratings. In other words, even individual members would appear to have an electoral incentive to be responsive to public evaluations of Congress.

At this point, it is important to define what we mean by "responsive." First, to be considered responsive, any change in Congress should be related to the underlying source of public discontent. Because, as we have demonstrated, ideological compatibility with Congress is a significant evaluative criterion for the American public, congressional responsiveness should involve ideological change. If, instead, public disapproval leads to changes unrelated to the public's central complaints—a change in the manner of dress by members of Congress, for example— we would not consider such changes to be a sign of responsiveness to public evaluations.

Second, the direction of change should be logically related to the tenor of the public's evaluations. Specifically, we have shown that public disapproval of Congress is based in part on displeasure with the majority party's policy stance and actions. Therefore, congressional responsiveness implies that public disapproval should lead to policy movement away from the ideological stance held by the majority party and toward the stance of the minority party. Conversely, high levels of approval should minimize any movement away from the majority party's ideological stance and should perhaps even encourage greater convergence among members toward that position.

In this chapter, we systematically examine whether or not Congress is ideologically responsive to public evaluations of its job performance. There are two possible mechanisms through which public evaluations of Congress could change the ideological bent of Congress: member replacement and member adaptation. Member replacement generally takes place during an election when an incumbent member of Congress retires or is defeated. If the new member who takes that seat is more liberal or more conservative than the departing member, this will affect the overall ideology of Congress. The change is likely to be greatest in cases where control of a seat shifts from one party to another. Member adaptation, in contrast, describes the situation in which the occupant of a seat remains constant but the ideological views of that member shift in either a more liberal or a more conservative direction.

Both partisan seat change and incumbent ideological change have been the subject of considerable volumes of research, yet almost none of this research has examined the possible role played by public evaluations of Congress in effecting these changes. We here discuss each of these two aspects of congressional change in turn, seeking to integrate our arguments regarding public evaluations of Congress with the existing scholarly research, then testing the resulting hypotheses. After considering each of these avenues of change separately, we examine the overall effect of public evaluations on the ideological stance of Congress.

PARTISAN SEAT SWING

Existing research has identified a few key factors that affect shifts in the overall partisan balance of seats in elections, or "seat swing." Two of the main factors are the very same national forces thought to affect the behavior of voters and challengers in congressional elections. In fact, Edward Tufte's use of them in aggregate congressional election models predates their use in individual models of vote choice in congressional elections.[2] According to Tufte, "election outcomes represent a referendum on the incumbent administration's handling of the economy and other issues" (1978, 106). In other words, the better the national economic conditions are and the higher the president's approval is, the more seats the president's party stands to gain during congressional elections. Though Tufte's original focus was on midterm congressional elections only, his findings led to the use of variables for aggregate presidential approval and short-term economic change in virtually all models of congressional seat change. For the most part, these factors have demonstrated consistent and significant explanatory effects.

The other main explanatory variable used in many analyses of seat swing is a measure of seats at risk in the election (J. Campbell 1985; Gaddie 1997; Marra and Ostrom 1989; Newman and Ostrom 2002; Oppenheimer, Stimson, and Waterman 1986; Waterman, Oppenheimer, and Stimson 1991). Scholars have differed on precisely how to determine the number of seats at risk, but regardless of the measure, the basic idea is the same: if one party has relatively more seats that are marginal, that party is at greater risk of seat loss. Compared to the variables for national forces, the explanatory power of various variables measuring seats at risk has been much less consistent (e.g., Finocchiaro 2003).

As in the case of research on individual voters, quality challengers, and incumbents' retirement decisions in congressional elections, research on seat swing has largely ignored consideration of public evaluations of Congress. The one exception is an article by Charles Finocchiaro (2003). Finocchiaro does not discuss or test the argument we make here—that approval of Congress helps the electoral fortunes of the majority party. Instead, he tests whether approval of Congress boosts the number of seats gained by the president's party, and he finds evidence that it does. We have doubts, however, about the theoretical and empirical underpinning of this finding. First, neither Finocchiaro nor any other study has offered a theoretical argument as to why congressional approval would benefit the president's party, as opposed to Congress's majority party. Second, his model testing congressional approval does not control for presidential approval, which research suggests has its own important influence. Finally, there is no test of the alternative hypothesis that congressional approval more accurately predicts seat change for the majority party.

Our argument in this book has been that voters do, in fact, hold the ruling majority party in Congress responsible for the performance of Congress. As a result, we predicted that citizens who approve of Congress would be more likely to vote for majority party candidates and less likely to vote for minority party candidates, and we found that they are. We also predicted that quality candidates would be less likely to challenge majority party incumbents and more likely to challenge minority party incumbents when Congress receives high approval ratings, and we found that they are. Based on these findings, we hypothesize that the higher the public's approval rating of Congress is, the more seats the majority party is likely to gain, and the fewer seats it is likely to lose, all else being equal. Conversely, the lower the public's approval rating of Congress is, the fewer seats the majority party is likely to gain, and the more seats it is likely to lose.

To test for possible effects that congressional evaluations have on seat swing, we return to the quarterly index of congressional approval we created using every question on congressional job performance from 1974 to 2006 archived at the Roper Center at the University of Connecticut. In particular, we focus on the level of congressional approval in the third quarter of each election year—the closest quarter prior to the election. The average third-quarter election-year approval rating during this period is 37 percent. A simple, though admittedly rough, test of our argument is to compare the average seat gain for the majority party in years when congressional approval was above and below this average level. Doing so, we find that in the nine elections when approval of Congress was higher than average, the majority party gained an average of six seats. In the eight elections when approval of Congress was below average, the majority party lost thirteen seats on average—a difference of nineteen seats. While this difference matches our predictions, it is still necessary to check whether or not this result will hold up once other causal factors are taken into consideration.

Table 7.1 presents linear multiple regression analyses of seat swing for the majority party during this same period. In addition to third-quarter congressional approval, the models include standard variables used to explain seat swing:[3] the state of the national economy (change in disposable income from the third quarter), presidential approval (the average of Gallup's third-quarter ratings), and the number of seats at risk for the majority party (the number of preelection seats held by the majority party minus their historical average).[4] Because the literature says that the president's party—not always the majority party—is supposed to be advantaged or disadvantaged by economic and presidential performance, both variables are multiplied by −1 when the president's party is the minority party in Congress.[5] This interaction requires that the models also include a dichotomous dummy variable capturing when the president's party is the majority party.

The first model in table 7.1 shows the effects of the traditional explanatory variables during this period, excluding congressional approval. The coefficients for all of the variables are in the expected direction, though the number of seats at risk does not appear to be a significant factor for these elections.[6] The second model adds our congressional approval measure to the equation. This addition not only substantially improves the overall explanatory power of the model—from 43 percent of variance explained to 78 percent—but also strengthens the estimated effects of the variables representing the economy and presidential approval.

The most important finding for our purposes is that even after taking into account the effects of the national economy and presidential approval, congressional approval has a significant, positive effect on the number of House seats gained by the majority party. Specifically, the model estimates that for every additional ten points in congressional approval, the majority party gains approximately seventeen additional House seats, all else being equal. Conversely, for every ten-point drop in the public's rating of congressional performance, the majority party loses seventeen House seats. For example, if approval of the Republican-led Congress in 2006 had been merely average prior to the election (at 37 percent, rather than the 27 percent it actually was), the model predicts that Republicans would have lost seventeen fewer House seats than they did that year.

We also tested variations on this second model. First, to rule out the possibility that congressional approval's real effect is on seat gain by the

TABLE 7.1. Explaining Seat Swing for the Majority Party in House Elections, 1974–2006

	MODEL 1	MODEL 2
Congressional approval		1.70°°°
		(.38)
Presidential approval (negative when	.62°	.71°°
nonpresidential majority)	(.39)	(.24)
Economy (negative when	4.25°°	6.46°°°
nonpresidential majority)	(2.15)	(1.42)
Seats at risk	.02	.04
	(.19)	(.12)
Majority party president	−103.60°°	−112.93°°°
	(40.10)	(24.92)
Constant	49.95°°	−5.35
	(21.37)	(18.05)
Adjusted R^2	.43	.78

Note: Table entries are regression coefficients (robust standard errors in parentheses). Number of cases is 17.
°$p \leq .10$ °°$p \leq .05$ °°°$p \leq .005$ (one-tailed)

president's party and that the results in the second model are merely spurious, we ran another regression using seat swing for the presidential party as the dependent variable. However, congressional approval did not display any significant effect on seat swing for the presidential party.[7] Second, we tried adding to the second model a variable representing the interaction between unified government and congressional approval, but this variable displayed no statistically significant difference in the effect of public evaluations of Congress during unified, as opposed to divided, government.[8]

While the effect of congressional approval on partisan seat change is important in and of itself, our ultimate interest here is in ideological change. Our argument assumes that when a previously Democratic seat is captured by a Republican, the new member will be more conservative than the old member; it similarly assumes that when a previously Republican seat is won by a Democrat, the new member will be more liberal than the old member. Merely because a seat changes party hands, however, does not necessarily mean that ideological change has taken place. In any given district, both the Democratic nominee and the Republican nominee might converge on the same ideological point in an effort to gain favor with the district's median voter (cf. Ansolabehere, Snyder, and Stewart 2001). If elected members simply represent the median voter in a district, changes in party label will not be systematically related to any particular ideological change.

To check the general proposition that a partisan seat change leads to a predictable ideological change, we examine the ideology of old and new members of Congress. As we have done previously in this book, we measure member ideology using Poole and Rosenthal's DW-NOMINATE scores. Their first-dimension scores capture a member's relative liberalism or conservatism based on roll call voting behavior while in office and are comparable across Congresses. During the sixteen elections between 1974 and 2004, 443 House seats changed party hands. Ideological scores are available for both the old and new member in 430 of these cases.[9] Among the 203 cases in which a previously Republican seat was won by a Democrat, the new member was more liberal than the old member 100 percent of the time. Among the 227 cases in which a previously Democratic seat was won by a Republican, the new member was more conservative than the old member 99.1 percent of the time.[10] As these figures demonstrate, partisan seat change is systematically related to ideological change in the expected direction.

Partisan seat change is one mechanism through which public evaluations of Congress can lead to ideological change in Congress. Before we
examine the overall effects of congressional approval on the collective
ideology of Congress, however, we need to consider the second possible
avenue of change in Congress: incumbent adaptation.

INCUMBENT ADAPTATION

Members of Congress do not change much ideologically throughout their
careers. Instead, as Poole and Rosenthal conclude, members largely "die
with their ideological boots on" (1997, 8). This same basic conclusion is
reached by multiple studies using different data, time periods, and methods (Carson et al. 2004; Lott and Bronars 1993; Poole and Romer 1993;
Poole 2007; cf. Rothenberg and Sanders 2000; Snyder and Ting 2003).
However, the explanation of this general stability is not that members of
Congress have inflexible personal ideological agendas: members do take
pains to reflect preferences of their constituents, and those who deviate
from constituency preferences are punished at the polls (e.g., Bender and
Lott 1996; Glazer and Robbins 1983; Johannes and McAdams 1981). Instead, central to the explanation of the general ideological stability of
members is that members' constituencies exhibit little systematic change
(Poole and Romer 1993). Small constituency deviations in a liberal direction one year may be followed by small deviations in a conservative direction in subsequent years, with the effect that little overall change is exhibited over a legislative career.

When clear changes in a member's constituency do occur, they produce significant changes in ideological voting behavior. For example,
House members who win reelection after being redistricted alter their
voting behavior to conform to the preferences of their new constituency.
Those facing a more liberal constituency move to the left ideologically in
their next Congress, while those facing a more conservative constituency
move to the right (Glazer and Robbins 1985; LeVeaux-Sharpe 2001;
Stratmann 2000). However, redistricting generally occurs only once
every decade and impacts relatively few districts.

Even members whose district boundaries do not change may still
observe differences in the mood of their constituency from one term in
office to the next. The literature cited in the previous paragraph suggests
that such members are likely to recalibrate their voting behavior to suit
the latest mood. We have already provided evidence that the public's

mood toward Congress is an important variable for reelection-oriented members to consider. We have also shown that public evaluations of Congress are related to ideological concerns. As a result, we can make specific predictions about the effect of congressional approval on ideological change among incumbents.

Low levels of congressional approval signal public dissatisfaction with the policy stance of the majority party. In cases like this, we expect that all incumbents—from both parties—will be more likely to increase their distance from the majority party's stance rather than stay put ideologically, all else being equal. Conversely, higher levels of congressional approval indicate a greater degree of public satisfaction with the stance of the majority party. As a result, we expect that higher congressional approval will make all incumbents more likely to decrease their distance from the majority party's stance (i.e., move toward the majority party), all else being equal.

To test these expectations, we first need to identify the location of each member in each Congress on an ideological scale. We do so using a customized version of Poole and Rosenthal's ideological scores, modified to specifically measure individual Congress-to-Congress variation by each member.[11] We then identify the majority party's ideological position in each Congress by using the average ideological position of all majority party members in that Congress.[12] To help us determine whether a reelected incumbent moves toward or away from the original (preelection) mean for the majority party, we measure, first, the absolute distance of the incumbent's original ideological location from the original mean and, second, the absolute distance of the incumbent's new ideological position (in the new Congress) from the original mean. If incumbents do not change at all, both of these measures will be exactly the same, and the original distance from the majority party will perfectly predict the subsequent distance. If the original distance does not perfectly predict the subsequent distance, however, it is possible that the remaining variation could be explained by the level of congressional approval during the election of the new Congress—with higher approval decreasing the member's distance from the majority party as the member shifts to more closely associate with the party responsible for high ratings, and with lower approval increasing the distance as the member seeks to separate from the party responsible for low ratings.

To measure our key independent variable, public approval of Congress, we once again employ our index of congressional approval using the third quarter of the election year.[13] In addition, the model controls for the fact that congressional observers have noted a distinct trend toward ideological polarization in Congress over the period we analyze, with members of both parties tending to move toward the extremes. We account for this reported tendency using a variable coded zero for the 1974 election and increasing by one for each subsequent election.[14]

Table 7.2 shows a linear regression analysis of the distance between the incumbent's location in the new Congress and the original mean of the majority party, explained as a function of the incumbent's distance before the election, a time trend, and congressional approval. The table presents separate results for majority party incumbents and minority party incumbents, to test our expectation that both are affected in the same way—increased distance from the majority mean when Congress is unpopular or reduced distance when Congress is popular. The results show that a member's distance from the majority party mean in the original Congress is a significant and substantial predictor of the comparable distance in the subsequent Congress. Given that incumbent ideology changes very little over time, this comes as little surprise.

Of greater interest, the results also demonstrate that after taking into account this relative stability in member ideology, congressional approval has a significant effect on whether an incumbent's distance from the majority party actually increases or decreases across Congresses. As we predicted, higher levels of congressional approval at the time of an election reduce an incumbent's distance from the majority party in the new

TABLE 7.2. Effects of Congressional Approval on Incumbent Ideological Distance from the Majority Party, 1974–2004

	MAJORITY PARTY INCUMBENTS	MINORITY PARTY INCUMBENTS
Congressional approval	−.10°°	−.03°
	(.01)	(.02)
Prior distance from majority party	.88°°	.92°°
	(.01)	(.01)
Time trend	−.02	.25°°
	(.02)	(.04)
Constant	5.49°°	5.87°°
	(.54)	(.70)
Adjusted R^2	.82	.93
Number of cases	3,237	2,272

Note: Table entries are regression coefficients (robust standard errors in parentheses).
°$p \leq .05$ °°$p \leq .001$ (one-tailed)

Congress, all else being equal. Conversely, lower levels of approval increase an incumbent's distance from the majority party, all else being
equal. Since the point of reference stays the same, this means that higher
levels of congressional approval prompt incumbents to move toward the
majority party, while lower levels prompt incumbents to move away from
the majority party. This is true for both majority party incumbents and
minority party incumbents—both move in relation to the majority party.

Despite the fact that most incumbents continue to be reelected during waves of public dissatisfaction with Congress, incumbents do appear
to take note of these public evaluations, recognize their potential impact
on future electoral prospects, and take steps to alter their legislative voting behavior accordingly. Put simply, individual incumbents seem to be
responsive to public evaluations of Congress.

Although this finding regarding incumbent concern over congressional approval is significant, it is important not to overstate the substantive dimensions of the effects on incumbent behavior. An incumbent
who continues to represent the same district under the same party label
does not change very much compared to what happens when the opposing party captures that seat. The average change in ideology when a seat
changes party hands is more than twelve times the average change of an
incumbent from one Congress to the next.[15] Nevertheless, even small
individual effects can have important aggregate consequences when
they occur in the same direction across numerous incumbents from
both parties. In the next section, we analyze the effects of public evaluations of Congress on the ideological stance and actions of the collective
Congress.

RESPONSIVENESS OF THE COLLECTIVE CONGRESS

While it is significant that disapproval of Congress produces change
within individual districts, district change does not appear to be Americans' main concern. After all, citizens are generally happy with their own
representative. What Americans who disapprove of Congress really want
is a change in Congress as a whole. Therefore, the most important question for us to address is whether public evaluations of Congress lead to
collective change.

Having demonstrated that their degree of ideological agreement or
disagreement with the policies pursued by Congress is a significant component of the public's evaluations of Congress, we are particularly inter-

ested in the responsiveness of Congress's collective policy stance. The policy stance of the collective Congress is determined by the ideological bent of its members. Since congressional approval affects House members through both elections and incumbent adaptation, it is reasonable to suspect that congressional approval will also affect the collective policy stance of the House.

A standard method of assessing the collective policy stance of a legislative body is to look at the average ideological position of its members. We predict that when public approval of Congress is low during an election period, the average ideological stance of House members in the new Congress will shift away from the previous majority party position, toward the previous minority party position.[16] Specifically, disapproval of a Republican Congress will lead to a liberal, or leftward, shift in the House average, and disapproval of a Democratic Congress will lead to a conservative, or rightward, shift in the House average. In contrast, approval of Congress is more likely to produce ideological movement toward the majority party. Approval of a Republican Congress may lead to a shift further rightward than its previous stance. Similarly, approval of a Democratic Congress may lead to a leftward shift in the House average.

Figure 7.1 provides a simple visual test of these expectations. The horizontal axis represents the public's evaluation of Congress in the third quarter of each election year, based on our index. The vertical axis represents change in the average ideological stance of the House in the following Congress, based on Poole and Rosenthal's ideological scores.[17] This axis is oriented such that change values above zero indicate movement toward the minority party, while those below zero indicate movement toward the majority party.

The data in figure 7.1 display a clear pattern consistent with our predictions. In the seven election years when congressional approval was below average—those to the left of the dotted line—the ideology of the new House shifted toward the minority party in all but one case (1982). In the nine election years when congressional approval was above average, the ideology of the new House shifted toward the majority party in all but two instances (1984 and 1998)—one being a case of no net change. Thus the overall trend in the figure is a negative relationship between the two variables: with higher levels of public approval of Congress, we see less ideological movement toward the minority party and more toward the majority party.

While the relationship between congressional evaluations and House

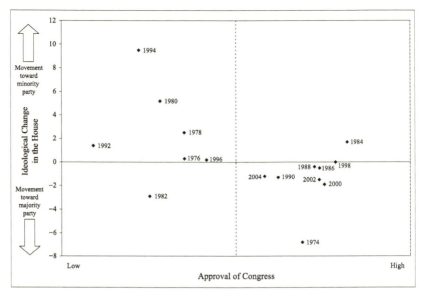

Fig. 7.1. Congressional approval and ideological change in the House, 1974–2004. (Data on approval from archive at the Roper Center for Public Opinion Research; data on ideology from Poole and Rosenthal's Web site, http://voteview.com.)

ideological change displayed in figure 7.1 fits our expectations, we hesitate to draw strong inferences from the figure, because it does not control for any other factors that might affect ideological movement in the House. Since the key avenue of change in Congress is partisan seat swing, we must account for the other variables that explain seat swing: presidential approval and the national economy.[18] Table 7.3 presents a regression analysis of the relationship presented in figure 7.1, controlling for effects of presidential approval and the national economy. Even after controlling for these other factors, congressional approval has a significant, negative effect on movement of the House's ideological average toward the minority party—the same relationship found in figure 7.1.[19]

Unlike in the case of seat change, it is a bit difficult to get an intuitive sense of just how much of an effect congressional approval has on ideological change simply by looking at its coefficient in the table. One method for doing so is to express its effect as a proportion of the average Congress-to-Congress change that occurs in the data. In this case, compared to a situation in which all the variables in the model predicted no shift, a ten-point decrease in congressional approval would produce a shift toward the minority party that would be 37 percent greater than the average shift. Another method is to express the effect of congressional approval in relation to well-known ideological shifts in congressional history. One of the most famous examples of a dramatic ideological shift in the House is the one that occurred after the 1994 elections bringing conservatives to power. Compared to a situation in which all variables in the model predicted no shift, a ten-point decrease in congressional approval would produce a shift toward the minority party equivalent to one-third of the shift that occurred after the 1994 elections.

While the average ideological stance of House members is one way of gauging the collective policy stance of the chamber, we can also use Poole and Rosenthal's measure of the average location of winning policy in a legislative chamber.[20] Congressional approval has a strikingly similar effect when we use this measure of the House's policy stance as when we use the average location of members. On a simple bivariate level, the average change in the location of winning policy for the seven Congresses with the lowest approval was toward the minority party, while the average change in the nine Congresses with the highest approval was toward the majority party. To increase our confidence in this observation, table 7.4 repeats the regression analysis from table 7.3, this time using change in the average location of winning policy as the dependent variable.[21]

TABLE 7.3. Effects of Congressional Approval on Ideological Shift toward the Minority Party in Average Member Location, 1974–2004

	AVERAGE MEMBER
Congressional approval	−.32°°
	(.07)
Presidential approval (negative when nonpresidential majority)	−.12°
	(.04)
Economy (negative when nonpresidential majority)	−.89°°
	(.23)
Majority party president	17.64°°
	(4.28)
Constant	3.11
	(3.06)
Adjusted R^2	.77

Note: Table entries are regression coefficients (robust standard errors in parentheses). Number of cases is 16.
°$p \leq .05$ °°$p \leq .005$ (one-tailed)

TABLE 7.4. Effects of Congressional Approval on Ideological Shift toward the Minority Party in Average Location of Winning Policy, 1974–2004

	AVERAGE WINNING POLICY
Congressional approval	−.70°
	(.37)
Presidential approval (negative when nonpresidential majority)	−.42
	(.24)
Economy (negative when nonpresidential majority)	−1.33
	(1.29)
Majority party president	51.45°
	(24.34)
Constant	−.33
	(17.41)
Adjusted R^2	.22

Note: Table entries are regression coefficients (robust standard errors in parentheses). Number of cases is 16.
°$p \leq .05$ (one-tailed)

Here again, we find that congressional approval has a significant, negative relationship with movement toward the minority party when we control for the effects of presidential approval and the economy.[22] Compared to a situation in which all the variables in the model predicted no shift, a ten-point decrease in congressional approval would produce a shift toward the minority party that would be 12 percent larger than the size of the average shift from Congress to Congress, or approximately one-fifth the size of the shift that occurred after the 1994 elections.

CONCLUSION

It is true that, on average, incumbents in the House are reelected at strikingly high rates and usually do not change their ideological position much while they remain in office. However, instead of drawing conclusions about congressional responsiveness—or unresponsiveness—from these average tendencies, we have looked deeper for patterns of covariation between congressional evaluations and changes in Congress over time. In doing so, we discovered evidence of significant congressional responsiveness to public approval ratings of Congress in three areas.

First, existing scholarship on partisan seat swing in House elections generally does not consider the public's evaluation of Congress to be a relevant explanatory factor. We find, however, that congressional approval does affect partisan seat swing. Specifically, the higher the public's approval of Congress is, the greater the number of House seats that the majority party will gain; the lower the public's approval of Congress is, the greater the number of seats that the minority party will gain. The dramatic improvement in the explanatory power of the model that includes congressional approval suggests that existing models have been overlooking a key component of seat swing. Put simply, models of House elections can do a better job explaining and predicting seat change once they begin to consider the role played by congressional approval. Additionally, since there are predicable ideological differences between members of the two main political parties, we are able to conclude that partisan seat swing is an important avenue through which the public's evaluation of Congress affects the ideological character of the House membership.

Second, the general consensus among congressional scholars has been that incumbents change their ideological stance very little while in office. Partly as a result, the existing literature contains no test of the potential influence of the public's congressional approval ratings on ideological change among incumbents. While we agree that incumbents are generally quite stable ideologically, our findings demonstrate that what movement incumbents do exhibit is less idiosyncratic than previously believed. In particular, it can be partially explained as a reaction to public opinion of Congress. The more positively the public rates Congress's performance prior to an election, the closer that incumbents from both parties will subsequently move toward the majority party's average position. The lower the public's congressional approval is, the farther that incumbents will move away from the majority party.

Third, previous academic research has done little to check for ideological responsiveness in the collective Congress. In fact, much scholarship has assumed that such responsiveness does not exist. The empirical analyses we present here demonstrate that through two avenues of change—partisan replacement and incumbent adaptation—public evaluations of Congress do have a cumulative effect on the collective policy stance of Congress. When there is greater disapproval of Congress, both the average member's ideological location and the average location of winning policy in the House shift toward the minority party. Conversely, greater approval shifts the ideological location of members and policies in the direction of the majority party.

144]   AMERICANS, CONGRESS, AND DEMOCRATIC RESPONSIVENESS

Overall, then, it appears that Congress is responsive to public evaluations of its performance. This does not, however, imply any benevolence on the part of Congress. Most of this responsiveness comes about unwillingly, through partisan seat changes in elections. The rest occurs as a result of individual members adapting in an effort to help their future electoral prospects.

Finally, it is important to reiterate that we find Congress to be responsive in terms of the very same characteristic that we have found citizens to consider when they evaluate Congress: its policy orientation. All things being equal, citizens prefer a Congress that represents their ideological preferences, disapproving when the majority party's policy orientation seems too distant from their own. This chapter demonstrates that Congress responds appropriately to public disapproval by shifting its policy stance away from the majority party.

CHAPTER 8

Conclusion

We began this book by arguing that the conventional wisdom in political science regularly underestimates both the American public's political abilities and the responsiveness of Congress to the public. The contribution we most hope to make is to encourage scholars to take a look at the democratic citizenry and institutions in this country in a new and more positive light. Unlike many studies on American government that conclude the system is broken—particularly in relation to the political capabilities of Americans and their Congress—our research provides welcome news. In our story, both Americans and their Congress display the type of responsiveness that a healthy democratic system requires. Americans are interested in and capable of making policy-based judgments of congressional job performance, and those evaluations have real consequences for the future policy performance of Congress. In other words, the public actually listens when its representatives speak, and representatives actually listen when the public speaks.

Because our conclusions run counter to much of the standard political science literature, we have taken great pains to demonstrate each step of our argument using the best empirical evidence that we could bring to bear. This evidence has included experimental, cross-sectional, and time series data. Our analyses have taken place at the levels of the individual voter, the congressional district, and the aggregate Congress. While we believe it was necessary to be as comprehensive as possible in testing our hypotheses—as well as the prominent alternatives—we also recognize that this strategy can sometimes distract the reader from the overall story.

In the following section, we bring together the key elements of the book to tell the full story about the role congressional evaluations play in

American politics. We highlight our main findings and how they both rely on and reinforce one another. Then, in the remainder of the chapter, we address three important, further issues. First, we discuss why Congress seems perennially unpopular, given that, as we demonstrate, Congress is responsive to the public's preferences. Second, we discuss whether our findings represent a temporal change in the relationship between Congress and the public. Third, we talk about the implications of our research for one vital area of governance: institutional reform. We discuss what our findings say about the various types of proposals that scholars and others have offered as ways to make the system more responsive.

THE ROLE OF CONGRESSIONAL APPROVAL IN AMERICAN POLITICS

This book's story is one of democratic responsibility. Democracy charges elements of society and government with certain tasks to make democracy work as it should. The people in a democracy have the dual responsibilities of civic knowledge and participation. Government representatives and institutions in a democratic system carry the charge of responsiveness to this public. What we have presented in this book, via a step-by-step analysis of this part of the democratic process, is evidence that both sides are, at least to some extent, upholding their end of the democratic bargain. We like to think that the picture this book paints of a working, albeit imperfect, democracy would please E. E. Schattschneider, who excoriated studies that expect too much from democratic citizens rather than looking at and defining democracy in the context of citizens' limitations (Schattschneider 1960).

Americans care about the policy representativeness of their Congress. Existing literature provides evidence that citizens' policy concerns correlate with their evaluations of Congress, and our survey experiment described in chapter 2 demonstrates that this is in fact a causal relationship. We find that citizens actually can and do react when presented with news about congressional policy action, incorporating this policy information into their evaluations of Congress's job performance. Our results make clear that the public wants their policy preferences to be represented not only by their own individual members of Congress, as others have shown (e.g., Canes-Wrone, Brady, and Cogan 2002), but also by the collective Congress. To the extent that citizens perceive adequate policy representation on the part of Congress, they are more likely to approve of how Congress is doing its job. To the extent that they do not, they are more likely to disapprove.

Additionally, Americans are able to acquire and retain information about congressional policy actions, even though standard measures of public knowledge suggest they cannot. As we demonstrate in chapter 3, when Congress changes its ideological course, citizens' evaluations also change in predictable ways. This is true not only for citizens who are able to answer informational questions about Congress—namely, which party has a majority of seats—but also for those whose knowledge of Congress appears low using standard measures. In other words, traditional measures of public knowledge do not fully capture citizens' true ability to "know" things about their government and to develop attitudes consistent with this knowledge. Whether intentional or accidental, citizens come across information about what policy direction Congress is pursuing, and they use that information to update their evaluations of congressional job performance. They retain the evaluations they make based on this information, even though many may subsequently forget the specific facts used to form that judgment at one time.

Citizens' ability to perceive and understand congressional policy direction provides them with the ability to judge Congress based on policy or ideological compatibility. Despite scholarly doubts about the ideological nature of Americans, we find that they not only have ideological preferences themselves but also judge the ideological orientation of Congress and use the relative degree of compatibility between the two when evaluating congressional performance. Just as political scientists have come to understand the role that party control of Congress has on legislative outcomes (e.g., Cox and McCubbins 2005), ordinary Americans also have a sense that it is primarily the majority party that is responsible for the policy direction of Congress. Chapter 4 demonstrates that across a variety of different political contexts, individuals' evaluations of congressional job performance are consistently negatively influenced by their perceived ideological distance from the majority party but not by distance from the minority party. Further, these ideological judgments by individuals have a cumulative effect on approval ratings of Congress. Aggregate approval of Congress is lower when the public's ideological mood is less compatible with Congress's general stance or when Congress's policy stance is too ideologically extreme for the general public.

Citizens' judgments of congressional job performance—based on

these ideological considerations—subsequently affect their choice between Republican and Democratic candidates in congressional elections.
Just as voters take into account other national forces, such as their evaluation of the performance of the president and the national economy, they
also base their electoral decisions on their evaluations of Congress.
Chapter 5 demonstrates that when individuals disapprove of Congress,
they are less likely to vote for majority party candidates for the House of
Representatives and more likely to vote for minority party candidates.
Conversely, when Americans are more positive about Congress's performance, they are more likely to vote for majority party candidates and
less likely to vote for minority party candidates. These tendencies among
individual voters also affect the actual vote margins in each House election. The greater the percentage of Americans who approve of Congress
is, the higher the vote percentage that the majority party candidate receives will be.

Savvy politicians, including both incumbents and quality challengers,
recognize when conditions are more favorable or less favorable for their
electoral success. They make strategic career decisions based on their
perceptions of these conditions. Chapter 6 indicates that a key consideration of these strategic politicians is our finding that majority party candidates receive fewer votes when the public disapproves of Congress and
more votes when it approves. When public approval of Congress is relatively low, potential challengers with prior electoral experience understand that this is a better electoral environment in which to try to unseat
a majority party incumbent and a less auspicious time to run against a
minority party incumbent. As a result, lower public approval of Congress
makes it more likely that majority party incumbents will face a quality
challenge and less likely that minority party incumbents will face one.
When congressional approval is higher, the opposite is true. This same
reasoning affects incumbents' decisions as well. For example, when congressional approval is low, majority party incumbents recognize that their
vote total is likely to drop, increasing their vulnerability. They also know
that this problem is compounded because they are more likely to face a
quality challenger. As a result, majority party incumbents have two increased incentives to retire when public dissatisfaction with Congress is
high. Overall, because public evaluations of congressional performance
affect voters, they also have an influence on which candidates decide to
run for Congress and which do not.

Citizens' evaluations of Congress also affect the resulting partisan makeup of the institution after an election. Election outcomes are determined by both the decisions made by voters and the decisions of strategic challengers and incumbents. Relatively negative evaluations of Congress make voters more likely to support minority party candidates. On top of this, lower approval ratings of Congress increase the quality of opposition to majority party incumbents, increasing the odds that they will be beat. Finally, lower approval of Congress increases the number of majority party incumbents who retire, leaving more vulnerable open seats for their party to try to defend. The result of these three processes is that greater disapproval of Congress increases the number of seats that will be lost by the majority party in House elections. Conversely, greater approval of Congress increases the majority party's prospects for holding or even widening its margin in the House. In this way, the analysis in chapter 7 shows that public evaluations of Congress have a significant impact on the partisan composition of Congress.

That seats are won or lost partly on the basis of public evaluations of Congress's job performance affects the subsequent behavior of members remaining in office after an election. Members who survive an election in which public evaluations of Congress constituted an electoral threat take affirmative steps to limit any further threat they might pose. At the same time, members who see their party's fortunes rise as a result of public evaluations of Congress seek to take advantage of this prevailing mood. Specifically, higher congressional approval ratings lead members to adopt voting patterns that are more in line with the average majority party position, while lower congressional approval ratings lead members to vote in ways that diverge from the average majority party position. While the extent to which incumbents can adjust their policy positions is limited, their documented efforts in this area demonstrate that public evaluations of Congress affect not only incumbents' strategic decisions whether or not to run but also their roll call voting behavior in office.

Finally, that the public's judgments of Congress affect both partisan seat changes in elections and changes in returning members' voting patterns has a significant effect on the collective Congress's overall policy stance. Specifically, low approval of Congress in the period leading up to an election leads to a new Congress in which the ideological location of both the average member and the average location of winning policy shifts away from the majority party position and toward the minority party position. In contrast, more positive public evaluations of Congress prior to an election lead to a new Congress that continues to support—

sometimes to an even greater degree—the policy positions of the previous Congress.

Overall, this story represents a continuing cycle of reciprocal democratic responsiveness on the part of Congress and the public. To this point, our presentation has focused primarily on one loop in the cycle: citizens evaluate Congress's policy stance; they hold it accountable in elections, then Congress changes its policy stance. However, the cycle does not stop there. Instead, it returns to the public again. When Congress's policy stance changes after an election—whether it changes radically or just moves in ideological degrees—the result comes back around for the public to judge once more, just as it judged the previous status quo and will judge those of the future. After each election, the public is faced with the Congress it creates, and individuals must then decide whether or not they approve of their handiwork or would like to try again. In sum, citizens express satisfaction or displeasure with congressional performance, and congressional policy responds; Congress adjusts its policy stance, and citizens' evaluations of Congress respond. Contrary to the excessive pessimism of many observers, both sides in this relationship hold up their end of the bargain, enabling our democratic system to function much as it is intended to function.

WHY ISN'T CONGRESS MORE POPULAR?

If Congress is responsive to public evaluations, as we claim, then why do its approval ratings not steadily climb or, at the very least, average better than 50 percent? We see three distinct reasons why we should not necessarily expect Congress to be popular simply because the public can obtain responsiveness from it. First, while representation of policy views is one of the key factors shaping public judgments of Congress, our results show that other factors can play a significant role as well. Even if Congress perfectly represented the policy preferences of all Americans, some of these same Americans may become frustrated with other aspects of government and take these frustrations out on Congress. For example, the public's feelings about government efficiency correlate with their attitudes toward Congress (see chap. 4), indicating some other effect at work. Even if this effect is relatively small, it could serve to offset, on a very regular basis, any increase in congressional approval caused by policy responsiveness. In all but three of the twelve election years in this study that are covered by the ANES, survey results show 60 percent or more of the public saying that the government wastes too much money, and there is relatively little variability in that figure overall. As a result, this may provide a constant negative drag on congressional approval.

A second reason our responsive Congress is frequently unpopular is that the overall level of ideological change in Congress from election to election is affected by other variables besides public evaluations of Congress. In chapter 7, we find that presidential approval and the national economy both have independent effects on policy shifts by Congress. If these other variables push Congress in the opposite direction than congressional approval does, the result may be a shift in policy that is "too small" for the public, relative to the degree warranted by congressional evaluations alone. For example, if the public is unhappy with Congress but is also unhappy with a president from the opposite party, the public's desire to punish the president's party may counteract its desire to punish the majority party, resulting in very little ideological change in Congress. That lack of overall ideological change may in turn mean that Americans continue to disapprove of Congress even after the election. In other scenarios, presidential approval or the national economy may push Congress in the same direction as congressional approval does, resulting in a shift that is "too large" for the public, relative to the degree warranted by congressional evaluations alone. Again, our theory would predict that many Americans would respond to the resulting Congress with disapproval.

But perhaps the main reason that congressional approval does not automatically climb as a result of congressional responsiveness is that it is simply impossible for Congress to simultaneously adopt all ideological stands to please all citizens. Americans have diverse policy preferences. Because of this, an ideological shift by Congress that mollifies the ideological concerns of one large segment of the public is almost certain to raise the ire of a countervailing segment of the public with opposing policy preferences. Thus, even if citizens only cared about policy concerns and if no other variables influenced ideological change in Congress, a significant proportion of the American public is almost always going to disapprove of Congress. In the case of policy, Congress simply cannot please all of the people at any given time. Our analysis in chapter 3 of the aftermath of the 1994 elections illustrates this point. While the public was clearly dissatisfied with the Democrats who controlled Congress before the election—a majority party that was more liberal at that point than they had been in over fifteen years—the dramatic shift to the right caused by the Republican takeover merely reversed which group of citizens approved of Congress and which disapproved. As a result, the Republican majority was only marginally more popular than the Democratic majority had been, and a majority of Americans still did not approve of Congress.

This observation may also help to explain Fenno's Paradox (1975, 1978)—the finding that Aemricans more often approve of their own member of Congress than they approve of the collective Congress. While Congress as a whole produces only one collective decision on any given policy issue—a position that is bound to disappoint many Americans from ideologically diverse districts around the country—individual members of Congress are better able to tailor their policy positions to reflect those held by their own particular constituency, which is often more homogeneous than the nation overall (see also Jones 2003).

CONTINUITY VERSUS CHANGE

In this section, we attempt to address whether or not our results represent a change in the way Americans think about Congress and the way Congress responds. Our ability to discern and analyze changing trends over time is necessarily dependent on the availability of requisite survey data. For this reason, we begin this section with a brief discussion of some of the key data limitations facing those who study public approval of Congress.

Looking backward in time, it quickly becomes clear that regular survey data on congressional approval do not extend nearly as far back as data on other aspects of the political system. For example, in the three decades prior to 1974—where this book's analysis begins—Gallup asked respondents to rate the performance of the president 391 times, including at least once in every year, but asked them to rate performance of Congress only fifteen times, missing twenty-one of those years. This historical data constraint severely limits our ability to compare our findings here to what might have been in the past.

Looking forward in time, a related problem is emerging. Ironically, while commercial surveys have dramatically increased their polling on approval of Congress (Gallup asked this question thirteen times in 2007), the main source of academic research on public opinion and voting behavior, the ANES, has moved in the opposite direction. In 2006, for the first time in half a century, the ANES discontinued its time series on midterm congressional elections. As a result, none of their detailed survey data are available to researchers for study of the 2006 election, one of the most important and dramatic congressional elections in recent history. Given the important role that the ANES has played in the discipline's understanding of the relationship between Americans and their Congress, it is our strong hope that it will be able to restart this time series before more potential knowledge is lost to history.

Despite the constraints imposed by data limitations, it is nevertheless possible to speculate on what trends might exist, based on both the literature and the data we do have. We begin by looking for trends within our data range of 1974–2006. While extrapolating backward or forward from these dates may lead to some erroneous conclusions, at least such guesses will be based on a solid foundation.

We are particularly interested in the answers to two questions. First, has the effect of ideological concerns on approval of Congress changed systematically over the period of our study? The simple answer to this question is no. This is clear even to the naked eye as one looks at the individual-level data we present in chapter 4. The size of the effect of ideological distance is sometimes higher and sometimes lower, but there is no clear increasing or decreasing trend during this period.

Second, has the effect of congressional approval on elections changed systematically over the period of our study—elections being the primary means for achieving congressional responsiveness? Here, the answer is less clear. On the one hand, there is some evidence that the magnitude of congressional approval's effect on vote margins at the level of the congressional district may have increased during this period (Jones 2010). On the other hand, we find no significant evidence that the effect of congressional approval on overall seat swing has increased (or decreased) during this period.[1] On this particular point, the jury is still out.

Overall, then, it does not appear that the relationships we have identified have undergone extreme changes during the period studied here. Nevertheless, our findings dramatically diverge from virtually all of the major scholarship written before 1980 on these issues. On the subject of public opinion, whether one looks at *The American Voter* (A. Campbell et al. 1960) or the Congress-specific work of Stokes and Miller (1962), the consensus was that most Americans do not think about politics or Congress in ideological terms. On the subject of members of Congress, classic works by Fenno (1975, 1978) and Mayhew (1974) argued that at least for electoral purposes, members did not need to concern themselves with the public's views of the collective Congress. Given the combined scholarly weight behind all of these opinions, it seems unlikely to us that they were simply wrong. Instead, the fact that this older scholarship paints such a different picture suggests that these relationships may very well have undergone an important transformation by the end of the 1970s. It is understandable if researchers writing during this time might have missed the fact that changes were already underway, as change is usually only recognizable with the benefit of hindsight.

Since we cannot be sure whether such a transformation actually occurred, any guesses as to what might have caused it are purely speculative. Nevertheless, a few key changes in both Congress and in the public stand out as plausible contributors. On the congressional side of the equation, three important interrelated dynamics were developing in the mid-1970s. First, Congress was attempting to formally reassert its institutional power vis-à-vis the executive branch for the first time in many decades (Sundquist 1982). For example, in highly public battles with the White House, Congress enacted such new legislative tools as the War Powers Act of 1973 and the Congressional Budget and Impoundment Control Act of 1974. Second, the ideological difference between the two parties' delegations in Congress started to become more pronounced in this period (McCarty, Poole, and Rosenthal 2006). In particular, the election of the "Watergate class" of Democratic freshmen in 1974 resulted in Congress projecting a distinctly more liberal image than it had in the past. Third, the House instituted a series of internal reforms from 1973 to 1975 that had the effect of centralizing authority in the majority party leadership (Dodd and Oppenheimer 1977). Together, these changes may have led many Americans who previously did not often think about Congress and its policy stance to begin to do so. Once the public viewed Congress as having its own identity independent of the president, perceived its policy leanings more clearly, and associated these policies with the majority party in particular, it would have been easier and more relevant to use these evaluations of Congress, consciously or not, when casting ballots on election day.

On the citizen side of the equation, public opinion scholars have documented other dynamics that may have played an important role. Page and Shapiro (1992) demonstrate important demographic changes leading into the 1970s that could have impacted political awareness and involvement, such as the dramatic increase of female independence and entrance into the workforce and significant increases in education. Multiple studies document substantial changes in individuals' political thinking and behavior from the 1950s to the 1970s that include, among other things, a rise in issue consistency among the public and resultant increases in ideo-logical coherence, consistency, and use (e.g., Nie, Verba, and Petrocik 1980). Some of these effects in the electorate may have come about partly as a result of the previously described changes in Congress (Abramowitz and Saunders 1998).

These concurrent developments—an increase in the political capac-ities of Americans and clearer political signals from Congress—had the potential to produce substantial change in the relationship between the public and Congress. While we cannot be sure, it is easy to imagine that these occurrences led to newfound importance both for ideology in ex-plaining public evaluations of Congress and for public evaluations of Congress in explaining congressional elections.

IMPLICATIONS FOR DEMOCRATIC GOVERNMENT

We need to address a final issue regarding democracy and responsive-ness. The notion that the American public does not hold Congress accountable and that Congress does not act accountably to the public has been around for so long that it has fostered the belief among many that our democratic system itself is inadequate (e.g., Mann and Ornstein 2006). Our finding that Congress actually is responsive to the public is important because observers have proposed numerous changes to the political system designed to address a supposed lack of responsiveness. These proposed reforms have taken quite disparate—and often even opposing—forms. Our findings have implications for each of them.

One segment of the political science community has lamented that weak, noncohesive parties have prevented operation of a classic respon-sible two-party system in the United States (e.g., Committee on Political Parties of the American Political Science Association 1950; Committee on the Constitutional System 1985; Sundquist 1992, 1993, 1995). According to the Committee on the Constitutional System, "divided government and party disunity . . . lead to diffused accountability" (1985, 6). In this view, only parties that consistently vote together as a team during unified party control of government can provide citizens with the ability to hold government accountable. These assumptions of scholars of responsible party government are reflected in the reforms they have proposed. Some have argued in favor of changes to make voting straight tickets easier or even mandatory in an attempt to reduce the chances of divided govern-ment. To increase cohesion within political parties, some have argued in favor of changes that would give national parties control over a greater share of campaign money, which could then be used to help elect the most loyal party members into office.

Our research shows, however, that under the existing system, Americans are not as helpless as the reformers for responsible party government assume. Citizens are already capable of assigning responsibility for the policy direction of Congress to the majority party. Furthermore, unified or divided control of government appears to make little difference in the ability of Americans either to understand who is responsible in Congress or to hold them accountable on election day.

In contrast to advocates of responsible party government, some recent political observers have argued that the parties in Congress have grown too internally cohesive, suggesting that this ideological polarization along party lines is preventing effective representation of the public's will (e.g., Mann and Ornstein 2006). From this point of view, the obvious solution would be measures to reduce the ideological difference between the average Democrat and average Republican in Congress. For example, these reformers have championed making House districts more competitive in an effort to put more moderate members of each party into office. Indeed, some states, such as Ohio and California, have attempted to do just that in recent years.

We have demonstrated that the current electoral system already permits citizens to obtain responsiveness from Congress—in part because of distinct ideological differences between the parties, differences that the public perceives. These partisan differences mean that when the public disapproves of Congress and punishes the majority party for it in elections, the resulting partisan seat swing will help change the policy direction of the next Congress. If the parties were to grow very similar to one another, partisan replacement would not have the same ability to effect change in congressional policy. It is true that Congress sometimes seems quite static. But this could be because Americans feel, at such times, relatively satisfied with its performance and not desirous of large policy changes. When public frustration with Congress rises, however, changes in the character of Congress can and do occur—some of them quite dramatic, as the case of 2006 illustrates.

Still other reform advocates who are worried about a lack of citizen impact on lawmaking have suggested that legislative power be shifted from Congress more directly to the people. Specifically, some have proposed that the United States adopt a national system of initiative and referenda (e.g., Committee on the Constitutional System 1985; Cronin 1989; Gerber 1999; Phillips 1994). In one version of such measures, Congress would vote to put a proposal for a new law on a national ballot, and citizens would then have the opportunity to make the final decision at the polls.

It is certainly possible that a form of direct democracy would make the system more responsive. It would, however, seem to require a more detailed level of policy knowledge on the part of citizens than our model requires. We have shown that under the current system, Americans are able to obtain policy responsiveness from the collective Congress simply by having a general impression of which party is in power and of the general policy direction it pursues—information most already possess and use in elections, according to our research. National initiative and referenda may offer a potential improvement to governmental responsiveness, but it is also possible that they would place unrealistic demands on citizens. Our work demonstrates that reforms of this type are neither the simplest nor the only way to obtain responsiveness.

The story we tell in this book does not claim that our current form of government is perfect. Indeed, it is quite likely that many useful reforms could be made. Some of the reforms previously listed may provide worthy benefits beyond responsiveness, such as increased efficiency on the part of government or increased participation on the part of citizens. Nevertheless, the law of unintended consequences cautions that changes meant to make things better in theory can often end up making things worse in reality. In this context, we feel, based on the research we have presented, that the United States should not rush into reforms under the mistaken premise that responsiveness from Congress is sorely lacking. While it is not necessarily ideally designed to do so, our current system does provide Americans with a measure of congressional responsiveness.

CHAPTER 9

The 2008 Congressional Elections:
An Afterword

The preceding chapters of this book present our theory and evidence of how the public judges Congress ideologically and how Americans express their resulting frustrations or (much more rarely) satisfaction with Congress's performance in the form of votes against or for the majority party's candidates in elections. These chapters were written primarily after the 2006 congressional elections but before the 2008 congressional elections. Writing books on elections is always difficult because another election has often passed by the time the book is in press. In our case, this difficulty was compounded because the election that passed—2008—was unprecedented in many ways and posed a potentially strong challenge to our theory. After the election, we were, naturally, extremely curious about how the results related to our theorized relationship between Congress's performance and the American public. This chapter, for the paperback edition of the book, presents what we found.

PUZZLES POSED BY THE 2008 ELECTION

According to public opinion polls, Americans' views of Congress sunk to all-time record lows in 2008. Specifically, in July 2008, Gallup reported that just 14 percent of the public approved of Congress's performance—the lowest rating in the thirty-four-year history of Gallup polling on the question.[1] Similarly, a CBS News Poll conducted in September 2008 found that only 15 percent of Americans approved of Congress—the lowest rating in that organization's thirty-one years of polling on congressional performance.[2]

Our work has argued that all else being equal, low congressional approval is harmful to the electoral fortunes of the majority party in Congress. In particular, individual voters are less likely to support majority party candidates for the House than they would be otherwise. As a result, the majority party is less successful in terms of the overall partisan seat swing in the chamber than it would be otherwise.

In chapter 1, we presented the results of the 2006 election as an intuitive example of our theory at work. In 2006, approval of Congress was the lowest it had been in over a decade. Partly as a consequence, we argued, Republicans in the majority party suffered a dramatic thirty-seat loss in the House, giving way to a new Democratic majority. In contrast to the 2006 election, it is not immediately clear to see how the results of the 2008 election could possibly fit our theory. Despite the fact that approval levels were even lower in 2008, the Democratic majority did not see any net loss of seats in the House. In fact, Democrats were able to increase their majority by twenty-one seats. This was the largest seat gain by a majority party in the House since 1982.

This level of increase in seats for the majority party amid record lows in approval in 2008 seems to pose a challenge to our theory. In particular, this apparent disconnect between theory and evidence raises two important issues—one specific to 2008 and one that is more general. First, the fact that the 2008 elections saw Republicans, who were in the minority party, lose seats suggests the possibility that voters may have held President Bush, a Republican, solely responsible for the poor performance of government. This would mean that voters in 2008 did not hold Congress and its Democratic majority at all responsible for its performance. Therefore, an initial question for this chapter is whether or not there is any evidence that Democratic candidates for the House in 2008 suffered some electoral consequences for the record disapproval of Congress. We believe that public disapproval of Congress did harm Democrats in 2008. Observing these effects, however, requires an analysis that takes into account other, typical electoral factors, some of which were particularly prominent in 2008.

Beyond the narrow question surrounding the specific circumstances of 2008, there is also a broader issue regarding accountability for congressional performance during divided partisan control of government as opposed to unified government. The fact that the 2008 election results occurred during divided government raises the question of whether, as a rule, divided governments limit the ability of citizens to hold the majority party in Congress responsible for its performance. Indeed, some scholars have suggested that divided government makes it difficult for citizens to hold anyone accountable for governmental performance (Cutler 1988; Nicholson and Segura 1999; Sundquist 1988). In chapters 5 and 7, we note that separate analyses of ours fail to find any significant differences in the effects of congressional approval during divided, as opposed to unified, government. However, it is not necessarily intuitive how this could be the case when one looks at the overall results of 2006 and 2008. By presenting a closer analysis of the 2008 election in comparison with that of 2006, we hope to be able to demonstrate more clearly how it is that even though the aggregate results may look different, Americans hold Congress equally accountable for poor performance during divided government as they do during unified government.

DEMOCRATS' RELATIVE SUCCESS (OR FAILURE) IN 2008

It is indisputable that Democrats gained twenty-one House seats in the 2008 elections. It is also true that a twenty-one-seat gain is impressive when compared to recent historical standards. The question of whether or not that number represented a successful achievement for Democrats is, however, a relative one. Elections are, after all, a game of expectations, and expectations prior to this particular election were that Democrats would perform significantly better than a twenty-one-seat gain. Before the election, some of the political world's most respected experts, including Charlie Cook and Stuart Rothenberg, predicted gains for Democrats as large as thirty seats. The thirty-seat expectation even became conventional wisdom for journalists. For example, Paul Kane (2008) of the *Washington Post* wrote about "the roughly 30 seats that are expected to flip to Democrats," and respected political reporters David Broder, Dan Balz, and Chris Cillizza (2008) wrote of an expected gain of "25 to 30 seats."

In this context of an expected thirty seats, what was an objectively large gain of twenty-one seats was actually viewed by many as somewhat of a failure on the part of the majority party. A *New York Times* headline from the day after the election, "Democrats Increase Their Strength in the House, but Lose Some Races" (Hulse 2008), demonstrates nicely how the Democrats' victory was qualified by the preelection expectations. Election coverage in other political news outlets echoed this theme that Democrats had not done as well as they could or should have.

The *National Journal* pondered "Obama's Short Coattails," and *Roll Call* declared, "Republicans Avoid Worst-Case Scenario."[3]

The view that a historic performance by the Democrats was not really as historic as it could have been may seem like typically cynical talk from the political elite. In this particular instance, however, there was ample reason to believe that Democrats had the potential to do much better than a twenty-one-seat gain. A major reason for the nearly universal expectation of high Democratic gains was the fact that the Republican president's job rating in 2008 also set records: in mid-October, public disapproval of Bush's performance hit 71 percent in the *USA Today*/Gallup Poll, the worst rating in Gallup Poll history. In addition, the same survey measured that around 80 percent of the public held negative views of the economy.[4] Given that both the academic literature and historical experience consistently show the negative effect that public disapproval of presidential and economic performance have on the electoral prospects of the president's party in Congress (e.g., Tufte 1975), it was clear that Americans' perceptions of Bush's performance were a potential disaster for all Republicans in 2008 and a huge boon for Democrats, all else being equal.

What the journalistic accounts of Democratic underperformance leave unexplained is the reason for this underperformance. How did Democrats fail to take full advantage of Bush's unpopularity? In his November 6, 2008, article analyzing the congressional results, Charlie Cook essentially threw up his hands and concluded, "The only thing that is really clear . . . is that this was a very complicated election that will take some time for us to really understand what happened and why."

Based on the theory we have put forward in this book, however, it is not so hard to understand why the Democrats were unable to fully capitalize on Bush's unpopularity and, as a result, underperformed relative to expectations. At the heart of our explanation is our general theory regarding the importance of public evaluations of Congress in congressional elections. Put simply, while Bush's low approval ratings may have played a leading role in the 2008 congressional elections, they were not the only significant factor in this drama. As discussed previously, Congress, too, was subject to abysmally low public evaluations leading up to the 2008 elections. As a result, the boost Democrats were expected to garner as a result of low approval of a Republican president was partially offset by the drag produced by the record low approval of a Democratically controlled Congress. In other words, the majority party did suffer electorally as a result of Congress's low approval ratings in 2008: it suffered by not achieving as much as it could have, given the other contextual factors in the political environment. The remainder of this chapter analyzes the evidence for this argument.

THE ROLE OF PUBLIC EVALUATIONS OF CONGRESS IN 2008

We test our argument—that disapproval of Congress caused Democratic candidates relative harm at the polls in 2008—using the same models of voting and elections presented in previous chapters. Specifically, we begin by testing our model of individual voting behavior from chapter 5 using national survey data from the 2008 elections. We then analyze the Democrats' twenty-one-seat gain in 2008 in the context of chapter 7's model of aggregate seat swing. Finally, we conclude this section by briefly discussing, as a case study, a race from the 2008 election that we think helps to illustrate how public disapproval of Congress hurt Democratic seat gains—a race that Democrats should have been able to win in 2008, absent the abysmal congressional approval numbers, but did not.

As we proceed through the analyses, we will often evaluate the evidence from the 2008 elections alongside comparable results from 2006 as a point of reference. As noted previously, this is a useful comparison because the 2006 elections were another example of simultaneously low congressional and presidential approval, but one in which both branches were controlled by the same political party instead of opposite political parties. Through this comparison, we hope to more clearly illustrate some general points regarding the effects of congressional approval across unified and divided forms of government.

Individual Voting Behavior

In order to understand the results of any election, one needs to start by understanding individual voting decisions. At the level of the individual voter, our theory predicts that after holding all other factors constant, a voter who approves of Congress will be more likely to vote for a majority party candidate, while a voter who disapproves will be less likely to do so. To analyze whether or not this hypothesized relationship continued to hold true in the 2008 election, we turn to data collected by the ANES. Though the ANES suspended its time series survey in midterm election years in 2006, it continues to conduct this survey in presidential election years. Using the data from 2008, we test the model of individual voting used in chapter 5. Specifically, we use logistic regression to estimate the impact that approval of Congress had on voting for a majority party candidate in 2008, while simultaneously controlling for other known influences on congressional vote choice, including voters' evaluations of other national forces, such as presidential job performance and the state of the nation's economy; whether a majority or minority party incumbent was running; voters' evaluations of that incumbent's performance; voters' ability to recognize the names of each candidate; and voters' party identification.

The results of the multivariate analysis, presented in the first data column in table 9.1, are fully consistent with our argument. Despite a twenty-one-seat gain nationally, Democratic candidates were negatively affected by citizens' disapproval of Congress in 2008. The significant coefficient on the congressional approval variable indicates that approving of Congress made a voter more likely to cast a ballot for the majority party (Democratic) candidate and that disapproving of Congress made a voter more likely to cast a ballot for the minority (Republican) party candidate. Because the election involved historically high public dissatisfaction with Congress, public evaluations of Congress were a net negative for Democrats overall, thus helping to explain Democrats' poorer-than-expected showing when the votes were totaled.

For purposes of comparison, table 9.1 also displays estimates of the effects of congressional evaluations and other variables on House voting in 2006 and from 1980–2004.[5] To analyze the 2006 elections, we needed to find an alternative to the discontinued ANES midterm time series. Our previous work (Jones and McDermott 2004) finds that the National Election Pool (NEP) exit poll conducted for the networks on election day produces results that are highly comparable (though not identical) to those of the ANES. One drawback of the exit poll is that it does not ask respondents to evaluate the performance of their own incumbent. However, when we tested a similarly reduced model using 2008 ANES data, we found that the estimated effect of congressional approval was not substantially affected by this difference.[6]

Results in the top row of table 9.1 show several things. First, the pattern of effects is similar for all three models: in the 1980–2004 period, in 2006, and in 2008. In each case, approving of Congress has a positive and significant effect on voting for majority party candidates. This is true during unified government in 2008, during divided government in 2006, and throughout the previous quarter century. In other words, as we have suggested elsewhere in this book (see also Jones and McDermott 2004), voters are able to hold Congress accountable for its performance regardless of the partisan composition of government. Second, the magnitude of the effect of congressional evaluations was no smaller in 2008 than in 2006—when it was touted by many pundits as a major factor explaining Democratic success—or than in the 1980–2004 period analyzed in chapter 5. In fact, a third observation from this comparison is that while congressional

TABLE 9.1. Effects of Congressional Approval on Individual Voting for Majority Party Candidates in House Elections

	2008	2006[a]	1980–2004[b]
Congressional approval	.34°°	.21°°	.17°°
	(.12)	(.06)	(.03)
Approval of majority party president		.93°°	.53°°
		(.06)	(.07)
Approval of minority party president	−.41°°		−.60°°
	(.12)		(.05)
Economy (majority party president)		.36°°	.07
		(.05)	(.09)
Economy (minority party president)	.29		−.29°°
	(.25)		(.06)
Approval of incumbent from majority party	2.00°°		1.77°°
	(.23)		(.07)
Approval of incumbent from minority party	−1.75°°		−1.80°°
	(.19)		(.09)
Party identification	1.92°°	1.92°°	1.32°°
	(.16)	(.07)	(.05)
Recognize majority party candidate/experienced (2006)	2.29°°	.36°	1.15°°
	(.33)	(.19)	(.09)
Recognize minority party candidate/experienced (2006)	−2.38°°	.01	−1.16°°
	(.38)	(.14)	(.08)
Majority party incumbent	−.27	.22	−.04
	(.28)	(.19)	(.10)
Minority party incumbent	−.19	−.65°°	.19°
	(.27)	(.21)	(.11)
Majority party president			−.44°
			(.18)
Constant	.75	−.09	.22
	(.49)	(.21)	(.16)
Pseudo-R^2	.74	.75	.68
Number of cases	1,236	5,349	9,891

Source: Data from ANES 2009, NEP 2007, and ANES 2005 (respectively).

Note: Table entries are logistic regression coefficients (standard errors in parentheses).

[a]Data from 2006 are from NEP, not ANES, and so certain variables use alternative constructions (see appendix).

[b]Results from 1980–2004 are reprinted from table 5.2.

°$p < .05$ °°$p < .005$ (one-tailed)

evaluations have played a significant role throughout, it is possible that they have been playing an even larger role in recent elections. While this cannot be definitively confirmed with the data presented here, it is a notion that has received support elsewhere (Jones 2010).

Translating our estimates from table 9.1 into predicted probabilities helps to more clearly illustrate the similarities and differences in effects across elections. As noted in the introduction to this section, it is particularly useful to compare the effects in 2008 to those in 2006. While the slight differences in models and data sources between these two elections mean that this is not a pure comparison, it is nevertheless possible to compare the basic pattern of effects, and the probability transformations allow us to do this in less abstract terms than we have up to this point. Because the majority party was different in each of these two elections, we facilitate the comparison by focusing on the predicted probability of voting for a Democratic candidate in each instance. All other predictors besides congressional approval are set at their mean values in the data.

Independent of congressional evaluations, both 2006 and 2008 were, on average, relatively favorable years for Democrats running for Congress. Table 9.2 shows that when we hold congressional evaluations at their neutral midpoint, the average voter in 2008 had a .61 probability of voting for a Democrat, while the average voter in 2006 was indifferent between the two parties—an improvement over the status quo of a Republican majority at that time. A major reason for the Democrats' relative advantage in each case was the consistent unpopularity of President Bush.

The key question here is, how were these generally favorable electoral environments for Democrats affected by public perceptions of Congress? In 2006, because Republicans controlled Congress, an otherwise average citizen who disapproved of Congress was even more likely to vote Democratic—increasing from a .50 probability to a .55 probability. In other words, with unified party control of government, disapproval of Congress

TABLE 9.2. Likelihood of Voting for a Democratic House Candidate, 2006 and 2008

	CONGRESSIONAL EVALUATION			EFFECT OF DISAPPROVAL ON LIKELY DEMOCRATIC VOTE
	APPROVE	NEUTRAL	DISAPPROVE	
Republican Congress (2006)	.45	.50	.55	+.10
Democratic Congress (2008)	.68	.61	.52	−.16

Source: Entries represent probability transformations of the estimates in table 9.1.

compounded the electoral dynamic of an unpopular president. As a result, generally negative perceptions of Congress that year helped turn a close contest for control of Congress into a Democratic tsunami.

The effect of congressional disapproval for Democrats in 2008, however, was the opposite of its effect in 2006, due to the change in party control. With a new, Democratically controlled Congress in 2008, an otherwise average citizen who disapproved of Congress was less likely to vote Democratic—dropping from a .61 probability to a .52 probability. In other words, with divided party control of government, disapproval of Congress helped offset the electoral dynamic of an unpopular president, not compound it as it did in 2006. As a result, even though Democrats won more votes than Republicans did in 2008, they could have won even more votes—and potentially more seats—if public perceptions of Congress had not been so negative.

It is important to note that the probabilities in table 9.2 represent an average voter in an average district. Democrats' unexpected losses (or expected pickups that failed to materialize) in 2008 did not occur in such districts, however. Rather, they occurred in Republican-leaning districts with vulnerable incumbents or open seats. In such a situation (a Republican-leaning, open-seat race), the model predicts that a neutral opinion of Congress would produce a .51 probability of voting Democratic (a potential gain), while disapproval would produce a .43 probability of voting Democratic (a likely loss). In other words, disapproval of Congress could have meant the difference between the average voter supporting or not supporting the Democratic candidate in competitive districts. We analyze one such district, Wyoming's single House seat, in more depth later in this chapter, to demonstrate how this appears to have been the case in at least one race.

This section has demonstrated that congressional evaluations affected voting in the 2008 election and that disapproval of Congress generally hurt Democrats' support among voters. The winning or losing of votes is important, but because we also care about congressional responsiveness, it is even more important to look at the winning and losing of seats. In the next section, we examine the role of congressional evaluations in the 2008 House elections from an aggregate perspective.

Partisan Seat Swing

In chapter 7, we used data from 1974–2006 to estimate both a traditional model of partisan seat swing and our own model. The traditional model took into account only presidential approval ratings, a measure of past economic performance, and the number of exposed seats a party has in the House. Our model added a measure of congressional approval ratings. The results of the estimations (see table 7.1) demonstrated that over the previous sixteen elections, a model incorporating data on congressional approval is much better at explaining election outcomes than is the traditional model. Specifically, the addition of congressional approval data increased explanatory power by more than 80 percent, raising the adjusted R^2 from .43 to .78. But fitting a model to existing data is one thing; using it to predict subsequent data points is another. The question here is how useful each of these models is in predicting the 2008 elections.

Our argument is threefold. First, we argue that if economic and presidential performance alone drive seat swing, as in the traditional model, then the poor economy and low presidential ratings in 2008 should have resulted in Democrats gaining more than the twenty-one seats they actually did. In other words, we believe that the pundits' lofty expectations for Democrats did in fact largely reflect the traditional view of congressional elections, rather than merely being pie-in-the-sky predictions. Second, we argue that our model incorporating congressional approval helps explain why the Democrats' actual seat gain was lower than that predicted by the traditional model. Specifically, poor congressional approval ratings generally reduce seat gain for the majority party, and congressional approval was sufficiently low in 2008 to have a sizable negative impact on seat gains for the Democratic majority. Finally, we argue that our model incorporating congressional approval does a better job than the traditional model in predicting the actual seat swing that occurred in 2008.

We test our argument by analyzing the specific predictions made by each model for 2008. We do this by using the coefficients presented in table 7.1 for each of the two models and simply plugging in the values that each independent variable took on during the 2008 election.[7] There is one important caveat about deriving predictions in this manner. The predictions are based on plugging in values for presidential and congressional approval that, in the case of 2008, are lower than any of the preelection values of those variables from 1974–2006. In other words, for both models, the predictions will be based on extrapolations of the effects of these variables beyond the range of values used to estimate their effects. Methodologically speaking, this is a situation that should be avoided if possible because the effects of a variable may not be strictly linear. For example, it is conceivable that at extremely low levels, presidential approval ratings either have effects that begin to increase exponentially or, conversely, have diminishing marginal effects. Since we cannot know whether one of these possible deviations from the (extrapolated) expected effect is present, our predictions derived from each model are likely to be less accurate than predictions made based on values within the range used to estimate the models. Because both models are subject to this same drawback, however, comparisons between the two are still useful even if the predictions may be less than ideal in and of themselves.

We begin by examining the prediction made by the traditional model. If our argument is correct, we would expect to find that this model predicts a seat swing toward Democrats that is substantially larger than the actual Democratic seat gain. Otherwise, there would be no "underperformance" by Democrats to explain. Our calculation reveals that based on the level of presidential approval, economic performance, and seat exposure in the 2008 election, the traditional model predicts that Democrats would win about thirty-four seats. As expected, this prediction is much higher than the actual gain of twenty-one seats—thirteen seats too high. In other words, if presidential and economic performance were the only important factors determining seat swing, Democrats would indeed have been likely to win more seats than the twenty-one they actually did. Also, note that the traditional model's prediction is roughly comparable to the pundits' predictions prior to the election. This suggests that the claims that Democrats underperformed were not an overblown media creation but were instead a product of academia's conventional wisdom on congressional elections.

Next, we test our argument that taking into account congressional approval ratings, as our model does, helps to explain why Democrats did worse in 2008 than the prediction made by the traditional model. If we are correct, we would expect to find that our model predicts a level of seat swing for 2008 that is lower than the level predicted by the traditional model. Otherwise, congressional approval cannot explain the specific finding of (relative) underperformance. For the moment, then, we set aside the question of predictive accuracy and instead focus on whether the predictions of the two models are different and, if so, the direction of this difference. Doing the requisite calculations, we find, as expected, that our model's prediction is indeed lower than that of the traditional model. Specifically, our model predicts a Democratic seat gain of only twelve as opposed to the thirty-four-seat gain predicted in the model without congressional evaluations. In other words, the public's low regard for Congress in 2008 can explain why Democrats gained fewer seats than predicted by the traditional model.

Finally, we compare the relative accuracy of our model versus the traditional model in predicting the 2008 election outcome. The actual seat gain by Democrats was twenty-one seats, the traditional model predicted thirty-four seats, and our model predicted twelve seats. Both models' predictions miss the mark—the traditional model by thirteen seats and ours by nine. This is understandable for both models, particularly given our earlier caveat about extrapolating effects of variables beyond the values previously examined. Nevertheless, our model does display better predictive accuracy in this comparison. While both predictions contain error, the error in the traditional model is more than 40 percent greater than the error in our model. This finding supports our argument that, overall, the 2008 election results for the House are better understood as a function not only of presidential and economic performance but also of congressional performance.[8]

A remaining point of interest is identifying precisely which seats Democrats failed to capture as a result of Congress's low ratings. Unfortunately, the model is not useful for this purpose. However, a brief case study of a competitive district that Democrats did not win but could have won can help to illustrate the kinds of races in which less dismal congressional approval ratings could have made a crucial difference in Democrats' favor.

Case Study: Wyoming's At-Large Congressional District

In this section, we analyze the 2008 race for Wyoming's single House seat. This was a race in which most signs pointed to a Democratic victory: it was a contest for an open seat in which a well-funded, quality Democratic candidate was running for the second consecutive time, having almost defeated the (now-retired) Republican incumbent in the previous election. Despite these advantageous conditions, however, the Democratic candidate lost. We readily acknowledge that a case study of this type is not appropriate for drawing broad inferential conclusions, for multiple reasons,[9] but that is not our purpose here. In the two previous sections, we have already demonstrated the effects of congressional approval on both individual voting behavior and aggregate seat swing. Here, our aim in presenting this case study is merely to illustrate the kind of practical impact that our theory could have on individual elections for Congress.

To understand the context of the 2008 race for Wyoming's House seat—an at-large district encompassing the entire state—it is useful to first review the 2006 contest for this seat. Wyoming is a traditionally Republican-leaning state that President George W. Bush carried by an overwhelming forty-point margin in his 2004 reelection. Despite this natural Republican advantage, the 2006 House race in Wyoming was surprisingly close. Incumbent Republican congresswoman Barbara Cubin faced Democrat Gary Trauner, an inexperienced and underfinanced challenger, and beat him by a mere 1,012 votes out of 193,369 cast—less than one percentage point. Undoubtedly, the country's anti-Republican mood in 2006 (Republicans lost thirty seats nationwide) contributed to this unexpected photo finish.

In October 2007, Trauner announced that he would run again in 2008, and many stars aligned in his electoral favor. First, in November 2007, incumbent Barbara Cubin decided to retire rather than seek reelection. In the 2008 Republican primary to replace her, Cynthia Lummis won a punishing race in which she was outspent four-to-one by her opponent. Lummis then moved on, substantially bloodied and bruised, to face Trauner, who had been unopposed in his Democratic primary. Trauner also had the money advantage this time around, outspending Lummis in the general election. Finally, Lummis was saddled with an unpopular president from her own party (as were all Republicans in 2008). Even in Wyoming, Bush had only a 42 percent approval rating in 2008.[10] Given these advantages in Trauner's favor, many political observers had Wyoming's House seat on their list of seats that could change hands from Republican to Democratic. In other words, this was one of the seats contributing to predictions of high seat gains for Democrats in the 2008 election. In its final prerace ratings, CQ Politics labeled the race "no clear favorite"—an unfamiliar label for Wyoming when it comes to partisan politics. Despite these expectations, however, Trauner ended up losing by a relatively large margin—nearly ten percentage points.

Why did Trauner fare more poorly in 2008, despite having many traditional (from an academic perspective) electoral advantages? In our analysis of the 2008 ANES, we found, in general, that Americans who disapproved of Congress were less likely to support Democratic candidates. Our question here is whether there is any evidence that Wyomingites' evaluations of Congress in 2008 contributed, in a similar fashion, to the poor showing for the Democratic candidate in their state, Gary Trauner. Analyzing this question requires appropriate district-level survey data.

Unfortunately, publicly available survey data for individual House races are notoriously difficult to come by, and those asking about congressional approval are even rarer. Nevertheless, we did find marginal results from a survey that was conducted by SurveyUSA in Wyoming during the closing weeks of the campaign and that included a congressional approval question.[11] This survey does have a couple of noteworthy drawbacks, but in each case, we do not feel that these drawbacks are crippling concerns. First, the survey measures preelection voting intentions rather than asking about actual votes. In theory, if the dynamics of the race changed before election day, the results may not accurately reflect actual votes. However, the survey's reported 50 percent to 44 percent lead for Lummis was close to the actual 51.3 to 41.7 margin on election day, indicating some continuity in preferences and potential accuracy in measurement. A second drawback is that we have only the publicly reported, partly disaggregated results of the survey, rather than the complete raw data set.[12] This prevents us from simultaneously controlling for a host of alternative causal factors as we look at the effects of congressional evaluations. However, we feel this is less of a concern here since we have already conducted a rigorous multivariate analysis of individual voting using the 2008 ANES data and since our limited purpose in this section is simply to illustrate these demonstrated effects at work in the context of a single House race.

Consistent with our overall theory and the results found elsewhere in this chapter and in this book, we expect to find that citizens in Wyoming who disapproved of Congress in 2008 were less likely to support the candidate from the majority party in Congress—in this case, Trauner—than were those who approved. To test this expectation, table 9.3 presents the relationship between Wyoming voters' evaluations of Congress and their

TABLE 9.3. Congressional Evaluations and 2008 House Vote Intention, Wyoming (at large)

| CANDIDATE | ALL VOTERS | VOTERS' CONGRESSIONAL EVALUATIONS | | |
		APPROVE	NEUTRAL	DISAPPROVE
Cynthia Lummis (R)	50%	27%	27%	57%
Gary Trauner (D)	44%	66%	66%	37%
W. David Herbert (L)	4%	4%	2%	4%
Undecided	2%	3%	5%	2%
Number of cases	604	70	82	452

Source: Data from SurveyUSA poll of likely Wyoming voters, conducted October 20, 2008.

preference for the Democratic House candidate (Trauner) or the Republican House candidate (Lummis) in 2008. The figures show that among those who approved of Congress, 66 percent favored the Democrat, while among those who disapproved, only 37 percent favored the Democrat, much as expected. Congressional disapproval appears to have had the same basic relationship in Wyoming as it did in the rest of the country in 2008.

If we assume, for the sake of argument, that this basic relationship would hold true regardless of the overall level of congressional approval among voters, it then becomes possible to calculate how much better the Democratic candidate might have done if Wyoming voters had been less negative (more positive) in their evaluations of Congress. In 2008, 12 percent of Wyoming voters approved of Congress, and 75 percent disapproved. In this scenario, a shift of only 10 percent of Wyoming voters from disapproval of Congress to approval could have been enough to give Trauner a narrow victory rather than a defeat.[13] But because, like the rest of the country, Wyoming's actual congressional approval rating was unusually low in 2008, the Democrat was not able to capture this otherwise winnable seat from the Republicans.

Congressional approval was also notably low (nationally) in 2006, so why did Trauner do so much better that year than in 2008? While there are many factors to consider, one that we believe is crucial is the difference in partisan control of Congress. In 2008, the Democratic Party controlled Congress, leading many Wyoming voters to hold Democratic candidates, including Trauner, accountable for the institution's poor performance. In 2006, however, Trauner's opponent's party was in charge, and while we have no survey data comparable to those from 2008, our national results suggest that this led Wyoming voters to hold Republican candidates accountable for the institution's poor performance. In this way, low congressional approval among Wyoming voters in 2006 helps explain Trauner's surprisingly high vote totals that year, and the subsequent change in party control of Congress, along with even lower congressional approval, helps to explain why Trauner then underperformed, in relative terms, in 2008.

While this case study cannot add very much in terms of statistical support for our argument, it does help to illustrate several important points regarding the 2008 House elections. First, the Wyoming case shows that even though Democrats gained seats overall in 2008, there were other winnable seats on which they were unable to capitalize.

Wyoming's congressional district represents one part of the underperformance in aggregate seat swing by Democrats that was reported by pundits and demonstrated in our aggregate analysis. Second, the pattern we found in Wyoming—lower support for the Democratic candidate among those who disapproved of Congress—meshes well with our analysis of the 2008 ANES data. In doing so, it helps to demonstrate more concretely the mechanism behind our argument. Specifically, it shows how, if public approval of Congress had been higher, Democrats could have captured more toss-up races of this type. Finally, this example further illustrates that even during divided government, voters can and do hold the party in charge of Congress accountable for its specific performance as distinct from presidential performance. In particular, rather than public disappointment in government being targeted solely at the president and his party, we find that, just as in the 2008 ANES data, voters in this race who disapproved of Congress took this frustration out on the candidate from the majority party in Congress. This may have helped to partially offset the boost that the Democratic candidate was getting from Bush's low performance ratings, thus ultimately shaping the final election outcome in Wyoming.

EVALUATIONS OF CONGRESS IN THEORY AND PRACTICE

We began this chapter with two primary goals. First, we wanted to explore the counterintuitive notion that low congressional approval caused Democrats to suffer electorally in 2008 even though they actually gained seats in the House. Consistent with our expectations, we found evidence that Democrats underperformed electorally when one considers the favorable political environment caused primarily by widespread public disapproval of President Bush. Furthermore, we demonstrated empirically that the source of Democratic underperformance was negative public evaluations of Congress combined with the fact that Congress was now controlled by Democrats. While no one source of evidence is definitive, our findings were consistent whether looking at national survey data containing many House districts, models of aggregate seat swing, or even a single House contest.

Our second, related goal was to use the example of the 2008 election in comparison to the 2006 election to show that while partisan control of the branches of government determines the manner in which congressional evaluations affect elections, divided government per se does not reduce or eliminate their effect. Even when Congress and the White House are controlled by different parties, Americans have the ability to hold each branch accountable for its own performance. When one party controls both branches, it will often be the case that the effect of congressional evaluations compounds the effect of presidential evaluations. This appears to have been the case in 2006, when low ratings for both led to a dramatic shift in power and policy direction in Congress. When the branches are controlled by different parties, the effects of congressional and presidential evaluations will partially offset one another. This appears to have been the case in the 2008 elections, as we have demonstrated.

Looking ahead, we can use the lessons learned here to make some general, preliminary predictions regarding the 2010 election cycle. The one thing we know for certain as the expanded version of this book goes to press is that because Barack Obama won the presidency and because Democrats held onto control of Congress in 2008, the 2010 election will once again take place in the context of unified party control of government. The significance of this observation is that, as 2006 and 1994 demonstrated, the potential dangers for the ruling party will be quite large. If Americans are dissatisfied with the performance of both Obama and Congress when the election rolls around, it is likely that Republicans will significantly increase the proportion of seats they hold in the House. If, however, the public feels pleased with the performance of both Congress and the president in 2010, Democrats could avoid the common phenomenon of midterm loss for the party in control of the White House and may actually gain additional seats.

There is also the possibility that the public will see Congress in a different light than they see Obama. One version of this scenario would be a situation in which Obama is reasonably popular, but Congress receives poor marks for its performance. In this case, even if the low ratings are a result of obstructionism caused by the minority party, our theory would likely predict that the potential benefits to Democrats of a popular president from their own party would be at least partially offset by the unpopularity of the party's management of Congress. Alternatively, the president's popularity may sink while Congress manages to keep its own ratings at reasonable levels. This might be achieved, for example, if Democrats in Congress were willing and able to publicly distance themselves from an unpopular Obama. Republicans appeared largely unwilling (or unable) to do this to their unpopular president in 2006, which may have helped seal their electoral fate. In a scenario where Democrats are able to pull off this unlikely feat, our theory suggests that this would serve to limit some of the damage caused by low ratings for a president from their own party.

Regardless of the particulars of any given election, our analysis in this chapter has reinforced one of the core messages of this book: the performance of Congress and public perceptions of that performance play an important role in congressional elections. Moreover, through elections, perceptions of congressional performance play an important role in shaping the composition and subsequent policy direction of Congress.

METHODOLOGICAL APPENDIX

Coding of Variables Used in Table 2.3

Congressional approval: Respondent's approval of the way Congress is handling its job. Scores range from −2 (strongly disapprove) to +2 (strongly approve).

Ideology: Respondent's self-reported ideology. Scores range from 1 (strong liberal) to 7 (strong conservative).

Liberal condition: Dummy variable coded 1 for respondents randomly selected into the liberal condition, 0 otherwise.

Party identification: Respondent's self-reported party identification. Scores range from 1 (strong Democrat) to 7 (strong Republican).

Member approval: Respondent's approval of the way her or his own member of Congress is handling her or his job. Scores range from −2 (strongly disapprove) to +2 (strongly approve).

Education: Coded as 1 = high school degree or less, 2 = some college, 3 = college degree or higher.

Income: Gross household income. Coded as 1 = under $15,000; 2 = $15,000–$24,999; 3 = $25,000–$34,999; 4 = $35,000–$49,999; 5 = $50,000–$74,999; 6 = $75,000 or more.

Gender: Coded as 1 = male, 2 = female.

Age: Respondent's age in years.

White: Dummy variable coded 1 for white respondents, 0 otherwise.

Author-Commissioned Survey Questions (chap. 3)

OCTOBER 2002 AND MAY 2003 SURVEYS

In general, do you approve or disapprove of the job Congress is doing?
   Approve
   Disapprove
   Don't know (volunteered)
   Refused (volunteered)

ROTATE NEXT TWO

Specifically, do you approve or disapprove of the job the U.S. (United States) Senate is doing?
   Approve
   Disapprove
   Don't know (volunteered)
   Refused (volunteered)

Specifically, do you approve or disapprove of the job the U.S. (United States) House of Representatives is doing?
   Approve
   Disapprove
   Don't know (volunteered)
   Refused (volunteered)

MAY 2003 SURVEY

Do you happen to know which party has the most members in the U.S. (United States) House of Representatives—the Democrats or the Republicans?
   Democrats
   Republicans
   Don't know (volunteered)
   Refused (volunteered)

Coding of Variables Used in Table 4.1

Congressional approval: Respondent's approval of the way Congress has been
handling its job. Coded as 1 = approve, 0 = neutral, −1 = disapprove.

Ideological distance from Democratic/Republican Party: Absolute value of the
difference between a respondent's rating of self and of party on a seven-point
liberal-to-conservative scale. Scores range from 0 (no distance) to 6 (most
distant).

Economy: The degree to which the respondent thinks the economy has gotten
better or worse over the past year. Scores range from −2 (much worse) to
+2 (much better).

Government efficiency: The degree to which the respondent thinks the government wastes money that people pay in taxes. Coded as 1 = a lot, 2 = some,
3 = not much.

Government fairness: A dichotomous variable measuring whether the respondent thinks government is run for the benefit of all the people (= 1) or by a
few big interests (= 0).

Efficacy: Additive scale summarizing the respondent's level of disagreement
with each of the following statements (coded as 0 = agree, 1 = neutral, 2 =
disagree): "I don't think public officials care much what people like me
think" and "People like me don't have any say about what the government
does." Summed scores range from 0 (low efficacy) to 4 (high efficacy).

Interest in politics: How often the respondent reports following public affairs.
Scores range from 1 (hardly at all) to 4 (most of the time).

Income: Respondent's self-reported household income. Categories range from 1
(low income) to 5 (high income).

Member approval: Respondent's approval of the way her or his own member of
Congress is handling her or his job. Coded as −1 = disapprove, 0 = neutral,
1 = approve.

Democrat: Respondent's self-reported party identification. Coded as 1 = Democrat, 0 = otherwise.

Republican: Respondent's self-reported party identification. Coded as 1 = Republican, 0 = otherwise.

Presidential approval: Respondent's approval of the way the president is handling
his job. Coded as −1 = disapprove, 0 = neutral, 1 = approve.

Ruling Out the Existence of Projection Effects in Table 4.1

Table A4.1 reestimates the model presented in table 4.1, with one significant difference. Instead of measuring the absolute difference between an individual's ideological self-rating and his or her rating of a party, we measure the absolute difference between an individual's self-rating and the sample-wide average rating of
that party—an assessment of that party's location that is essentially independent of

TABLE A4.1. Effects of Ideological Distance from the Sample's Mean Majority Party Rating on Congressional Approval, 1980–2004

INDEPENDENT VARIABLES	DEMOCRATIC CONGRESSES					REPUBLICAN CONGRESSES				DEM. HOUSE/REP. SEN.		
	1980	1988	1990	1992	1994	1996	1998	2000	2004	1982	1984	1986
Ideological distance from Democratic Party	−.20° (.09)	−.42°° (.05)	−.24°° (.05)	−.18° (.05)	−.13# (.08)	.19° (.08)	.11 (.09)	.08 (.07)	−.01 (.09)	−.17# (.09)	−.16° (.07)	−.24°° (.07)
Ideological distance from Republican Party	.02 (.08)	.09 (.07)	.20° (.08)	.17° (.07)	.01 (.08)	−.21°° (.08)	−.19° (.09)	−.04 (.07)	−.15# (.09)	.20° (.06)	.19° (.08)	.12 (.07)
Economy	.03 (.11)	.12 (.07)	.09 (.07)	.02 (.07)	.01 (.07)	−.05 (.07)	−.03 (.07)	.05 (.05)	.21°° (.08)	.03 (.08)	.04 (.06)	.21°° (.05)
Government efficiency	.73°° (.19)	.32°° (.12)	.46°° (.12)	.53°° (.11)	.58°° (.13)	.37°° (.12)	.43°° (.12)	.53°° (.12)	.23 (.14)	.63°° (.16)	.26° (.11)	
Government fairness	.29 (.20)	.64°° (.14)	.62°° (.14)	1.04°° (.14)	.93°° (.16)	.61°° (.14)	.83°° (.15)	.44°° (.13)	.70°° (.15)	.42° (.18)	.62°° (.12)	
Efficacy	.10° (.05)	.13°° (.04)	.04 (.05)	.09° (.04)	−.03 (.04)	.07# (.04)	−.01 (.04)	.09° (.04)	.09# (.05)	.17° (.05)	.11°° (.04)	
Interest in politics	−.28°° (.09)	−.23°° (.07)	−.25° (.06)	−.45°° (.07)	−.39°° (.07)	−.25°° (.07)	−.33°° (.07)	−.21° (.07)	−.24°° (.08)	−.30°° (.09)	−.24°° (.06)	−.23°° (.05)
Income	.04 (.07)	.07 (.06)	−.13°° (.05)	−.08 (.05)	−.09# (.06)	.00 (.06)	−.03 (.06)	.06 (.06)	−.01 (.06)	−.02 (.07)	.04 (.06)	−.00 (.04)
Member approval	.10# (.05)	.21°° (.04)	.09°° (.04)	.13°° (.04)	.13°° (.04)	.12°° (.04)	.07# (.04)	.10°° (.04)	.08# (.04)	.12# (.05)	.15°° (.04)	.14°° (.03)
Presidential approval	.30°° (.09)	.10 (.07)	.29°° (.07)	.26°° (.07)	.45°° (.07)	−.01 (.08)	−.07 (.08)	.15° (.07)	.31°° (.10)	.52°° (.10)	.22°° (.08)	.23°° (.06)
Democrat	.19 (.19)	.45°° (.15)	.24# (.13)	.51°° (.13)	−.04 (.15)	.14 (.15)	.09 (.15)	−.27# (.14)	.02 (.18)	.53°° (.20)	.53°° (.14)	.52°° (.12)
Republican	−.22 (.21)	−.25 (.15)	−.24 (.15)	−.38° (.17)	−.17 (.17)	.59°° (.16)	.53°° (.17)	.36° (.17)	−.34# (.20)	−.33 (.22)	−.03 (.15)	.27° (.12)
Pseudo R^2	.15	.15	.13	.19	.22	.11	.12	.10	.16	.18	.11	.07
Number of cases	699	1,293	1,443	1,598	1,349	1,236	1,090	1,154	878	715	1,378	1,735

Source: Data from ANES 2005.

Note: Table entries are ordered logistic regression estimates (standard errors in parentheses).

#p ≤ .05 (one-tailed)   °p ≤ .05   °°p ≤ .01 (two-tailed)

any individual's personal views. Since individuals are not rating the parties them-selves, each individual's distance score is not a product of projection.

The results in table A4.1 are strikingly similar to those in table 4.1. In all twelve estimations, our key coefficients of interest are still in the correct direction. Their sizes vary a bit from table 4.1, but half of these differences are actually slight increases in impact. Finally, in all but one of these twelve alternative estimations (2000), the key coefficient is still statistically significant, at $p \leq .05$ (one-tailed).

Testing the Effect of Ideological Distance from the Majority Party in Congress Using a 1998 Gallup Survey (chap. 4)

Here, we provide evidence in support of our assertion in chapter 4 that ideolog-ical distance from the party that has a majority in Congress (in 1998, "the Re-publican Party") is a suitable surrogate for ideological distance from the majority party as represented specifically in Congress ("Republican leaders in Con-gress"). We do this by estimating a model similar to that in table 4.1, but with an alternative measure of ideological distance. In the Gallup survey used here, re-spondents are asked whether Republican congressional leaders are too liberal, too conservative, or about right. We code "about right" as low ideological differ-ence (1) and each of the other responses as higher ideological difference (2). While the range of control variables is more limited than in the ANES surveys, we include comparable measures of those that are available. We control for ide-ological difference from the minority party leadership ("Democratic leaders in Congress") in the same manner as for the majority party. Income is a seven-point scale from low (1) to high (7). Dummy variables are used for Democratic Party and Republican Party identification. Presidential approval and congressional ap-proval are measured as approve (1), neutral (0), and disapprove (−1). As in chapter 4, we employ ordinal regression analysis.

The results of the estimation, presented in table A4.2, demonstrate that even when a survey measurement refers specifically to party representatives in Con-gress, the effect of ideological difference from the majority party—in this case, Republicans—is still negative and significant, as with our general party measure in table 4.1. As a result, there is little reason to believe that the ANES party mea-sure is not capturing the effect of the party in Congress.

Coding of Variables Used in Table 4.2

Congressional approval: Percentage approving of Congress, from table A4.3.

Public liberalism: Stimson's (1999) "mood" data, updated on his Web site: http://www.unc.edu/~jstimson.

Congressional policy extremism: A weighted average of Poole and Rosenthal's means for winning policy for the House and Senate, multiplied by 100 and then multiplied by −1 for Democratic Congresses.

TABLE A4.2. Effects of Ideological Difference from the Majority Party
in Congress on Congressional Approval, 1998

INDEPENDENT VARIABLES	EVALUATION OF CONGRESS
Ideological difference from Democratic leaders in Congress	−.42°
	(.15)
Ideological difference from Republican leaders in Congress	−1.04°°
	(.15)
Income	−.01
	(.06)
Democrat	.05
	(.18)
Republican	−.51°
	(.19)
Presidential approval	.59°°
	(.09)
Pseudo R^2	.14
Number of cases	870

Source: Gallup poll, January 16–18, 1998 ($N = 1,004$).

Note: Table entries are ordered logistic regression estimates (standard errors in parentheses).
°$p \leq .05$ °°$p \leq .005$ (one-tailed)

Prior quarter approval of Congress: Congressional approval variable, lagged one
quarter.

National economic conditions: Predicted values obtained by regressing the University of Michigan's Index of Consumer Sentiment on unemployment, quarterly and yearly change in unemployment, quarterly and yearly change in the consumer price index, and quarterly and yearly change in real per capita disposable income.

Presidential approval: Average approval from Gallup polls taken during that
quarter.

Presidential vetoes, veto overrides: Total number in each quarter.

Intra-Congress conflict: Number of cloture votes in each quarter.

Major bills: Measured using David Mayhew's (1991) series, updated on his Web
site: http://pantheon.yale.edu/~dmayhew.

Scandals: Dummy variables representing (year:quarter) Koreagate (1976:4–
1978:4), ABSCAM (1980:3–1982:1), the Jim Wright scandal (1989:2), the
Keating Five (1990:3–1991:4), the House Bank scandal (1991:3–1992:3),
and the Post Office scandal (1992:2–1992:4) were tested in the model, with
insignificant variables removed.

Presidencies: Dummy variables representing each presidency were tested in the
model, with insignificant variables removed.

TABLE A4.3. Quarterly Congressional Approval Values from Figure 4.2

YEAR	QUARTER	APPROVAL	YEAR	QUARTER	APPROVAL	YEAR	QUARTER	APPROVAL
1974	1	33.62	1985	1	47.72	1996	1	29.10
1974	2	32.15	1985	2	53.00	1996	2	29.87
1974	3	42.54	1985	3	55.21	1996	3	33.65
1974	4	35.38	1985	4	51.03	1996	4	34.72
1975	1	32.41	1986	1	51.26	1997	1	36.66
1975	2	31.71	1986	2	46.04	1997	2	36.61
1975	3	27.82	1986	3	44.28	1997	3	37.68
1975	4	26.37	1986	4	43.80	1997	4	38.97
1976	1	25.22	1987	1	41.63	1998	1	44.98
1976	2	31.74	1987	2	49.75	1998	2	43.36
1976	3	31.60	1987	3	42.81	1998	3	45.90
1976	4	31.39	1987	4	41.28	1998	4	42.53
1977	1	33.93	1988	1	44.14	1999	1	41.31
1977	2	34.35	1988	2	45.62	1999	2	41.28
1977	3	31.13	1988	3	43.83	1999	3	39.77
1977	4	30.70	1988	4	44.88	1999	4	39.13
1978	1	29.85	1989	1	47.30	2000	1	42.43
1978	2	30.68	1989	2	45.68	2000	2	40.65
1978	3	31.39	1989	3	44.35	2000	3	44.50
1978	4	32.59	1989	4	43.17	2000	4	47.51
1979	1	30.11	1990	1	43.23	2001	1	46.56
1979	2	25.61	1990	2	44.35	2001	2	46.99
1979	3	21.64	1990	3	40.55	2001	3	47.79
1979	4	19.65	1990	4	32.68	2001	4	55.66
1980	1	26.48	1991	1	38.67	2002	1	50.81
1980	2	23.49	1991	2	37.95	2002	2	46.64
1980	3	29.60	1991	3	31.37	2002	3	44.79
1980	4	29.48	1991	4	29.27	2002	4	43.81
1981	1	35.70	1992	1	22.70	2003	1	42.69
1981	2	43.13	1992	2	20.07	2003	2	41.46
1981	3	48.95	1992	3	22.75	2003	3	39.57
1981	4	44.61	1992	4	24.89	2003	4	39.34
1982	1	41.64	1993	1	27.26	2004	1	41.90
1982	2	34.74	1993	2	27.15	2004	2	39.88
1982	3	32.95	1993	3	26.37	2004	3	39.34
1982	4	34.68	1993	4	27.16	2004	4	39.39
1983	1	33.68	1994	1	29.47	2005	1	38.65
1983	2	37.39	1994	2	31.50	2005	2	34.64
1983	3	42.80	1994	3	27.01	2005	3	32.39
1983	4	42.99	1994	4	25.93	2005	4	31.00
1984	1	43.06	1995	1	31.97	2006	1	30.31
1984	2	46.10	1995	2	33.12	2006	2	26.87
1984	3	47.17	1995	3	30.77	2006	3	27.36
1984	4	47.56	1995	4	29.48	2006	4	26.51

Coding of Variables Used in Table 5.2

Vote: Coded as 1 = majority party candidate, 0 = minority party candidate.

Congressional approval: Coded as 1 = approve, 0 = don't know, −1 = disapprove.

Approval of majority party president: Coded as 1 = approve, 0 = don't know or no majority party president, −1 = disapprove.

Approval of minority party president: Coded as 1 = approve, 0 = don't know or no minority party president, −1 = disapprove.

Economy (majority party president): Coded as 1 = better, 0 = same, don't know or no majority party president; −1 = worse.

Economy (minority party president): coded as Coded as 1 = approve, 0 = same, don't know or no minority party president, −1 = worse.

Approval of majority party incumbent: Coded as 1 = approve, 0 = don't know or no majority party incumbent, −1 = disapprove.

Approval of minority party incumbent: Coded as 1 = approve, 0 = don't know or no minority party incumbent, −1 = disapprove.

Party identification: Coded 1 if the voter is the same party as majority party candidate, 0 if the voter does not identify with either major party, −1 if the voter is same party as the minority party candidate.

Recognize majority/minority party candidate name: Coded 1 if the voter recognizes the candidate's name, 0 if the voter does not recognize the candidate's name.

Majority/minority party incumbent: Coded 1 for yes, 0 for no.

Majority party president: Coded 1 for yes, 0 for no.

Year: Dummy variables for 1980–2002 are also included in the model but are not shown in the results (2004 is included in the constant term).

Note: This analysis is restricted to races with candidates from both major parties and excludes respondents who voted in a different (unknown) district than the one in which they were interviewed. In 2002, the question on incumbent approval was not asked. For that year only, we replace these specific missing data with the data-wide sample mean. Results are virtually identical if 2002 is simply dropped from the analysis.

Coding of Variables Added in the Alternative Specifications for Table 5.2 (table A5.1)

Number of contacts with majority/minority candidate: Number of contacts out of seven possible types (0–7 range).

Incompatibility with majority/minority party candidate (services/spending issue): Absolute difference between the respondent's ratings of self and of the candidate on the seven-point ANES scale of preference on services vs. spending (0–6 range).

TABLE A5.1. Alternative Specifications for Table 5.2

	ORIGINAL MODEL FROM TABLE 5.2	WITH "CANDIDATE CONTACT" ITEM	WITH "SERVICES/ SPENDING ISSUE" ITEM	WITH "CANDIDATE IDEOLOGY" ITEM
Congressional approval	.17°°	.22°°	.20°	.22°°
	(.03)	(.05)	(.09)	(.07)
Approval of majority party president	.53°°	.37°°	.54°°	.45°°
	(.07)	(.09)	(.15)	(.12)
Approval of minority party president	−.60°°	−.54°°	−.36°°	−.41°°
	(.05)	(.06)	(.12)	(.11)
Economy (majority party president)	.07	−.02	−.12	−.09
	(.09)	(.12)	(.18)	(.15)
Economy (minority party president)	−.29°°	−.38°°	−.38°	−.31°
	(.06)	(.07)	(.17)	(.14)
Approval of majority party incumbent	1.77°°	1.68°°	1.85°°	1.68°°
	(.07)	(.09)	(.21)	(.15)
Approval of minority party incumbent	−1.80°°	−1.64°°	−1.62°°	−1.60°°
	(.09)	(.11)	(.22)	(.18)
Party identification	1.32°°	1.25°°	1.30°°	1.33°°
	(.05)	(.06)	(.12)	(.10)
Recognize majority party candidate name	1.15°°	.77°°	.75°	.75°°
	(.09)	(.11)	(.31)	(.27)
Recognize minority party candidate name	−1.16°°	−.83°°	−.94°	−1.23°°
	(.08)	(.11)	(.41)	(.28)
Majority party incumbent	−.04	−.22°	−.32	−.30
	(.10)	(.12)	(.26)	(.21)
Minority party incumbent	.19°	.47°°	.33	.51°
	(.11)	(.14)	(.29)	(.23)
Majority party president	−.44°	−.27°	−.43	−.57°
	(.18)	(.15)	(.36)	(.30)
Number of contacts with majority candidate		.35°°		
		(.03)		
Number of contacts with minority candidate		−.39°°		
		(.04)		
Incompatibility with majority party candidate (services/spending issue)			−.41°°	
			(.07)	
Incompatibility with minority party candidate (services/spending issue)			.35°°	
			(.07)	
Incompatibility with majority party candidate (ideology)				−.12°
				(.05)
Incompatibility with minority party candidate (ideology)				.28°°
				(.05)
Constant	.22	.03	.36	.39
	(.16)	(.17)	(.57)	(.43)
Pseudo R^2	.68	.69	.69	.64
Number of cases	9,891	6,017	1,466	1,946

Source: Data from ANES 2005.
Note: Table entries are logistic regression coefficients (standard errors in parentheses).
°$p \leq .05$ °°$p \leq .005$ (one-tailed)

Incompatibility with majority/minority party candidate (ideology): Absolute difference between the respondent's ratings of self and of the candidate on the seven-point ANES ideology scale (0–6 range).

Coding of Variables Used in Table 5.3

Vote: Percentage of the two-party vote received by the majority party candidate.

Congressional approval: Congressional approval in the third quarter of each election year, from table A4.3.

Approval of majority party president: Average approval from Gallup polls in the third quarter of the election year, multiplied by 1 for a majority party president, 0 otherwise.

Approval of minority party president: Average approval from Gallup polls in the third quarter of the election year, multiplied by 1 for a minority party president, 0 otherwise.

Economy (majority party president): Percentage change in real disposable per capita income over the year ending in the third quarter of the election year, multiplied by 1 for a majority party president, 0 otherwise.

Economy (minority party president): Percentage change in real disposable per capita income over the year ending in the third quarter of the election year, multiplied by 1 for a minority party president, 0 otherwise.

Previous vote percentage in district: Percentage of the two-party congressional vote received by the majority party in the last general election.

Experienced majority party candidate: Coded 1 if the majority party candidate has previously held an elected public office, 0 otherwise. Source: Gary Jacobson, personal communication.

Experienced minority party candidate: Coded 1 if the minority party candidate has previously held an elected public office, 0 otherwise. Source: Gary Jacobson, personal communication.

Majority/minority party incumbent: Coded 1 for yes, 0 for no.

Majority/minority party freshman incumbent: Coded 1 for yes, 0 for no.

Majority/minority party candidate spending: Inflation adjusted (2004 = 1) dollars, in units of 100,000.

Majority party president: Coded 1 for yes, 0 for no.

Coding of Variables Used in Table 6.1

Quality challenge: Coded 1 if the incumbent faces a challenger who has previously held an elected public office, 0 otherwise. Source: Gary Jacobson, personal communication.

Congressional approval: Congressional approval in the second quarter of the election year, from table A4.3.

Presidential approval (incumbent from president's party): Average approval from Gallup polls in the second quarter of each election year, multiplied by 1 if the incumbent is from the president's party, 0 otherwise.

Presidential approval (incumbent not from president's party): Average approval from Gallup polls in the second quarter of each election year, multiplied by 1 if the incumbent is not from the president's party, 0 otherwise.

Economy (incumbent from president's party): Percentage change in real disposable per capita income over the year ending in the third quarter of the election year, multiplied by 1 if the incumbent is not from the president's party, 0 otherwise.

Economy (incumbent not from president's party): Percentage change in real disposable per capita income over the year ending in the third quarter of the election year, multiplied by 1 if the incumbent is not from the president's party, 0 otherwise.

Incumbent from president's party: Coded 1 for yes, 0 for no.

Previous vote percentage for incumbent: Percentage of the two-party vote received by the incumbent in the last general election.

Note: This analysis excludes incumbents who were not elected in the previous national election. It also excludes House seats with two incumbents running in the general election due to redistricting.

Coding of Variables Used in Table 6.3

Voluntary retirement: Coded 1 for an incumbent who voluntarily left the House, 0 otherwise. Source: Inter-university Consortium for Political and Social Research and Carroll McKibbin (1997), and *Almanac of American Politics* (1998–2006).

Congressional approval: Congressional approval in the second quarter of the election year, from table A4.3.

Presidential approval (incumbent from president's party): Average approval from Gallup polls in the second quarter of the election year, multiplied by 1 if the incumbent is from the president's party, 0 otherwise.

Presidential approval (incumbent not from president's party): Average approval from Gallup polls in the second quarter of the election year, multiplied by 1 if the incumbent is not from the president's party, 0 otherwise.

Economy (incumbent from president's party): Percentage change in real disposable per capita income over the year ending in the third quarter of the election year, multiplied by 1 if the incumbent is not from the president's party, 0 otherwise.

Economy (incumbent not from president's party): Percentage change in real disposable per capita income over the year ending in the third quarter of the election year, multiplied by 1 if the incumbent is not from the president's party, 0 otherwise.

Incumbent from president's party: Coded 1 for yes, 0 for no.

Previous vote percentage for incumbent: Percentage of the two-party vote received by the incumbent in the last general election.

Incumbent age: Incumbent's age in years at the beginning of that Congress.

Note: Members who seek higher office are excluded from this analysis. The analysis also excludes incumbents who were redistricted into a seat with another incumbent, who were not previously elected during a regular national election, and/or who have served less than a majority of their term.

Coding of Variables Used in Table 7.1

Seat swing for the majority party: Number of seats gained or lost (if negative) by the party holding a majority of seats prior to the election.

Congressional approval: Congressional approval in the third quarter of the election year, from table A4.3.

Presidential approval: Average approval from Gallup polls in the third quarter of the election year, multiplied by 1 for a majority party president, −1 for a minority party president.

Economy: Percentage change in real disposable per capita income over the year ending in the third quarter of the election year, multiplied by 1 for a majority party president, −1 for a minority party president.

Seats at risk: Difference between the number of seats the majority party held before the election and its historical average from the previous eight elections.

Majority party president: Coded 1 for yes, 0 for no.

Coding of Variables Used in Table 7.2

Distance from the majority party: Absolute difference between the ideological location of the incumbent in the postelection Congress and the average majority party location in the Congress prior to the election.

Congressional approval: Congressional approval in the third quarter of the election year from table A4.3.

Prior distance from majority party: Absolute difference between the ideological location of the incumbent in the Congress prior the election and the average majority party location in the Congress prior to the election.

Time trend: Coded 0 for the 1974 election and increasing by 1 for each subsequent election.

Note: For this analysis only, ideological scores are derived from a specially modified version of Poole and Rosenthal's scores. Our modification follows the general procedure recommended for this purpose in Poole and Romer 1993 (195 n. 13) and Poole and Rosenthal 1997 (268 n. 17). We take the first-dimension scores obtained when each Congress is scaled separately (W-NOMINATE) and regress these scores on the corresponding scores obtained from the dynamic scaling procedure (DW-NOMINATE). We use the estimated coefficients to linearly transform the original static (W-NOMINATE) scores. This has the effect of putting each pair of Congresses on the same metric, while retaining the individual Congress-to-Congress variation permitted by W-NOMINATE scores (members are not restricted to linear movement averaged over a career). For presentational purposes, we multiply the resulting scores by 100 so the scale ranges from −100 to +100. At the time of our analysis, scores were not yet available for incumbents returning in the 109th Congress. In addition, we necessarily exclude incumbents who cast too few roll call votes to be scaled by Poole and Rosenthal. The original (untransformed) data can be found online at http://www.voteview.com.

Coding of Variables Used in Tables 7.3 and 7.4

Shift toward the minority party in average member location (table 7.3 only): Calculated as the average first-dimension DW-NOMINATE (conservatism) score of members in the Congress following the election minus the average first-dimension DW-NOMINATE score of members in the Congress before the election, reversing the sign for all Congresses with a Republican House majority and multiplying the scale by 100.

Shift toward the minority party in average location of winning policy (table 7.4 only): Calculated as the average location of winning policy in the Congress following the election minus the average location of winning policy in the Congress before the election, using first-dimension DW-NOMINATE scores, reversing the sign for all Congresses with a Republican House majority, and multiplying the scale by 100.

Congressional approval: Congressional approval in the third quarter of the election year, from table A4.3.

Presidential approval: Average approval from Gallup polls in the third quarter of the election year, multiplied by 1 for a majority party president, −1 for a minority party president.

Economy: Percentage change in real disposable per capita income over the year ending in the third quarter of the election year, multiplied by 1 for a majority party president, −1 for a minority party president.

Majority party president: Coded 1 for yes, 0 for no.

Coding of Variables Used in Table 9.1

For 1980–2004 and 2008 ANES data, coding follows that of table 5.2. Coding for 2006 NEP data is as follows.

Vote: Coded as 1 = majority party candidate, 0 = minority party candidate.
Congressional approval: Coded as 1 = approve, 0 = no answer, −1 = disapprove.
Presidential approval: Coded as 1 = approve, 0 = no answer, −1 = disapprove.
Economy: Coded as 1 = good/excellent, 0 = no answer, −1 = not so good/poor.
Party identification: Coded 1 if the voter is the same party as the majority party candidate, 0 if the voter does not identify with either major party, −1 if the voter is the same party as the minority party candidate.
Experienced majority party candidate: Coded 1 if the majority party candidate has previously held an elected public office, 0 otherwise. Source: Gary Jacobson, personal communication.
Experienced minority party candidate: Coded 1 if the minority party candidate has previously held an elected public office, 0 otherwise. Source: Gary Jacobson, personal communication.
Majority/minority party incumbent: Coded 1 for yes, 0 for no.

Note: This analysis is restricted to races with candidates from both major parties. This model uses a measure of candidate experience in place of a measure of candidate name recognition, because the NEP, unlike the ANES, does not measure voters' ability to recognize candidate names.

NOTES

CHAPTER 1

1. Democrats needed to capture fifteen Republican seats to retake the majority. Among researchers who developed academic models not driven by poll numbers on the generic congressional ballot, Brandt and Brunell (2006) predicted a Democratic pickup of about twelve seats; Campbell (2006), about thirteen seats; Cuzan and Bundrick (2006), about twenty seats; Klarner and Buchanan (2006), about twenty-two seats; and Abramowitz (2006), about twenty-five seats.

2. Democrats needed to capture five Republican seats to retake the majority and ended up losing seven of their own. Erikson and Bafumi (2002) predicted a Democratic pickup of twenty-five seats; Abramowitz (2002), fourteen seats; Tamas (2002), twelve seats; and Lewis-Beck and Tien (2002), eight seats.

3. Gallup polls conducted November 2–5, 2006 ($N = 1,500$), and October 3–6, 2002 ($N = 1,502$).

4. Preliminary analysis of the 2008 election outcomes, conducted as this book went to press, shows a similar situation. Traditional academic models greatly overestimated the number of seats the Democratic Party would gain in the House. Historically low public evaluations of Congress appear to have tempered what would otherwise have been an even stronger Democratic year (Jones and McDermott 2009).

5. But see Born 1990.

6. According to the authors, 1994 is an exception to this rule.

7. Personal communication with the authors.

8. Specifically, Lipinski's content analysis found that 70 percent of members sent messages about policy.

9. Our previous research comes closest to answering this question, and we more fully elaborate on it in this book.

10. Our previous research, which we expand on in this book, is one exception.

11. Similarly, Arnold's 2004 study of local media coverage of congressional incumbents finds members of the majority party to be much less critical of Congress.

CHAPTER 2

1. We refer to Hibbing and Theiss-Morse 1995, 118 n. 4. The authors use two-tailed significance testing and report that the variable has a greater than 90 percent probability of being significantly different from zero. Since our hypothesis is directional—that the effect of the variable will be in the negative direction—the appropriate significance test is a one-tailed test (Frankfort-Nachmias and Nachmias 2000), providing 95 percent confidence in the estimate.

2. Other work demonstrates that the public views Congress as a more important shaper of national policy than the president (e.g., Hibbing and Theiss-Morse 1995, 51–53).

3. They do not, however, test ideological distance's potential effects on performance evaluations. These two dependent variables have been shown to be conceptually distinct and not always explained by the same factors (Hibbing and Theiss-Morse 1998).

4. In recent work, scholars have argued that political scientists traditionally used the term *internal validity* as a catchall category for the appropriateness of the internal research design to the research question. For example, Shadish, Cooke, and Campbell (2002) provide four measures for study validity (rather than merely two): statistical conclusion validity, internal validity, construct validity, and external validity. According to Morton and Williams (2008), these first three measures comprise what political scientists have typically considered internal validity. For our purposes here, we consider internal validity to represent Shadish, Cook, and Campbell's more precise definition: whether the conclusions from the study can be accurately interpreted as causal.

5. National Science Foundation grant no. 0094964, Diana C. Mutz and Arthur Lupia, principal investigators.

6. This observation essentially replicates that of other standard cross-sectional surveys.

7. In each case, we computed the gamma statistic as an ordinal measure of association (and direction) in the relationship. These figures are reported in the table, along with their *p*-values.

8. Because our dependent variable had five categories, we used ordinal logistic regression. We included respondents with no definitive opinions ("don't know" responses) in the dependent variable of our regression model (as the middle value), as an N-saving measure to partially mitigate the N-losing effects of multiple independent variables. We have also run the model with these cases excluded and found virtually identical results.

9. In theory, random assignment of subjects to experimental and control groups ensures that the groups will not differ with respect to these other factors. But this is not always true in practice. We therefore feel that statistical controls are a necessary precaution.

10. We also tried including presidential approval in the model, but it was too highly correlated with both party identification and ideology. We removed the variable of presidential approval, rather than either of the other two variables, because it had the lowest tolerance score of the three. While the estimates for party identification and ideology were strongly impacted by the inclusion of presidential approval, the interaction variable at the heart of this test—respondent ideology multiplied by liberal policy condition—was unaffected.

11. Specifically, we plugged each value of the variables representing ideology and liberal condition into the model while holding all other independent variables constant at their median value in the data. We combined the probabilities for "strongly" and "somewhat" approve for an overall probability of approval.

CHAPTER 3

1. While we are not disputing this conclusion here, there are scholars who do. For example, Paul Goren (e.g., 2000) has repeatedly found evidence that political experts do not necessarily make better political belief connections and judgments than the public. We discuss Goren's research further in chapter 4.

2. The failure of these percentages to total 100 percent is due to rounding.

3. Poll conducted by Princeton Survey Research Associates, April 7–16, 2006 ($N = 1,501$).

4. This is, of course, a rather crude test of the public's use of ideology. Because the focus of this chapter is knowledge, we leave a fuller discussion of the role of ideology and the public's use of it for chapter 4.

5. Poll conducted by Princeton Survey Research Associates, November 28–December 4, 1995 ($N = 1,514$).

6. This is, admittedly, an oversimplification of the ideological and party concepts, and it makes some assumptions about citizens' ideological capacities. We do not think, however, that these issues undermine the simple question here of gauging whether citizens generally judge Congress in a manner consistent with their own preferences. See chapter 4 for a complete discussion of citizen ideology and ideological judgments, as well as a controlled, multiple regression analysis of the relationship between ideology and congressional evaluations.

7. Throughout this chapter, we use a dichotomous measure of congressional approval for ease of presentation. This excludes respondents who have no opinion of congressional performance, a number that is marginally higher among those not correctly answering the question of majority party control (15 percent versus 8 percent for those answering correctly). Including the group with no opinion in the analysis does not, however, change the pattern or statistical significance of the results reported here.

8. Liberals are those who described themselves as liberal in both 1994 and 1996, and conservatives are respondents who called themselves conservative in

both periods. These ideologically consistent respondents make up 76 percent of the 1996 sample. For the sake of our upcoming argument in chapter 4, it is worth noting that only 1 percent of panel respondents shifted completely from liberal to conservative or vice versa and that only 5 percent did not place themselves ideologically in one or both years. The remaining 18 percent moved within one step of their original position (e.g., from moderate to conservative).

9. The net change is calculated as the proportion of individuals moving from disapproval to approval minus the proportion moving from approval to disapproval.

10. Results are fundamentally the same if the "incorrect" group is split into three subgroups—those who did not answer correctly in both years, those who did not do so only in 1994, and those who were not correct in 1996 only. Due to the small size of each group and the similarity in the results, we combine the groups here.

11. Poll conducted by Princeton Survey Research Associates, June 13–17, 2001 ($N = 1,200$).

12. The 2002 survey unfortunately did not include a factual question on party control.

13. To ensure that the changes in approval levels are not due to differences in survey practices (e.g., question wording, question order, weighting), we use a single survey source. We chose the polls conducted by NBC News because, during this period, they conducted the most polls that included both a question on congressional approval and a question on ideology.

14. In a Gallup poll conducted that week, March 11–14, 2007 ($N = 1,009$), 35 percent of Americans volunteered that the Iraq War was the most important problem facing the country. No other issue was mentioned by more than 8 percent of Americans.

15. We thank Jennifer DePinto of the CBS News Election and Survey Unit for her help with these data.

CHAPTER 4

1. The difference in ordinal approval ratings between the "very liberal" and "somewhat liberal" groups is statistically significant in a one-tailed test, at $p <$ .05. Most other differences are also statistically significant.

2. Because the sheer volume of data restricts our ability to be comprehensive, we arrived at this figure by looking at the last poll in each election year from 1980 to 2006 for each of the following survey organizations (average placement percent in parentheses): ABC News (93%), CBS News (94%), and Gallup Poll (96%). Those missing include both "don't know" answers and refusals. Data were collected through the iPOLL database of the Roper Center for Public Opinion Research at the University of Connecticut.

3. This is the average proportion from the ANES cumulative file from 1984,

when the ANES survey began asking the follow-up question, to 2004, the year of the most recent ANES survey as of this writing.

4. The analysis presented here represents an update and expansion on our previously published work in this area (Jones and McDermott 2002).

5. We exclude the year 2002 from the analysis because the survey of that year did not ask questions about ideological placement of the parties—key questions necessary to test our hypothesis.

6. As in chapter 2, our regression here includes the respondents with no opinion ("don't know" responses) as an *N*-saving measure. We have also conducted the analysis excluding the "don't know" responses and found the same pattern of results (see Jones and McDermott 2002).

7. To ensure that our results are not merely an artifact of projection, we also ran the model in each year, measuring the ideological distance of each respondent from the entire sample's mean ideological placement of the majority party (see Wlezien and Carman 2001 for a similar strategy). Even when using this more "objective" measure of party placement, our expected relationships continue to hold in all years but one (see the appendix for complete results). Because a key point of our hypothesis is that individuals' perceptions are what matter, we here use their own placements rather than the sample mean.

8. Some respondents did not place themselves or the parties on the ideological scale. To address this issue, we also tested our model using a version of ideological distance that included these cases. Since those who cannot use the ideological scales necessarily cannot perceive any ideological differences between themselves and that party, we coded such individuals as perceiving no ideological difference (zero distance). With this expanded operational definition of ideological distance, we found that these nonraters behave the same as those who actually perceive zero ideological distance (a *t*-test shows no significant difference in mean approval of Congress between the two types of "zeros"). Accordingly, the results of our model actually become a bit stronger when these cases are included in the analysis. These results demonstrate that the model's central hypothesis applies not only to ideologues but also to nonideologues: the model expects those who see no ideological differences to be the most approving of Congress, and this is, in fact, what we find among both raters and nonraters.

9. Specifically, we regress individuals' ratings of the party that happens to be the House majority on the mean conservatism score for actual House majority members (using Poole and Rosenthal's first-dimension DW-NOMINATE scores found at http://voteview.com). This result holds true independent of which party controls the House.

10. The appendix contains coding details for all of the variables in the model.

11. We also ran the model with a seven-point party variable that accounts for differences in the strength of party attachment, but our basic results remained the same. See Jones and McDermott 2002.

12. Three of our control variables were not available in the 1986 ANES survey, so we ran a reduced model for that year.

13. We ran diagnostics for each year (using ordinary least squares) to ensure that multicollinearity was not responsible for the limited effects of party identification. The lowest tolerance value for either party variable (both of which generally had the lowest tolerance values in the models) was for Republican identification in 2004, at 0.53—still well above any threshold for concern. Overall, the tests demonstrated that both Democratic and Republican identifications were more than sufficiently independent from the other variables in the model.

14. The numbers represent an average American, with average perceived ideological distance from the minority party and with middling positions on all other variables.

15. Our assumption would be violated if the average American viewed Congress as "too moderate." However, the limited evidence we have suggests otherwise. In 1992, Americans rated the Democratic Congress significantly more liberal than themselves (Hibbing and Theiss-Morse 1995); in 1997, they rated the Republican Congress significantly more conservative than themselves (Wlezien and Carman 2001). While some individuals may view Congress as too moderate, the mass public is unlikely to do so.

16. Also, as discussed shortly in text, difficulty in placing the public and Congress on the same policy scale prevents appropriate hypothesis testing.

17. The appendix reports the exact values of this measure, as well as details on the measurement of all variables in this analysis.

18. Looking at the untransformed scores on policy conservatism, Democratic Congresses have ranged between −0.167 and −0.040 during this period, while Republican Congresses have ranged between 0.100 and 0.270.

19. To our knowledge, there are no publicly available time series data that measure public ideology and congressional ideology on comparable scales.

20. We also tested the simpler idea that all divided governments have a uniform effect on congressional approval. But as in Durr, Gilmour, and Wolbrecht 1997, our results did not support this hypothesis.

21. Since congressional approval is theoretically affected by the overall ideological output from both chambers of Congress, we have no clear predictions for our variables in cases in which the chambers are controlled by different parties. For this reason, we exclude such cases from the analysis—specifically, 1981 through 1986 and 2001 (beginning in the third quarter) through 2002.

22. The economy does not reach statistical significance during Democratic Congresses, but it does if presidential approval is purged of its economic component. All the variables representing legislative activity are insignificant, similar to Rudolph's (2002) findings. Scandals are generally insignificant, with the House Bank as an exception, as found in other studies (Durr, Gilmour, and Wolbrecht 1997; Rudolph 2002). Presidential regimes are largely undifferentiated, with two

exceptions. Consistent with some scholarly views (e.g., Peters 2005, 231–32), Reagan appears to have served as a useful contrast for Democratic Congresses, while Clinton appears to have bested the Republican Congresses he faced.

CHAPTER 5

1. This overwhelming support led to an average House incumbent reelection rate of 96 percent during this period. We address aggregate election results more fully in chapter 7.

2. The idea that evaluations of Congress are meaningful is not new, but it does contrast with seminal works in this area such as Converse 1964.

3. All the figures supplied in this paragraph are based on two-party vote totals.

4. One notable exception is our country's "influence in the world"—an issue related to foreign policy—for which Americans found the president to be most responsible.

5. These observations are consistent with a study by Thomas Rudolph (2003) regarding responsibility for the nation's economy in 1998 and with more general observations made by Hibbing and Theiss-Morse (1995) from their interviews in 1992.

6. In instances in which each chamber is controlled by a different party, we hypothesize that disapproval of Congress would translate into disapproval of the majority party in the House for House elections and in the Senate for Senate elections. We have chosen to focus on House elections (see n. 10).

7. It is also possible that the effects were driven primarily by respondents with House members from the majority party (presumably a larger proportion of the sample, since the majority party represents more districts). Neither study analyzes electoral effects.

8. For an exception, see McDermott and Jones 2003. The next section of this chapter expands on our previous work in this area.

9. Consistent with Lipinski's work, Arnold's (2004) analysis of local news coverage of incumbents in 1993 and 1994 finds thirteen times as many articles with minority party incumbents attacking Congress as opposed to those with majority party incumbents attacking Congress.

10. Each election year, the number of voters and the number of races potentially affected by congressional evaluations are greater in House contests than in Senate contests. We present evidence elsewhere of similar effects on voters in U.S. Senate races as those presented here for House races (Jones and McDermott 2004; McDermott and Jones 2005).

11. All of these differences are statistically significant.

12. For details on variable coding and model construction, see the appendix.

13. We also tested alternative models with variables for voter contact with candidates and for relative issue and ideological evaluations of the candidates.

None of these alternative specifications reduced the impact or significance of congressional approval. The model reported in the text was chosen because including any one of these alternative variables results in a loss of at least four elections from the analysis. See the appendix for details.

14. Specific probabilities depend on the value of every other variable in the model. For this example, we chose to set the dummy variable for year to the most recent election year.

15. Details on variable measurement are in the appendix.

16. As in the individual-level analysis, further testing finds no significant difference in effects between midterm and presidential-year elections. Testing for differences between unified and divided government is trickier, because there are only five values of the aggregate variables for national forces (i.e., approval and economy) during unified government. However, a reestimation using data only from divided government produces coefficients for congressional approval nearly identical to those presented in table 5.3.

17. Estimates use the average total two-party vote in contested elections across all seventeen election years in the analysis. Estimates of vote change are even higher for recent elections, since the electorate has grown over the period of the study.

CHAPTER 6

1. Research demonstrates that the kinds of electoral factors considered by incumbents and incumbents' challengers do not necessarily apply to experienced candidates deciding whether to run in open-seat races (Bianco 1984), and we do not address such decisions here.

2. See Carson 2005 for an attempt to integrate these research agendas.

3. Specific reelection percentages were 87 percent versus 98 percent.

4. We exclude races with two incumbents running against each other (an occasional result of redistricting) and races with incumbents not elected in a regular general election.

5. Details on variable measurement are in the appendix.

6. For a discussion of challenger timing, see Jacobson 1989, 779.

7. Unless otherwise noted, all other variables are held constant at their median value in the data.

8. Other contextual variables, such as holding a leadership position or being outside the mainstream of one's party, have also been tested but have not demonstrated the same consistent effects as majority party status (see Bernstein and Wolak 2002, table 1).

9. In contrast, we are aware of no comparable literature suggesting that challengers might be influenced by such concerns. Perhaps this is because challengers cannot perceive the scorn felt by the quoted member of Congress before they actually become members themselves.

10. A recent study by Wolak (2007) considers the effect of attitudes toward Congress, among other variables, at the aggregate level.

11. Details on variable measurement and model specification are in the appendix.

12. Additional tests demonstrate that the difference in effects between majority and minority parties is statistically significant.

13. All other variables are held constant at their median value in the data unless otherwise noted.

CHAPTER 7

1. This average was calculated over the period 1974–2006.

2. See Fiorina 1981 for a discussion of this lineage.

3. Details on variable measurement are in the appendix.

4. This is the measure used by Marra and Ostrom (1989) and Newman and Ostrom (2002). Gaddie (1997) proposes an alternative measure based on the difference in open seats held by each party. The results of our model are virtually identical regardless of which measure we employ.

5. This methodological technique is often used in models of seat swing, which have relatively few degrees of freedom. For example, see Jacobson 1989, table 7. The fit does not improve when separate variables for majority and minority party conditions are used instead.

6. Finocchiaro (2003) also finds no significant exposure effects during elections since 1974.

7. With the dependent variable measured as seat swing for the presidential party, we do not need to create any interaction for the variables representing the economy or presidential approval. As expected, they had a statistically significant effect on seat swing for the presidential party, whereas congressional approval did not. While this result differs from Finocchiaro 2003, there are a few potential explanations. First, our model includes four additional elections not considered by Finocchiaro. Second, Finocchiaro does not control for presidential approval, which we find to have its own significant effect.

8. Since there are only five cases of unified government in the data set, it is not possible to conduct a full Chow test. Nevertheless, if we estimate the second model using only data from elections that took place during divided government, the results for congressional approval are nearly identical to those found in table 7.1. This null finding is consistent with the null finding in the analysis in chapter 5.

9. Missing cases can occur when either the old or new member does not serve a full term and thus does not have enough roll call votes to be scaled. Final scores for members elected in 2006 were not available at the time of this writing.

10. The two exceptions (Louisiana's 6th district in 1974 and Virginia's 3rd

district in 1980) were both retiring conservative Southern Democrats who had voted with the Republican Party more often than with the Democratic Party while in office.

11. Details on this modification and on other variable measurements are in the appendix.

12. Our results are nearly identical if we use the party median instead.

13. Ideally, congressional approval would be measured at the district level for this test. Unfortunately, comprehensive survey data on congressional approval at the district level simply does not exist.

14. The model does not include measures of presidential approval or the economy, because we are not aware of any literature or theory predicting how these factors might affect an incumbent's ideology.

15. These figures do not take into account the relative impact of congressional approval on each type of change or their aggregate effect—topics addressed later in this chapter.

16. This would take place mainly because of the partisan seat change—but also because of the incumbent adaptation—associated with low congressional approval.

17. Details on the measurement of this variable and other variables discussed in this section are in the appendix.

18. We also tested for any time trend but found none. We do not include an index of liberalism/conservatism in public opinion, because our argument is that congressional approval itself includes an ideological component (see chap. 4) that would be difficult to test in the presence of a variable representing a summary of all ideological views.

19. We find the same results for congressional approval using an alternative specification that controls for partisan seat swing purged of its congressional approval component.

20. Details on this measure and the rest of the model are in the appendix. Stimson, MacKuen, and Erikson (1995) devised another method of placing policy on an ideological scale strongly correlated with Poole and Rosenthal's scale ($r = .51, p < .05$). We have chosen to use the Poole and Rosenthal data because it provides a more direct measure.

21. The major difference between our two measures of change in House policy stance is that only the average location of winning policy takes into account the agenda-setting powers of the majority party. If we control for change in majority party status, the effect of congressional approval is essentially identical for both dependent variables. We have here chosen not to control for change in majority party status, since this itself is influenced by congressional approval via seat swing. We also tried controlling for change in the presidency and in the Senate, but neither variable was significant.

22. Again, we find the same results for congressional approval using an alter-

native specification that controls for partisan seat swing purged of its congressional approval component.

CHAPTER 8

1. Specifically, a variable representing the interaction between congressional approval and time, which we added to the model in table 7.1, was not statistically significant.

CHAPTER 9

A version of this chapter was presented at the annual meeting of the Midwest Political Science Association in Chicago, April 2–5, 2009.

1. Gallup poll conducted July 10–13, 2008 ($N = 1,016$). For accompanying analysis, see http://www.gallup.com/poll/108856/Congressional-Approval-Hits -RecordLow-14.aspx.

2. Poll conducted by the CBS News Election and Survey Unit, September 27–30, 2008 ($N = 1,257$). For accompanying analysis, see http://www.cbsnews .com/stories/2008/10/01/opinion/polls/main4492043.shtml.

3. Cook 2008; Drucker 2008.

4. Gallup poll conducted October 10–12, 2008 ($N = 1,269$). For accompanying analysis, see http://www.gallup.com/poll/111169/Americans-Satisfaction-New -AllTime-Low.aspx. Although Bush's accompanying 25 percent approval rating was higher than congressional approval, it represents just as significant a drop from average approval. Using figures since 1974, both congressional and presidential approval levels were about two standard deviations lower than their three-decade averages.

5. The results for 1980–2004 are reprinted from table 5.2.

6. The exit poll also does not test whether respondents can recognize candidate names. We compensate by using an objective measure of candidate quality in place of the missing subjective one: previous elective office experience (see Jones and McDermott 2004). Because they measure similar concepts, we report the estimated effect of the experience variable in the same row as the variable for name recognition. Despite these differences in the 2006 model, it provides a good fit to the data (explaining 75 percent of the variance in the vote) and a pattern of effects similar to that found in the other periods. See the appendix for details on coding of all variables in the 2006 model.

7. Obtaining the appropriate value for congressional approval in the third quarter of 2008 requires that we rerun the Stimson algorithm (used to create the original 1974–2006 time series in chapter 4), incorporating the raw 2007–8 approval data. Unfortunately, doing so slightly changes the previous values in the series that were used to estimate the coefficients in table 7.1. To allow us to use the original coefficients, we translated the newly obtained 2008 data point onto the original scale based on a regression of the old scale onto the new one.

8. We also reran the models from table 7.1, adding the 2008 data. As expected, the refitted traditional model had a larger residual for 2008 than did our refitted model with congressional approval.

9. These reasons include the fact that we have specifically chosen the case on the dependent variable rather than at random, as well as the fact that each election's dynamics are shaped by its own unique context, thus making generalizations risky.

10. Survey conducted by SurveyUSA among likely voters, October 18–19, 2008 ($N = 604$), with a margin of error of plus or minus 4.1 points.

11. See n. 10 for survey details. While SurveyUSA has been criticized for potential methodological problems (e.g., Traugott 1995), they have also been cited for electoral poll accuracy (e.g., Kenner and Selatan 2004; Silver 2008). See the appendix of Brown 2007 for a discussion of issues with SurveyUSA methodology and for an argument in favor of the validity of their data.

12. While we had permission from the survey's sponsor, *Roll Call,* to use the raw data, our repeated requests to SurveyUSA and its CEO, Jay Leve, to obtain the raw data went unheeded.

13. (22 [approval %] × .66) + (14 [don't know %] × .66) + (65 [disapproval %] × .37) = 47.81 (total Democratic %); (22 [approval %] × .27) + (14 [don't know %] × .27) + (65 [disapproval %] × .57) = 46.77 (total Republican %). A 10 percent shift from disapproval to a neutral ("don't know") opinion would have the same effect.

BIBLIOGRAPHY

Abramowitz, Alan I. 1981. "Choices and Echoes in the 1978 U.S. Senate Elections: A Research Note." *American Journal of Political Science* 25 (1): 112–18.

Abramowitz, Alan I. 1985. "Economic Conditions, Presidential Popularity, and Voting Behavior in Midterm Elections." *Journal of Politics* 47 (1): 31–43.

Abramowitz, Alan I. 2002. "Who Will Win in November: Using the Generic Vote Question to Forecast the Outcome of the 2002 Midterm Election." Paper presented to the online Symposium on Mid-Term Elections sponsored by the Elections, Public Opinion, and Voting Behavior Subsection of the American Political Science Association.

Abramowitz, Alan I. 2006. "National Conditions, Strategic Politicians, and U.S. Congressional Elections: Using the Generic Vote to Forecast the 2006 House and Senate Elections." *PS: Political Science and Politics* 39 (4): 863–66.

Abramowitz, Alan I., and Kyle L. Saunders. 1998. "Ideological Realignment in the U.S. Electorate." *Journal of Politics* 60 (3): 634–52.

Abramowitz, Alan I., and Kyle L. Saunders. 2000. "Ideological Realignment and U.S. Congressional Elections." Paper presented at the annual meeting of the American Political Science Association, Washington, DC.

Abramowitz, Alan I., and Kyle L. Saunders. 2006. "Exploring the Bases of Partisanship in the American Electorate: Social Identity vs. Ideology." *Political Research Quarterly* 59 (2): 175–87.

Abramson, Paul R., John H. Aldrich, and David W. Rohde. 2007. *Change and Continuity in the 2004 and 2006 Elections.* Washington, DC: CQ Press.

Aldrich, John. H. 1995. *Why Parties? The Origin and Transformation of Party Politics in America.* Chicago: University of Chicago Press.

American National Election Studies. 2005. 1948–2004 ANES Cumulative Data File. Stanford, CA: Stanford University; Ann Arbor: University of Michigan.

American National Election Studies. 2009. American National Election Study, 2008: Pre- and Post-Election Survey. Ann Arbor, MI: Inter-university Consortium for Political and Social Research.

Ansolabehere, Stephen, James M. Snyder Jr., and Charles Stewart III. 2001. "Candidate Positioning in U.S. House Elections." *American Journal of Political Science* 45 (1): 136–59.

Arnold, R. Douglas. 2004. *Congress, the Press, and Political Accountability.* Princeton: Princeton University Press.

Atkeson, Lonna R. 1999. "'Sure I Voted for the Winner!' Overreport of the Primary Vote for the Party Nominee." *Political Behavior* 21 (3): 197–215.

Bartels, Larry M. 2002. "Beyond the Running Tally: Partisan Bias in Political Perceptions." *Political Behavior* 24 (2): 117–50.

Baum, Matthew A. 2002. "Sex, Lies, and War: How Soft News Brings Foreign Policy to the Inattentive Public." *American Political Science Review* 96 (1): 91–109.

Bender, Bruce, and John R. Lott. 1996. "Legislator Voting and Shirking: A Critical Review of the Literature." *Public Choice* 87:67–100.

Bennett, Stephen Earl. 1995. "Americans' Knowledge of Ideology, 1980–1992." *American Politics Research* 23 (3): 259–78.

Berelson, Bernard, Paul F. Lazarsfeld, and William N. McPhee. 1954. *Voting: A Study of Opinion Formation in a Presidential Campaign.* Chicago: University of Chicago Press.

Berke, Richard L. 1995. "Washington Talk; For G.O.P., Moderation Is Becoming Intolerable." *New York Times,* March 7, sec. A.

Bernstein, Jeffrey L., and Jennifer Wolak. 2002. "A Bicameral Perspective on Legislative Retirement: The Case of the Senate." *Political Research Quarterly* 55 (2): 375–90.

Bianco, William T. 1984. "Strategic Decisions on Candidacy in U.S. Congressional Districts." *Legislative Studies Quarterly* 9 (2): 351–64.

Billiet, Jacques, and Geert Loosveldt. 1988. "Improvement of the Quality of Responses to Factual Survey Questions by Interviewer Training." *Public Opinion Quarterly* 52 (2): 190–211.

Binder, Sarah, Forrest Maltzman, and Lee Sigelman. 1998. "Senators' Home-State Reputations: Why Do Constituents Love a Bill Cohen So Much More Than an Al D'Amato?" *Legislative Studies Quarterly* 23 (4): 545–60.

Black, Gordon S. 1972. "A Theory of Political Ambition: Career Choices and the Role of Structural Incentives." *American Political Science Review* 66 (1): 144–59.

Born, Richard. 1990. "The Shared Fortunes of Congress and Congressmen: Members May Run from Congress, but They Can't Hide." *Journal of Politics* 52 (4): 1223–39.

Box-Steffensmeier, Janet, Gary C. Jacobson, and J. Tobin Grant. 2000. "Question Wording and House Vote." *Public Opinion Quarterly* 64 (3): 257–70.

Brace, Paul. 1985. "A Probabilistic Approach to Retirement from the U.S. Congress." *Legislative Studies Quarterly* 10 (1): 107–23.

Brandt, Patrick T., and Thomas L. Brunell. 2006. "Forecasting the 2006 House Election." Paper submitted in the Pollyprize competition held by the International Institute of Forecasters.

Broder, David. 1996. "Parceling Out Power to Both Parties." *Washington Post*, November 6, sec. A.

Broder, David S., Dan Balz, and Chris Cillizza. 2008. "Polls Show Obama Leading in States Whose Electoral Votes Total Nearly 300, and the Democrats Heading Toward Expanded House and Senate Majorities." *Washington Post*, November 2, sec. A.

Brown, Adam R. 2007. "Gubernatorial Approval and Strategic Entry in the 2006 Elections." Paper presented at the annual meeting of the Midwest Political Science Association, Chicago, Illinois, April 2–15.

Campbell, Angus, Phillip E. Converse, Warren E. Miller, and Donald E. Stokes. 1960. *The American Voter.* New York: Wiley.

Campbell, James E. 1985. "Explaining Presidential Losses in Midterm Congressional Elections." *Journal of Politics* 47 (4): 1140–57.

Campbell, James E. 1986. "Forecasting the 1986 Midterm Elections to the House of Representatives." *PS: Political Science and Politics* 19 (1): 83–87.

Campbell, James E. 2006. "Forecasting the 2006 National Elections to the U.S. House of Representatives." *Forum* 4 (2): article 2.

Canes-Wrone, Brandice, David W. Brady, and John F. Cogan. 2002. "Out of Step, Out of Office: Electoral Accountability and House Members' Voting." *American Political Science Review* 96 (1): 127–40.

Cannon, David T. 1999. *Race, Redistricting, and Representation.* Chicago: University of Chicago Press.

Carson, Jamie L. 2005. "Strategy, Selection, and Candidate Competition in U.S. House and Senate Elections." *Journal of Politics* 67 (1): 1–28.

Carson, Jaime L., Michael H. Crespin, Jeffery A. Jenkins, and Ryan J. Vander Wielen. 2004. "Shirking in the Contemporary Congress: A Reappraisal." *Political Analysis* 12:176–79.

Committee on Political Parties of the American Political Science Association. 1950. *Toward a More Responsible Two-Party System. American Political Science Review* 44 (3), Part 2, Supplement: i–xi.

Committee on the Constitutional System. 1985. *Reforming American Government: The Bicentennial Papers of the Committee on the Constitutional System.* Boulder: Westview.

Conover, Pamela Johnston, and Stanley Feldman. 1984. "How People Organize the Political World: A Schematic Model." *American Journal of Political Science* 28 (1): 95–126.

Conover, Pamela Johnston, and Stanley Feldman. 1986. "Emotional Reactions to the Economy: I'm Mad as Hell and I'm not Going to Take it Anymore." *American Journal of Political Science* 30 (1): 50–78.

Converse, Philip E. 1964. "The Nature of Belief Systems in Mass Publics." In *Ideology and Discontent*, ed. David E. Apter. New York: Free Press.

Cook, Charlie. 2007. "Poll Track: Delayed Gratification." *National Journal*, June 9.

Cook, Charlie. 2008. "Obama's Short Coattails." *National Journal*, November 6.

Cook, Timothy E. 1979. "Legislature vs. Legislator: A Note on the Paradox of Congressional Support." *Legislative Studies Quarterly* 4 (1): 43–52.

Cox, Gary W., and Jonathan N. Katz. 1996. "Why Did the Incumbency Advantage in U.S. House Elections Grow?" *American Journal of Political Science* 40 (2): 478–97.

Cox, Gary W., and Mathew D. McCubbins. 2005. *Setting the Agenda: Responsible Party Government in the U.S. House of Representatives.* New York: Cambridge University Press.

Cronin, Thomas. 1989. *Direct Democracy.* Cambridge, MA: Harvard University Press.

Cutler, Lloyd N. 1988. "Some Reflections about Divided Government." *Presidential Studies Quarterly* 17 (3): 485–92.

Cuzan, Alfred G., and Charles M. Bundrick. 2006. "Will the Republicans Retain Control of the House of Representatives in 2006?" Paper presented at the annual meeting of the Northeastern Political Science Association, Boston.

Dao, James. 1999. "Long Island Congressman Quits G.O.P., Citing 'Extremists,'" *New York Times,* July 18, sec. 1.

Delli Carpini, Michael X., and Scott Keeter. 1996. *What Americans Know about Politics and Why It Matters.* New Haven: Yale University Press.

Dodd, Lawrence C., and Bruce I. Oppenheimer. 1977. "The House in Transition." In *Congress Reconsidered,* ed. Lawrence C. Dodd and Bruce I. Oppenheimer. New York: Praeger.

Downs, Anthony. 1957. *An Economic Theory of Democracy.* New York: Harper.

Drucker, David M. 2008. "Republicans Avoid Worst-Case Scenario." *Roll Call,* November 5. Available online at http://www.rollcall.com/news/29876-1.html (accessed Oct. 19, 2009).

Druckman, James N., and Arthur Lupia. 2000. "Preference Formation." *Annual Review of Political Science* 3:1–24.

Durr, Robert H., John B. Gilmour, and Christina Wolbrecht. 1997. "Explaining Congressional Approval." *American Journal of Political Science* 41 (1): 175–207.

Erikson, Robert S., and Joseph Bafumi. 2002. "Generic Polls, Late Balancing Acts, and Midterm Outcomes: Lessons from History for 2002." Paper presented to the online Symposium on Mid-Term Elections sponsored by the Elections, Public Opinion, and Voting Behavior Subsection of the American Political Science Association.

Erikson, Robert S., Michael B. MacKuen, and James A. Stimson. 2002. *The Macro Polity.* New York: Cambridge University Press.

Feldman, Stanley. 1988. "Structure and Consistency in Public Opinion: The Role of Core Beliefs and Values." *American Journal of Political Science* 32 (2): 416–40.

Feldman, Stanley, and Pamela Johnston Conover. 1983. "Candidates, Issues, and

Voters: The Role of Inference in Political Perception." *Journal of Politics* 45 (4): 810–39.

Fenno, Richard F., Jr. 1975. "If, as Ralph Nader Says, Congress Is 'the Broken Branch,' How Come We Love Our Congressmen So Much?" In *Congress in Change: Evolution and Reform,* ed. Norman J. Ornstein. New York: Praeger.

Fenno, Richard F., Jr. 1978. *Home Style.* Boston: Little, Brown.

Finocchiaro, Charles J. 2003. "An Institutional View of Congressional Elections: The Impact of Congressional Image on Seat Change in the House." *Political Research Quarterly* 56 (1): 59–65.

Fiorina, Morris P. 1981. *Retrospective Voting in American National Elections.* New Haven: Yale University Press.

Fiorina, Morris P. 1990. "Information and Rationality in Elections." In *Information and Democratic Processes,* ed. John Ferejohn and James Kuklinski. Urbana: University of Illinois Press.

Fiorina, Morris P. 1992. *Divided Government.* New York: Macmillan.

Fiske, Susan T., Richard R. Lau, and R. A. Smith. 1990. "On the Varieties and Utilities of Political Expertise." *Social Cognition* 8 (1): 31–48.

Frankfort-Nachmias, Chava, and David Nachmias. 2000. *Research Methods in the Social Sciences.* 6th ed. New York: Worth.

Gaddie, Ronald Keith. 1997. "Congressional Seat Swings: Revisiting Exposure in House Elections." *Political Research Quarterly* 50 (3): 699–710.

Gamson, William A. 1992. *Talking Politics.* Cambridge: Cambridge University Press.

Gant, Michael M., and Dwight F. Davis. 1984. "Mental Economy and Voter Rationality: The Informed Citizen Problem in Voting Research." *Journal of Politics* 46 (1): 132–53.

Gerber, Elisabeth. 1999. *The Populist Paradox: Interest Group Influence and the Promise of Direct Legislation.* Princeton: Princeton University Press.

Gilens, Martin. 2001. "Political Ignorance and Collective Policy Preferences." *American Political Science Review* 95 (2): 379–96.

Glazer, Amihai, and Marc Robbins. 1983. "Voters and Roll Call Voting: The Effect on Congressional Elections." *Political Behavior* 5 (4): 377–89.

Glazer, Amihai, and Marc Robbins. 1985. "Congressional Responsiveness to Constituency Change." *American Journal of Political Science* 29 (2): 259–73.

Goodstein, Laurie. 1995. "Gingrich Vows to Pursue Christian Coalition Agenda; Gingrich Vows Action on Group's 'Blueprint.'" *Washington Post,* May 18, sec. A.

Goren, Paul. 2000. "Political Expertise and Principled Political Thought." *Political Research Quarterly* 53 (1): 117–36.

Goren, Paul. 2004. "Political Sophistication and Policy Reasoning: A Reconsideration." *American Journal of Political Science* 48 (3): 462–78.

Graber, Doris A. 2006. "Government by the People, for the People—Twenty-First Century Style." *Critical Review* 18 (1–3): 167–78.

Green, Donald Philip. 1988. "On the Dimensionality of Public Sentiment toward Partisan and Ideological Groups." *American Journal of Political Science* 32 (3): 758–80.

Groeling, Tim, and Samuel Kernell. 2000. "Congress, the President, and Party Competition Via Network News." In *Polarized Politics: Congress and the President in a Partisan Era,* ed. John R. Bond and Richard Fleisher. Washington, DC: CQ Press.

Hager, Gregory L., and Terry Sullivan. 1994. "President-Centered and Presidency-Centered Explanations of Presidential Public Activity." *American Journal of Political Science* 38 (4): 1079–1103.

Hall, Richard L., and Robert P. Van Houweling. 1995. "Avarice and Ambition in Congress: Representatives' Decisions to Run or Retire from the U.S. House." *American Political Science Review* 89 (1): 121–36.

Hamill, Ruth, Milton Lodge, and Frederick Blake. 1985. "The Breadth, Depth, and Utility of Class, Partisan, and Ideological Schemata." *American Journal of Political Science* 29 (4): 850–70.

Harwood, John. 2005. "Washington Wire: The NBC News/*Wall Street Journal* Poll." *Wall Street Journal,* April 8, sec. A.

Hetherington, Marc J. 2001. "Resurgent Mass Partisanship: The Role of Elite Polarization." *American Political Science Review* 95 (3): 619–31.

Hibbing, John R. 1982a. "Voluntary Retirement from the U.S. House of Representatives: Who Quits?" *American Journal of Political Science* 26 (2): 467–84.

Hibbing, John R. 1982b. "Voluntary Retirement from the U.S. House: The Costs of Congressional Service." *Legislative Studies Quartlerly* 7 (1): 57–74.

Hibbing, John R., and Christopher W. Larimer. 2005. "What the American Public Wants Congress to Be." In *Congress Reconsidered,* ed. Lawrence C. Dodd and Bruce I. Oppenheimer. 8th ed. Washington, DC: CQ Press.

Hibbing, John R., and Elizabeth Theiss-Morse. 1995. *Congress as Public Enemy: Public Attitudes towards American Political Institutions.* New York: Cambridge University Press.

Hibbing, John R., and Elizabeth Theiss-Morse. 1998. "The Media's Role in Public Negativity toward Congress: Distinguishing Emotional Reactions and Cognitive Evaluations." *American Journal of Political Science* 42 (2): 475–98.

Hibbing, John R., and Elizabeth Theiss-Morse. 2002. *Stealth Democracy: Americans' Beliefs about How Government Should Work.* New York: Cambridge University Press.

Hibbing, John R., and Eric Tiritilli. 2000. "Public Disapproval of Congress Can Be Dangerous to Majority Party Candidates: The Case of 1994." In *Continuity and Change in House Elections,* ed. David W. Brady, John Cogan, and Morris P. Fiorina. Stanford, CA: Stanford University Press.

Holm, John D., and John P. Robinson. 1978. "Ideological Identification and the American Voter." *Public Opinion Quarterly* 42 (2): 235–46.

Huckfeldt, R. Robert, and John Sprague. 1995. *Citizens, Politics, and Social Communication: Information and Influence in an Election Campaign.* New York: Cambridge University Press.

Huckfeldt, Robert, Jeffrey J. Mondak, Michael Craw, and Jeanette Morehouse. 2002. "Terms and Conditions of Candidate Choice: Partisan versus Ideological Heuristics." Paper presented at the annual conference of the American Political Science Association, Boston.

Hulse, Carl. 2008. "Democrats Increase Their Strength in the House, but Lose Some Races." *New York Times,* November 5, sec. P.

Hurwitz, Jon, and Mark Peffley. 1987. "How Are Foreign Policy Attitudes Structured? A Hierarchical Model." *American Political Science Review* 81 (4): 1099–1120.

Inter-university Consortium for Political and Social Research and Carroll McKibbin. 1997. Roster of United States Congressional Officeholders and Biographical Characteristics of Members of the United States Congress, 1789–1996: Merged Data [Computer file]. 10th ICPSR ed. Ann Arbor, MI: Inter-university Consortium for Political and Social Research.

Jacobson, Gary C. 1989. "Strategic Politicians and the Dynamics of U.S. House Elections, 1946–1986." *American Political Science Review* 83 (3): 773–93.

Jacobson, Gary C. 1990. *The Electoral Origins of Divided Government.* San Francisco: Westview.

Jacobson, Gary C. 2000. "The Electoral Basis of Partisan Polarization in Congress." Paper presented at the annual meeting of the American Political Science Association, Washington, DC.

Jacobson, Gary C. 2004. *The Politics of Congressional Elections.* 6th ed. New York: Longman.

Jacobson, Gary C., and Michael A. Dimock. 1994. "Checking Out: The Effects of Bank Overdrafts on the 1992 House Elections." *American Journal of Political Science* 38 (3): 601–24.

Jacobson, Gary C., and Samuel Kernell. 1983. *Strategy and Choice in Congressional Elections.* 2nd ed. New Haven: Yale University Press.

Jacoby, William G. 1986. "Levels of Conceptualization and Reliance on the Liberal-Conservative Continuum." *Journal of Politics* 48 (2): 423–32.

Jacoby, William G. 1988. "The Impact of Party Identification on Issue Attitudes." *American Journal of Political Science* 32 (3): 643–61.

Jamieson, Kathleen. 1988. *Eloquence in an Electronic Age.* New York: Oxford University Press.

Jerit, Jennifer, Jason Barabas, and Toby Bolsen. 2006. "Citizens, Knowledge, and the Information Environment." *American Journal of Political Science* 50 (2): 266–82.

Johannes, John R., and John C. McAdams. 1981. "The Congressional Incumbency Effect: Is It Casework, Policy Compatibility, or Something Else? An

Examination of the 1978 Election." *American Journal of Political Science* 25 (3): 512–42.

Jones, David R. 2003. "Joint Evaluations of Legislature and Legislator." *Journal of Legislative Studies* 9 (1): 77–93.

Jones, David R. 2010. "Partisan Polarization and Congressional Accountability in House Elections." *American Journal of Political Science* 54 (2): 323–37.

Jones, David R., and Monika L. McDermott. 2002. "Ideological Distance from the Majority Party and Public Approval of Congress." *Legislative Studies Quarterly* 27 (2): 245–64.

Jones, David R., and Monika L. McDermott. 2004. "The Responsible Party Government Model in House and Senate Elections." *American Journal of Political Science* 48 (1): 1–12.

Jones, David R., and Monika L. McDermott. 2009. "Disapproval of Congress and the 2008 House Elections." Paper delivered at the annual meeting of the Midwest Political Science Association, Chicago.

Judd, Charles M., and James W. Downing. 1990. "Political Expertise and the Development of Attitude Consistency." *Social Cognition* 8 (1): 104–25.

Kam, Cindy D. 2005. "Who Toes the Party Line? Cues, Values, and Individual Differences." *Political Behavior* 27 (2): 163–83.

Kane, Paul. 2008. "GOP Slide in Michigan Hews to Economy; Democrats Say They Expect to Gain." *Washington Post,* November 2, sec. A.

Kenner, David, and William Saletan. 2004. "Let's Go to the Audiotape: Who Nailed the Election Results? Automated Pollsters." *Slate,* December 9. Available online at http://slate.msn.com/id/2110860 (accessed Oct. 19, 2009).

Key, V. O., Jr. 1966. *The Responsible Electorate: Rationality in Presidential Voting, 1936–1960.* New York: Vintage.

Kiewiet, D. Roderick, and Langche Zeng. 1993. "An Analysis of Congressional Career Decisions, 1947–1986." *American Political Science Review* 87 (4): 928–41.

Kimball, David C., and Samuel C. Patterson. 1997. "Living Up to Expectations: Public Attitudes toward Congress." *Journal of Politics* 59 (3): 701–28.

Klarner, Carl, and Stan Buchanan. 2006. "Forecasting the 2006 Elections for the U.S. House of Representatives." *PS: Political Science and Politics* 39 (4): 849–56.

Knight, Kathleen. 1985. "Ideology in the 1980 Election: Ideological Sophistication Does Matter." *Journal of Politics* 47 (3): 828–53.

Kuklinski, James H., and Paul J. Quirk. 2001. "Conceptual Foundations of Citizen Competence." *Political Behavior* 23 (3): 285–311.

Lau, Richard R, and David P. Redlawsk. 2001. "Advantages and Disadvantages of Cognitive Heuristics in Political Decision Making." *American Journal of Political Science* 45 (4): 951–71.

Lawrence, David G. 1994. "Ideological Extremity, Issue Distance, and Voter Defection." *Political Research Quarterly* 47 (2): 397–421.

Leveaux-Sharpe, Christine. 2001. "Congressional Responsiveness to Redistricting Induced Constituency Change: An Extension to the 1990s." *Legislative Studies Quarterly* 26 (2): 275–86.

Levine, Jeffrey, Edward G. Carmines, and Robert Huckfeldt. 1997. "The Rise of Ideology in the Post–New Deal Party System, 1972–1992." *American Politics Quarterly* 25 (1): 19–34.

Levitin, Theresa, and Warren E. Miller. 1979. "Ideological Interpretation of Presidential Elections." *American Political Science Review* 73 (3): 751–71.

Levitt, Steven D., and Catherine D. Wolfram. 1997. "Decomposing the Sources of Incumbency Advantage in the U.S. House." *Legislative Studies Quarterly* 22 (1): 45–60.

Lewis-Beck, Michael S., and Tom W. Rice. 1992. *Forecasting Elections.* Washington, DC: CQ Press.

Lewis-Beck, Michael, and Charles Tien. 2002. "Mid-Term Election Forecast: A Democratic Congress." Paper presented to the online Symposium on Mid-Term Elections sponsored by the Elections, Public Opinion, and Voting Behavior Subsection of the American Political Science Association.

Lipinski, Daniel. 2004. *Congressional Communication: Content and Consequences.* Ann Arbor: University of Michigan Press.

Livingston, Steven G., and Sally Friedman. 1993. "Reexamining Theories of Congressional Retirement: Evidence from the 1980s." *Legislative Studies Quarterly* 18 (2): 231–53.

Lodge, Milton, Kathleen M. McGraw, and Patrick Stroh. 1989. "An Impression-Driven Model of Candidate Evaluation." *American Political Science Review* 83 (2): 399–419.

Lodge, Milton, Marco R. Steenbergen, and Shawn Brau. 1995. "The Responsive Voter: Campaign Information and the Dynamics of Candidate Evaluation." *American Political Science Review* 89 (2): 309–26.

Lodge, Milton, and Patrick Stroh. 1993. "Inside the Mental Voting Booth: An Impression-Driven Process." In *Explorations in Political Psychology,* ed. Shanto Iyengar and William J. McGuire. Durham, NC: Duke University Press.

Lott, John R., Jr., and Stephen G. Bronars. 1993. "Time Series Evidence on Shirking in the U.S. House of Representatives." *Public Choice* 74:461–84.

Luttbeg, Norman R., and Michael M. Gant. 1985. "The Failure of Liberal/Conservative Ideology as a Cognitive Structure." *Public Opinion Quarterly* 49 (1): 80–93.

Macdonald, Stuart Elaine, George Rabinowitz, and Ola Listhaug. 1995. "Political Sophistication and Models of Issue Voting." *British Journal of Political Science* 25:453–83.

Maisel, L. Sandy, Walter J. Stone, and Cherie Maestas. 2001. "Quality Challengers to Congressional Incumbents: Can Better Candidates Be Found?" In *Playing Hardball: Campaigning for the U.S. Congress,* ed. Paul S. Herrnson. Upper Saddle River, NJ: Prentice Hall.

Mann, Thomas E., and Norman J. Ornstein. 2006. *The Broken Branch: How Congress Is Failing America and How to Get It Back on Track.* New York: Oxford University Press.

Marra, Robin F., and Charles W. Ostrom Jr. 1989. "Explaining Seat Change in the U.S. House of Representatives, 1950–1986." *American Journal of Political Science* 33 (3): 541–69.

Mayhew, David R. 1974. *Congress: The Electoral Connection.* New Haven: Yale University Press.

Mayhew, David R. 1991. *Divided We Govern: Party Control, Lawmaking, and Investigations, 1946–1990.* New Haven: Yale University Press.

McCarty, Nolan M., and Keith T. Poole. 1995. "Veto Power and Legislation: An Empirical Analysis of Executive and Legislative Bargaining from 1961 to 1986." *Journal of Law, Economics, and Organization* 11:282–312.

McCarty, Nolan, Keith Poole, and Howard Rosenthal. 2006. *Polarized America: The Dance of Unequal Riches.* Cambridge, MA: MIT Press.

McDermott, Monika L., and David R. Jones. 2003. "Do Public Evaluations of Congress Matter? Retrospective Voting in Congressional Elections." *American Politics Research* 32 (2): 155–77.

McDermott, Monika L., and David R. Jones. 2005. "Congressional Performance, Incumbent Behavior, and Voting in Senate Elections." *Legislative Studies Quarterly* 30 (2): 235–57.

McGraw, Kathleen. 2000. "Contributions of the Cognitive Approach to Political Psychology." *Political Psychology* 21 (4): 805–32.

McGraw, Kathleen M., Milton Lodge, and Patrick Stroh. 1990. "On-Line Processing in Candidate Evaluation: The Effects of Issue Order, Issue Importance, and Sophistication." *Political Behavior* 12 (1): 41–58.

Miller, Warren, E. 1991. "Party Identification, Realignment, and Party Voting: Back to the Basics." *American Political Science Review* 85 (2): 557–68.

Mondak, Jeffery J., Edward G. Carmines, Robert Huckfeldt, Dona-Gene Mitchell, and Scot Schraufnagel. 2007. "Does Familiarity Breed Contempt? The Impact of Information on Mass Attitudes toward Congress." *American Journal of Political Science* 51 (1): 34–48.

Mondak, Jeffrey J., and Belinda Creel Davis. 2001. "Asked and Answered: Knowledge Levels When We Will Not Take 'Don't Know' for an Answer." *Political Behavior* 23 (3): 199–224.

Moore, Michael K., and John R. Hibbing. 1998. "Situational Dissatisfaction in Congress: Explaining Voluntary Departures." *Journal of Politics* 60 (4): 1088–1107.

Morton, Becky, and Kenneth Williams. 2008. "Experimentation in Political Science." In *The Oxford Handbook of Political Methodology,* ed. Janet M. Box-Steffensmeier, Henry E. Brady, and David Collier. Oxford: Oxford University Press.

Mutz, Diana C., and Gregory N. Flemming. 1999. "How Good People Make Bad Collectives." In *Congress and the Decline of Public Trust,* ed. Joseph Cooper. Boulder: Westview.

Nadeau, Richard, and Richard G. Niemi. 1995. "Educated Guesses: The Process of Answering Factual Knowledge Questions in Surveys." *Public Opinion Quarterly* 59 (3): 323–46.

Nagourney, Adam. 2006. "For Democrats, Lots of Verses, But No Chorus." *New York Times,* March 6, sec. A

Nagourney, Adam, and Janet Elder. 2006. "Only 25% in Poll Voice Approval of the Congress." *New York Times,* September 21, sec. A.

National Election Pool, Edison Media Research, and Mitofsky International. 2007. National Election Pool General Election Exit Polls, 2006. Somerville, NJ: Edison Media Research; New York: Mitofsky International; Ann Arbor, MI: Inter-university Consortium for Political and Social Research.

Neuman, Russell. 1986. *The Paradox of Mass Politics: Knowledge and Opinion in the American Electorate.* Cambridge, MA: Harvard University Press.

Newman, Brian, and Charles Ostrom Jr. 2002. "Explaining Seat Changes in the U.S. House of Representatives, 1950–98." *Legislative Studies Quarterly* 27 (3): 383–406.

Nicholson, Stephen P., and Gary M. Segura. 1999. "Midterm Elections and Divided Government: An Information-Driven Theory of Electoral Volatility." *Political Research Quarterly* 52 (3): 609–29.

Nie, Norman H., Sidney Verba, and John R. Petrocik. 1980. *The Changing American Voter.* Enlarged ed. Cambridge, MA: Harvard University Press.

Oppenheimer, Bruce I., James Stimson, and Richard W. Waterman. 1986. "Interpreting U.S. Congressional Elections: The Exposure Thesis." *Legislative Studies Quarterly* 11 (2): 227–47.

Page, Benjamin I., and Robert Y. Shapiro. 1992. *The Rational Public: Fifty Years of Trends in Americans' Policy Preferences.* Chicago: University of Chicago Press.

Parker, Glenn R. 1977. "Some Themes in Congressional Unpopularity." *American Journal of Political Science* 21 (1): 93–109.

Parker, Glenn R. 1996. *Congress and the Rent-Seeking Society.* Ann Arbor: University of Michigan Press.

Parker, Glenn R., and Roger H. Davidson. 1979. "Why Do Americans Love Their Congressmen So Much More Than Their Congress?" *Legislative Studies Quarterly* 4 (1): 53–61.

Patterson, Samuel C., and Gregory A. Caldeira. 1990. "Standing Up for Congress: Variations in Public Esteem since the 1960s." *Legislative Studies Quarterly* 15 (1): 25–47.

Patterson, Samuel C., Randall B. Ripley, and Stephen V. Quinlan. 1992. "Citizens' Orientations toward Legislatures: Congress and the State Legislature." *Western Political Quarterly* 45:315–38.

Peters, Ronald M., Jr. 2005. "The Changing Speakership." In *The Cannon Centenary Conference: The Changing Nature of the House Speakership*, ed. Walter J. Oleszek. Washington DC: Joint Committee on Printing.

Phillips, Kevin. 1994. *Arrogant Capital: Washington, Wall Street, and the Frustration of American Politics*. Boston: Little, Brown.

Pierce, Greg. 2006. "McCain's Warning." *Washington Times,* April 14, sec. A.

Poole, Keith T. 2007. "Changing Minds? Not In Congress!" *Public Choice* 131 (3–4): 435–51.

Poole, Keith T., and Thomas Romer. 1993. "Ideology, 'Shirking,' and Representation." *Public Choice* 77:185–96.

Poole, Keith T., and Howard Rosenthal. 1997. *Congress: A Political-Economic History of Roll Call Voting*. New York: Oxford University Press.

Popkin, Samuel L. 1991. *The Reasoning Voter: Communication and Persuasion in Presidential Campaigns*. Chicago: University of Chicago Press.

Popkin, Samuel L. 2006. "The Factual Basis of 'Belief Systems': A Reassessment." *Critical Review* 18 (1–3): 233–54.

Ragsdale, Lyn. 1991. "Strong Feelings: Emotional Responses to Presidents." *Political Behavior* 13 (1): 33–65.

Rahn, Wendy M. 1993. "The Role of Partisan Stereotypes in Information Processing about Political Candidates." *American Journal of Political Science* 37 (2): 472–96.

Ripley, Randall B., Samuel L. Patterson, Lynn Maurer, and Stephen V. Quinlan. 1992. "Constituents' Evaluations of U.S. House Members." *American Politics Quarterly* 20 (4): 442–56.

Robinson, John P., and John A. Fleishman. 1988. "Ideological Identification: Trends and Interpretations of the Liberal-Conservative Balance." *Public Opinion Quarterly* 52 (1): 134–45.

Rohde, David W. 1991. *Parties and Leaders in the Postreform House*. Chicago: University of Chicago Press.

Rosenbaum, David E. 1998. "The Speaker Steps Down: The Center; Complaint from a Mainstream District," *New York Times,* November 11, sec. A.

Rothenberg, Lawrence S., and Mitchell S. Sanders. 2000. "Severing the Electoral Connection: Shirking in the Contemporary Congress." *American Journal of Political Science* 44 (2): 316–25.

Rudolph, Thomas J. 2002. "The Economic Sources of Congressional Approval." *Legislative Studies Quarterly* 27 (4): 577–600.

Rudolph, Thomas J. 2003. "Who's Responsible for the Economy? The Formation and Consequences of Responsibility Attributions." *American Journal of Political Science* 47 (4): 698–713.

Schattschneider, E. E. 1960. *The Semisovereign People: A Realist's View of Democracy in America*. New York: Holt, Rinehart, and Winston.

Schuman, Howard, and Stanley Presser. 1996. *Questions and Answers in Attitude Surveys*. Beverly Hills, CA: Sage.

Schwarz, Norbert. 1999. "Self-reports: How the Questions Shape the Answers." *American Psychologist* 54 (2): 93–105.

Shadish, William R., Thomas D. Cook, and Donald T. Campbell. 2002. *Experimental and Quasi-Experimental Designs for Generalized Causal Inference.* Boston: Houghton Mifflin.

Sharp, Carol, and Milton Lodge. 1985. "Partisan and Ideological Belief Systems: Do They Differ?" *Political Behavior* 7 (2): 147–66.

Silver, Brian D., Barbara A. Anderson, and Paul R. Abramson. 1986. "Who Overreports Voting?" *American Political Science Review* 80 (2): 613–24.

Silver, Nate. 2008. "Pollster Ratings, V3.1.1." *FiveThirtyEight*, May 28. Available online at http://www.fivethirtyeight.com/2008/05/pollster-ratings-v311.html (accessed Oct. 19, 2009).

Smith, Eric R. A. N. 1989. *The Unchanging American Voter.* Berkeley: University of California Press.

Sniderman, Paul M., and Douglas B. Grob. 1996. "Innovations in Experimental Design in Attitude Surveys." *Annual Review of Sociology* 22:377–99.

Snowiss, Leo M. 1966. "Congressional Recruitment and Representation." *American Political Science Review* 60 (3): 627–39.

Snyder, James M., Jr., and Michael M. Ting. 2003. "Roll Calls, Party Labels, and Elections." *Political Analysis* 11:410–44.

Stimson, James A. 1975. "Belief Systems: Constraint, Complexity, and the 1972 Election." *American Journal of Political Science* 19 (3): 393–417.

Stimson, James A. 1999. *Public Opinion in America: Moods, Cycles, and Swings.* 2nd ed. Boulder: Westview.

Stimson, James A. 2004. *Tides of Consent: How Public Opinion Shapes American Politics.* New York: Cambridge University Press.

Stimson, James A., Michael B. Mackuen, and Robert S. Erikson. 1995. "Dynamic Representation." *American Political Science Review* 89 (3): 543–65.

Stokes, Donald E., and Warren E. Miller. 1962. "Party Government and the Saliency of Congress." *Public Opinion Quarterly* 26 (4): 531–46.

Stone, Walter J., Ronald B. Rapoport, and Alan I. Abramowitz. 1992. "Candidate Support in Presidential Nomination Campaigns: The Case of Iowa in 1984." *Journal of Politics* 54 (4): 1074–97.

Stratmann, Thomas. 2000. "Congressional Voting over Legislative Careers: Shifting Positions and Changing Constraints." *American Political Science Review* 94 (3): 665–76.

Sundquist, James L. 1982. *The Decline and Resurgence of Congress.* Washington, DC: Brookings Institution Press.

Sundquist, James L. 1988. "Needed: A Political Theory for the New Era of Divided Government in the United States." *Political Science Quarterly* 103 (4): 613–35.

Sundquist, James L. 1992. *Constitutional Reform and Effective Government.* Rev. ed. Washington, DC: Brookings Institution Press.

Sundquist, James L., ed. 1993. *Beyond Gridlock? Prospects for Governance in the Clinton Years—and After.* Washington, DC: Brookings Institution Press.

Sundquist, James L., ed. 1995. *Back to Gridlock? Governance in the Clinton Years.* Washington, DC: Brookings Institution Press.

Tamas, Bernard I. 2002. "The 2002 House Seat Swing in Historical Perspective." Paper presented to the online Symposium on Mid-Term Elections sponsored by the Elections, Public Opinion, and Voting Behavior Subsection of the American Political Science Association.

Taylor, Andrew J. 1996. "The Ideological Development of the Parties in Washington, 1947–1994." *Polity* 29 (2): 273–92.

Theriault, Sean M. 1998. "Moving Up or Moving Out: Career Ceilings and Congressional Retirement." *Legislative Studies Quarterly* 23 (3): 419–33.

Traub, James. 2006. "The Submerging Republican Majority." *New York Times,* April 18, sec. 8.

Traugott, Michael. 1995. "'CATS' dissected." *Public Perspective* 6 (August/ September): 1–3.

Tufte, Edward R. 1975. "Determinants of the Outcomes of Midterm Congressional Elections." *American Political Science Review* 69 (3): 812–26.

Tufte, Edward R. 1978. *Political Control of the Economy.* Princeton: Princeton University Press.

Waterman, Richard W., Bruce I. Oppenheimer, and James A. Stimson. 1991. "Sequence and Equilibrium in Congressional Elections: An Integrated Approach." *Journal of Politics* 53 (2): 372–93.

Wlezien, Christopher, and Christopher Carman. 2001. "Ideological Placements and Political Judgments of Government Institutions." *Public Opinion Quarterly* 65 (4): 550–61.

Wolak, Jennifer. 2007. "Strategic Retirements: The Influence of Public Preferences on Voluntary Departures from Congress." *Legislative Studies Quarterly* 32 (2): 285–308.

Wright, Gerald C., Jr. 1993. "Errors in Measuring Vote Choice in the National Election Studies." *American Journal of Political Science* 37 (1): 291–316.

Wright, Gerald C., Jr., and Michael B. Berkman. 1986. "Candidates and Policy in United States Senate Elections." *American Political Science Review* 80 (2): 567–88.

Zaller, John R. 1992. *The Nature and Origins of Mass Opinion.* Cambridge: Cambridge University Press.

Zaller, John, and Stanley Feldman. 1992. "A Simple Theory of the Survey Response: Answering Questions versus Revealing Preferences." *American Journal of Political Science* 36 (3): 579–616.

Zinni, Frank P., Jr., Franco Mattei, and Laurie A. Rhodebeck 1997. "The Structure of Attitudes toward Groups: A Comparison of Experts and Novices." *Political Research Quarterly* 50 (3): 595–626.

INDEX

ABOUT THE AUTHORS

David R. Jones is a professor of political science at the City University of New York's Graduate Center and Baruch College. His research focuses on the U.S. Congress, legislative behavior, and elections. He is the author of *Political Parties and Policy Gridlock in American Government* (2001). His work has also been published in such scholarly journals as the *American Journal of Political Science*, the *Journal of Politics*, *Legislative Studies Quarterly*, and *Political Research Quarterly*. He regularly serves as an exit poll analyst for such media outlets as CBS News and the *New York Times*.

Monika L. McDermott is an associate professor of political science at Fordham University, where she studies voting behavior, political psychology, and public opinion. Her research follows multiple lines of inquiry, including public opinion of Congress, as well as voting cues and information shortcuts—most recently with regard to religious stereotypes and elections. Her work has been published in some of the profession's top journals, such as the *American Journal of Political Science*, the *Journal of Politics*, *Political Research Quarterly*, and *Public Opinion Quarterly*. McDermott is also a survey researcher, having conducted election surveys for the *Los Angeles Times*, the CBS News Election and Survey Unit, and the Center for Survey Research and Analysis at the University of Connecticut. She has been an election and polling consultant for CBS News since 2002.